A Life in
Transition

A Life in
Transition

ALEX BORAINE

ZEBRA

Published by Zebra Press
an imprint of Struik Publishers
(a division of New Holland Publishing (South Africa) (Pty) Ltd)
PO Box 1144, Cape Town, 8000
New Holland Publishing is a member of Avusa Ltd

www.zebrapress.co.za

First published 2008

1 3 5 7 9 10 8 6 4 2

Publication © Zebra Press 2008
Text © Alex Boraine 2008

PUBLISHING MANAGER: Marlene Fryer
MANAGING EDITOR: Robert Plummer
EDITOR: Marléne Burger
COVER AND TEXT DESIGNER: Natascha Adendorff-Olivier
TYPESETTER: Monique van den Berg
INDEXER: Robert Plummer
PRODUCTION MANAGER: Valerie Kömmer

Set in 10.5 pt on 14.2 pt Minion

Reproduction by Hirt & Carter (Cape) (Pty) Ltd
Printed and bound by Paarl Print, Oosterland Street, Paarl, South Africa

ISBN 978 1 77022 012 6

To Jenny
Thank you for fifty years of love, support and joy

Contents

Foreword

WHEN PRESIDENT NELSON MANDELA APPOINTED US TO THE Truth and Reconciliation Commission in 1995, we were expected to hit the ground running.

The commission was deliberately designed to have a short shelf life. We had to start literally from scratch – no staff, no premises, absolutely no infrastructure. I really would not wish our plight on even my worst enemy. It just seemed all had been designed as a recipe for disaster.

What a wonderful gift to have had Alex Boraine as the deputy chair (quite a few had rightly thought he should have been the chair). He has formidable managerial and administrative skills in addition to his other admirable attributes. And so, almost as if he had been a consummate magician pulling rabbits nonchalantly out of a hat, we soon had a head office in Cape Town and four regional offices in Cape Town, Johannesburg, East London and Durban, almost all fully staffed and equipped. It was indeed almost magically that after our inaugural meeting – symbolically on the Day of Reconciliation, 16 December 1995 – we were able to hold our first public hearing in East London in April 1996. None of this would have happened had we not been blessed with an Alex Boraine. I want again to pay very warm tribute to him, especially for that crucial intervention then.

It would have been an excruciating hell had it been that his loyalty to the chair had been less than wholehearted and genuine. The work of the commission was traumatic and revealed just how we had all been damaged by apartheid. This was revealed starkly when a black commissioner was wrongfully implicated in a matter before the Amnesty Committee – the commission was split down the middle along racial lines, most blacks believing him to be innocent and most whites conversely thinking there could be no smoke without fire. So our warm friendship and Alex's undivided loyalty were not inevitable. Indeed, they were extraordinary phenomena. What a huge relief that I did not ever have to watch my back. It would have been so debilitating had it been otherwise. We were on the same wavelength on almost all issues. We had many tricky moments, but it was so invigorating to know that we shared the same perspectives and held dear the same values. We can never take that sort of thing for granted.

Alex has a formidable theological and philosophical intellect. After all, he was the youngest cleric to be elected president of the Methodist Conference. Clearly he was an impressive personality, and soon made his mark in the political arena as an MP for the Progressive Federal Party, where he and his few fellow party members proved a constant thorn in the flesh of the racist National Party. His impeccable integrity forced him to resign from parliament when he felt that his continued presence lent an undeserved credibility to what was no more than a cruel charade. Together with Van Zyl Slabbert, he founded IDASA, seeking to provide rational alternatives to what was so fundamentally irrational, cruel and inhumane. His own experience of deprivation (he started working at the age of fourteen) inspired his passion for justice and equity, as did his interaction with blacks when he traversed the length and breadth of South Africa as director of the Methodist Church's Department of Christian Education.

He was at the forefront of those who were already considering how South Africans would deal with the aftermath of conflict in the post-apartheid period, especially in the non-governmental organisation Justice in Transition, which he set up. With others they debated the various options. What a wonderful blessing that he should have been a dear friend of Dullah Omar, who, as minister of justice in the first post-apartheid government of Nelson Mandela, was to pilot through parliament the legislation setting up the TRC. Alex was prominent in drafting that legislation.

I have nothing but the highest praise for the outstanding work Alex did in the TRC. His contribution was invaluable and irreplaceable. He went on to found in New York the highly acclaimed International Center for Transitional Justice, of which he was president for the first four years. He has helped to make it the best of its kind, held in the highest possible esteem globally. He did this while a professor at the New York University Law School.

I am greatly honoured to have been asked to provide this foreword. You are about to be regaled with the story of one of South Africa's greatest sons, who has been so ably aided and abetted by his charming wife, Jenny. Enjoy it and be moved and inspired.

DESMOND TUTU
Archbishop Emeritus
December 2007

Preface

WHEN I STARTED WRITING THIS BOOK, IT WAS GOING TO BE a substantial study of transitional justice, drawing on many anecdotes from a number of the countries I have visited as president of the International Center for Transitional Justice. While in Bellagio on a fellowship from the Rockefeller Foundation in 2005, I spent a great deal of time researching the theory and practice of transitional justice and developed quite a large body of writing. But when I discussed this with a number of friends and family, and finally with my editors, there was a strong view that I should focus on the life that I have lived and the various professions in which I have served. Thus, the book is very much a story of my life, from early beginnings to the present. I have attempted to reflect on my life by sharing my understanding of transitional justice and some of my experiences in this field.

Inevitably, I have revisited South Africa's Truth and Reconciliation Commission, covered in depth in my previous book, *A Country Unmasked*, and some of the material from that book is repeated here.

I have many, many people to thank for helping me to write this book. Obviously, I am grateful to my parents and immediate family, who gave me a good and solid base on which to build, even though our economic and social situation was so restricted. I also want to thank so many family and friends who have shared my life over many years, challenging, advising and generally supporting me in every possible way.

It is very difficult to write about oneself, and much easier to focus on issues. Francis Wilson, an old friend, helped me get started by asking searching questions about my early childhood.

Every writer owes a debt of gratitude to his or her editors. I certainly could not have written this book without careful and thorough editing by Robert Plummer and Marléne Burger. Robert was the editor of my previous book, *A Country Unmasked*, and I was keen to renew that relationship. I would also like to thank Marlene Fryer and everyone at Zebra Press.

In particular, my thanks to Paddy Clark, who transcribed and typed every word of the manuscript and was also enormously helpful as a researcher.

I remain very much in her debt. When the going got quite tough and writing was difficult, she gave me a great deal of encouragement.

I am most grateful to Archbishop Emeritus Desmond Tutu for his over-generous foreword, and also for the example set by his life, and his abiding friendship.

My family has always been close and supportive, and while I wrote this book, they were there for me. I claimed a great deal of their time talking about some of the ideas and stories that I wanted to include, and they always listened patiently and with encouragement. Special thanks to Andrew, Jeremy, Kathy and Nick.

This book is dedicated to my wife, Jenny, who features throughout the book, because she is the centre of my life.

There are many friends from the church, business, politics and civil society in South Africa and further afield, especially in New York, who have been most generous in their support and time and encouragement. I want to thank in particular the staff of the International Center for Transitional Justice. In many ways, we started as a small family and have grown beyond my wildest dreams. I am thankful to be part of this ongoing, dynamic group, so many of whom have become not only colleagues, but also friends.

ALEX BORAINE
Cape Town
February 2008

Abbreviations

ANC	African National Congress
APLA	Azanian People's Liberation Army
AWB	Afrikaner Weerstandsbeweging
BOSS	Bureau of State Security
BPC	Black People's Convention
CEO	chief executive officer
CI	Christian Institute
COSATU	Congress of South African Trade Unions
CP	Conservative Party
DA	Democratic Alliance
DP	Democratic Party
DRC	Democratic Republic of Congo
FF	Freedom Front
ICC	International Criminal Court
ICTJ	International Center for Transitional Justice
ICTY	International Criminal Tribunal for the Former Yugoslavia
IDASA	Institute for a Democratic Alternative for South Africa
IFP	Inkatha Freedom Party
IJR	Institute for Justice and Reconciliation
JICA	Japan International Cooperation Agency
MDC	Movement for Democratic Change
MK	Umkhonto we Sizwe
MP	member of parliament
MPC	provincial council representative
MRI	magnetic resonance imaging
NATO	North Atlantic Treaty Organisation
NGO	non-governmental organisation
NIACRO	Northern Ireland Association for the Care and Resettlement of Offenders
NP	National Party
NRP	New Republic Party
NUSAS	National Union of South African Sudents

NYU	New York University
OSCE	Organisation for Security and Cooperation in Europe
PAC	Pan Africanist Congress
PFP	Progressive Federal Party
PKK	Kurdistan Workers' Party
PRP	Progressive Reform Party
PSA	prostate-specific antigen
SAAF	South African Air Force
SABC	South African Broadcasting Corporation
SACC	South African Council of Churches
SACP	South African Communist Party
SADF	South African Defence Force
SAP	South African Police
SAPS	South African Police Service
SASO	South African Students' Organisation
SRC	Student Representative Council
TRC	Truth and Reconciliation Commission
UDF	United Democratic Front
UN	United Nations
UP	United Party
USIP	United States Institute for Peace
WCC	World Council of Churches
WTC	World Trade Center
ZANU-PF	Zimbabwe African National Union – Patriotic Front

'Thou shalt not be a victim. Thou shalt not be a perpetrator. Above all, thou shalt not be a bystander.'
— YEHUDA BAUER

'Not all the wounds inflicted can be healed, but what matters is that there shall be no more wounds. Forgiveness in history can come only when the wound of guilt is healed, when violence has become justice, lawlessness has become order, and war has become peace.'
— DIETRICH BONHOEFFER

PART I

*From childhood
to the church*

Chapter 1

Humble beginnings

M Y MOTHER HAD A SAYING FOR EVERY SITUATION AND EVERY
occasion. She was usually right on the money with her proverbs,
aphorisms and witty sayings, drawn mainly from the biblical book of
Proverbs. Some of her favourites included 'Pride cometh before a fall', 'Waste
not, want not' and 'Blood is thicker than water'. But when she declared that
'Alex was born with a silver spoon in his mouth', she was altogether wide of
the mark.

We lived in a sub-economic housing estate, which had a profound effect
on my thinking from a young age. I was determined not to be trapped
there forever. Not that Brooklyn, Cape Town, which is where I grew up,
was a slum. The streets were paved and Clarendon Crescent – such a grand
name for a lowly thoroughfare – had a few trees growing along its length.
A Mr Le Roux seemed to appear every day to sweep the pavements and,
more than that, to terrorise me and the other children who ran and played
in the street. He was mean, leathery skinned and gaunt, his mouth framed
with a luxuriant moustache. He seemed very, very old but was probably
only in his early forties, an unhappy man who hated those who found simple
pleasure in climbing a tree and dangling from the strong branches. So, on
a fairly regular basis, he took his sharp saw and lopped off the lower limbs,
making it impossible for us to swing from branch to branch.

Our house, No. 39, was shabby, but not derelict. It was a box that sat
among a long row of similar boxes, but the roof didn't leak, it was fairly
solidly built and we even had a patch of lawn in front and a small garden at
the back, with a single fig tree and a small lean-to where my brother Aubrey
and I kept homing pigeons. I remember the fun we had and the anxiety in
our hearts as we released those pigeons and finally watched them return.
The birds shared a small space with several chickens and one rooster, which
woke us up every morning. Unfortunately, from time to time, one of the
chickens would end up in the pot!

The housing estate was built to accommodate poor whites rendered
jobless by the economic depression from 1930 onwards. The rent was very,
very low. My father had previously been employed by the South African

Railways and we lived in a railway cottage at No. 7 Range Road, Lansdowne, where I was born. We moved to Brooklyn soon afterwards, in 1931, all our furniture and meagre belongings piled onto a horse-drawn cart, and me, only a few months old, in my mother's arms.

My mother described our ten-kilometre journey to the Brooklyn estate often. She felt very depressed; her husband was out of work, she had lost the roof over her head and didn't know what she was going to do. She felt a loss of dignity. But what worried her even more was that she had lost her favourite black cat. He had disappeared when they were packing up, but several days later he appeared at our new home. How on earth he found his way we will never know, but his return gave my mother great joy and she told the story many, many times.

My father, Mike Boraine, was short and stocky, physically strong, with limited education, a handyman rather than a carpenter. He would leave home early in the morning with a small bag of tools on his back and look for work. It must have been demeaning and tiring but I can't remember him ever complaining. He would return to tell us about a gate that he had repaired, or a job that he had been promised. He had rough, tough hands and was a quiet man. He never once offered to teach me his craft – I had to sweep up the wood shavings, but was not allowed to use any of his tools. He had grown up on a farm in Oudtshoorn. His father died when he was only about twelve years old and he had to leave school after Standard 4, his strong arms needed on the farm in his father's absence. It didn't work out, and as a teenager he went to Cape Town and found employment on construction sites. He hardly ever read a book, but every day of his life he read the newspapers, both the *Cape Times* and the *Argus*.

My mother was Isa Blanche, more English than the English. Her father had served in the British army during the Anglo-Boer War and decided to settle in Cape Town afterwards. She was remarkably loyal to the British royal family and an ardent supporter of Winston Churchill during the Second World War. She was vital, comical, full of laughter, often singing at the top of her voice as she did her housework or waited for the kettle to boil. She had several sisters and they loved being together. Every Friday night, all the sisters visited their parents' home in Observatory. My grandmother, Mary Evans, who went by the name of Mama, was totally dominant and I remember her sitting in her chair, a light on a pulley pulled down close in front of her, her daughters hanging on her every word. Her husband Frank had found work with the railways when he settled in South Africa around the turn of the twentieth century, and after retirement he served as a barman at the Olympic Club in Rondebosch.

When we accompanied my mother on the occasional Friday night, we would go to the Observatory railway station to meet him. It was often clear, as he alighted from the train, that he had partaken generously of the drinks he had been serving earlier. He was a quiet, courteous and grand man, who walked somewhat slowly up the hill towards No. 6 Nuttal Road. He would always stop at a café, not to buy us sweets, but for a carrier bag full of fruit. We would take that to his house, where he would solemnly hand out the contents to us, take off his hat, sit in his big armchair, a silver chain across his somewhat ample stomach, and light his pipe. I adored him. He had silver hair and a moustache, blue eyes and a quiet spirit; hardly saying a word, he would just be there, and I know he cared for us.

When my mother went to visit her parents with her sisters and left us behind, my father looked after us. He always cooked something special – not merely the evening meal, but a bowl of spotted dick, a boiled pudding with raisins. Round about nine o'clock, we would sit down and devour this with homemade custard and then all of us would go to bed, waiting for the door to open on my mother's return.

In some strange way, although my mother did the bulk of the cooking, my father's meals seemed to have greater relish. He would cook breakfast early in the morning before setting off for work. I used to wake and smell the bacon frying and I would crawl into the kitchen and watch him cook one egg, eat that, and then cook another. Whenever I got a taste of his breakfast, it tasted so much better than everything else. When he made a stew, it seemed as if he worked from some special recipe that he never shared with me or anyone else, and it always tasted good.

My mother had left school at the age of fifteen after passing Standard 6. An intelligent woman and avid reader, she introduced me to the wonder of books long before I started school. This was a priceless gift, and my love of literature has stayed with me throughout my life. I remember walking with her to the library when I was very young. While she selected her books, I was allowed to choose mine, and in time I began reading some of hers as well as my own. She was old fashioned and house proud to a fault. The front door of our house was always locked. We had to use the back door, after carefully wiping our feet on the step. Her first words of greeting were, 'Take off your shoes.' These had to be preserved, because we could ill afford a new pair.

I recall vividly the first day I went to school. I was not at all pleased, but my mother walked with me to the Maitland Junior School and stayed with me for a while. But there came a time when she had to leave and I was left in the care of a very tall teacher called Miss Day. I didn't want my mother to go, but she took out her purse and from it removed a small coin, a tickey, encrusted with hardened dough, and said: 'This is very, very special. I found it in the Christmas pudding and I don't want to part from it, but you can keep it safe and you will know that I am with you, and you can give it back to me when you get home.' I immediately dried my tears and was quite happy for her to go. I looked at that little brown object many times during the day and happily parted with it that night. I never had any major problems going to school after that. In fact, without any real effort on my part, I seemed to take to studying, perhaps because I had been such an avid reader before I even went to school, and, six months into the first year, I was promoted to Standard 1. I had no difficulty doing well in all the subjects as I went through the standards.

I had two brothers: Ronnie, who was six years older than me, and Aubrey, who was nearly three years my senior. Ronnie was almost beyond my reach because of the age gap, but I worshipped him. He was a kind of golden boy, very good-looking, blond with touches of red in his hair. He always seemed to do the right thing – he was a Cub and a Scout and got every badge imaginable. He did very well at school and my mother absolutely adored him. But I don't remember playing with him much, because he was older and had his own group of friends.

From an early age, all three of us had to help with the housework. My brothers and I had to make our beds before we left for school, and in the evening we had to set the table for dinner and take turns to do the dishes, which involved washing, drying and putting them away. As the youngest, I was given the last of these chores, because it was the easiest.

Aubrey and I had an extremely difficult relationship. He had been a very sickly child and had a bout of scarlet fever when he was quite young. I understood vaguely, because everyone talked about it in hushed tones, that he had nearly died. Whether this had any effect on him or not or whether he was by nature a tough, quarrelsome, often violent boy, I will never know. But I certainly suffered at his hands. He was tough on me, and yet, when we were bullied by other children on our way home from school, he would defend me. He would stand between me and the others and take on as many as were there, often returning home with a bloody shirt and nose, or a black eye. I was a bit of a sissy. I didn't like fighting and I was a little scared of the other boys, but Aubrey was exactly the opposite. In later years, he became an excellent boxer and won many matches, reaching the Western Province finals in the Cape Town City Hall.

He persuaded me to take up boxing when we were at junior school, but that was a disaster. For some unknown reason, our boxing coach put the two of us in the ring together. As we advanced to the centre, my brother pushed out a left and then a strong right, which landed on my nose and left me in tears. I don't think I ever boxed against him again. My other bouts as a junior boxer were a lot easier, because I wasn't facing my brother, who actually terrified me in many ways. I managed to get to the finals of the Western Province junior light-heavyweight championship. My opponent didn't turn up for the fight, so I became champion by default! My last tournament was a total mismatch. I was sixteen years old and my opponent was a twenty-one-year-old railway ticket conductor. I managed a lucky punch in the first round and he was furious. He knocked me around from then on and I only just managed to survive the three rounds. I was so dazed they gave me a small glass of brandy to revive me. No more boxing for me.

When we were still in junior school, Aubrey and I got up to a lot of mischief together. He was very much the ringleader, but I followed dutifully. Stealing fruit was one of our favourite pastimes. One evening, we jumped out of our bedroom window and climbed up a high fence protecting a neighbour's fruit trees. Unfortunately we were spotted, and the owner used a salt and pepper gun to assail our backsides! We fell off the fence and ran as if Lucifer himself was in pursuit.

Another unforgettable incident involved us going into another neighbour's yard, which had wooden posts supporting a grapevine. There was nothing small about my brother. He produced a pair of scissors and cut off a branch bearing several bunches of grapes. We carried this back to our house, clambered through the window and dragged the laden branch into our room. We ate as many of the grapes as we could, but a lot were left over. My mother discovered the discarded branch and grapes, demanded an explanation, and we had to apologise to the neighbour. He was most gracious. 'If you had asked me, I would have given you as much as you could eat.' But forbidden fruit somehow tastes much better.

We always had cats, and also canaries, which caused a lot of problems. I had a stocky dog called Jock. When I felt out of sorts, I used to hug him and say, 'You're the only one who really loves me.' If we were very naughty or disobedient, my mother seldom punished us herself, but warned, 'Wait until your father comes home.' He, poor man, had to listen to the tale of our offences and mete out appropriate punishment, when all he wanted to do was rest after his very long day. Usually he used a strap, specially made for us by the local cobbler. I was quite scared but pulled a blanket over me, so the strap did very little damage. Looking back, it's clear to me that his heart wasn't in it, but the noise of the strap on the blanket satisfied my mother that we were being suitably chastised.

There were a couple of times when my mother wouldn't wait until my father came home. On one such occasion, while looking over the fence into our neighbour's property, I saw a little girl. She must have been about my age, nine or ten. I had no sisters and I was very curious about girls and what made them tick, and how they were different from me. So I asked her to pull down her panties and to wee, so that I could see what distinguished girls from boys. She did as I asked, but unfortunately my mother overheard me and was furious. She rushed me into the house, took me into my bedroom and told me to close the window, so that the neighbours couldn't hear me screaming while she punished me. Although I was terrified at the time, I realise, looking back, that she could hardly stop laughing, but felt she had to do something, so the old strap came out. But, once again, the blanket saved me.

My parents lived a fairly ordinary, mundane life. Their major purpose seemed to be to try to get enough money together to pay the rent, feed their children, clothe us and send us to school. We were a respectable family and my mother was not keen that we should mix too freely with some of the people who lived in the neighbourhood. Most of the neighbours spoke Afrikaans and, despite the fact that this was also my father's home language, seemed to resent our presence, often shouting derogatory comments in our direction. However, there were some exceptions.

On the corner of Clarendon Crescent lived Mrs De Wet, a widow, who made the most delicious *mosbolletjies* (soft rusks). I was sent once a week to buy these, hot out of the oven, and she and I would talk. I enjoyed that, listening to her telling me about life on her own, the loss of her husband and her fear of people breaking into her home. One of my favourites was Ouma Fullard, a distant relative on my father's side. She spoke only Afrikaans, but we got on very well. She always had a pot of delicious soup on her coal stove. I would walk along the railway line and pick up lumps of coal to take to this tall, grey-haired woman who always welcomed me into her cosy home.

There were also the Browns, who were Seventh Day Adventists. I hadn't the slightest idea what that meant, except that we could never play with Roy, their son, on a Saturday, which was regarded as a holy day. They seemed very strict, were vegetarian, and kept to themselves. The O'Learys were different – loud, full of fun, the father a traffic officer who rode a large motorcycle with a sidecar. On more than one occasion, I was allowed to sit in the sidecar and, although I was scared as he turned corners, I enjoyed this thoroughly. Mrs O'Leary was a short but large woman, as Irish as they come, with a broad accent. She and my mother were great friends. My mother used to visit her quite often, occasionally in the evenings. My father didn't really like this. He rose very early in the morning, worked hard and, after supper, read the *Argus* and was ready for bed. If my mother hadn't returned by nine o'clock, he would go out onto our tiny stoep, collect a few stones from the garden and throw them onto the roof of the O'Leary house, which was just across the road, as a signal that it was time to come home. My mother was furious when this happened, but she always responded by crossing the street and in no time was in bed and the lights were out.

Another family that I remember, the Morgans, were among our closest friends. I was intrigued that the father had a wooden leg, a legacy of the First World War. As he walked it creaked, and I couldn't keep my eyes off him.

There were a number of other children we played with occasionally, but ours was a fairly tight circle. I recall going with Aubrey to the small park that had a few swings. We waited for our turn, because there were only a few seats, and many children. Once, when Aubrey eventually swung high into the air, a young girl, older than us, tried to stop him after a while and demanded that he should give the swing up to her. He resisted. She slapped him and, being Aubrey, he slapped her back, a little harder. She was furious, yelled at us in Afrikaans, '*Jou vuilgoed*!' (You rubbish!) and ran off, presumably to tell her parents.

We didn't hang around, being a little scared, and said nothing of the incident at home. The next morning, Sunday, my father was up early. He had bathed and shaved and put on a clean white shirt, which he kept for church, when someone rapped on the front door. He opened the door and there was the young girl's father, who demanded that my father should punish Aubrey for hitting his daughter. My father called Aubrey and me and we told him the story and he responded, 'That seems fair enough. She started it and I think we should just leave it.'

At that, the girl's father leant forward, grabbed my father by his shirt – his clean white shirt, his church shirt! – and it tore as my father pulled back. Then my father launched a single blow to the other man's chin and, to my utter astonishment, it lifted the irate caller off his feet and sent him flying into our tiny garden, where he landed on his back. He was furious and used language I wasn't used to, but then brushed himself off and, possibly realising that he might be courting even more punishment, ran off, threatening to call the police. This didn't bother my father at all. He quietly replaced the shirt, put on his tie and took us off to church.

My father had joined the Salvation Army in the direst time of unemployment, and they were extremely kind and helpful to him and, indeed, to us. They tried to find a job for him, invited him to their services and always served a midweek supper, which was most welcome to a hungry family. They finally got him a job at the South African Museum. It was a fairly lowly position, but nevertheless regular employment, and my father would ride his bicycle from Brooklyn every morning to the museum and return around 5.30 p.m. He supplemented his income by doing small repair jobs in the neighbourhood.

My brothers and I walked to both junior and high school in Maitland, no matter what the weather. We had no car and we didn't ride our bikes to school, but I did cycle around the neighbourhood quite a lot. During the Cape winters, we often came home absolutely drenched, and of course we had to take off our shoes before we were allowed into the house, where my mother was waiting with a towel in her hand, and a steaming hot cup of cocoa for us. She told us to take off our school clothes and to hang them up, so they could dry and we could wear them again in the morning.

We had some rather strange teachers at Maitland. Mr Ross, the principal, was very strict and remote but straightforward, down the line. On one occasion, I was vying for the last place in the first cricket team against Bernard Kroger, a friend of mine, and somehow I managed to get that place. This was announced in the afternoon, when we were due to play a match against a neighbouring school. Bernard was furious, believing that he deserved to be in the team, and he verbally attacked me. Then the pushing and shoving started, and before long we were having a go at one another. I managed to throw him to the ground and fell on top of him. Unfortunately, his arm was underneath his body and without realising it I had broken it. There was a great to-do and the next morning Bernard arrived at school with his arm in a plaster cast. I was called into Mr Ross's office and got three cuts on my behind with a cricket stump. At least we had won the match and I had even made a few runs.

One of the oddest teachers was Mr Meintjies, who was loud and vocal and danced around the classroom. But what made him stand out for me was that, every day, he examined all the sandwiches we had brought from home, and whatever he fancied he would confiscate. We tried to hide our lunch in our desks or behind our backs, but to no avail. One boy, Maurice Goodman, always brought lovely rye sandwiches with Gouda cheese that Mr Meintjies loved. When he tried to hide them, the teacher simply chased him around the classroom, took one of the sandwiches and quietly ate it. Nothing happened. I was astonished at this performance.

My own favourite school sandwich was corned beef out of a tin, the leftover mashed potato from the night before, salt and pepper, all mixed together and spread thickly on the bread. A lot of boys were quite envious of this concoction, and sometimes I had to share my sandwiches, at other times exchanging them for something not nearly as interesting.

The most peculiar teacher of all was Mr Swanepoel. He was a man of moods: smiling and happy and warm one moment, the Devil incarnate the next. His whole face seemed to change and he would become very, very angry and rail against us. On one occasion he was extremely critical of a boy called Lionel Munn. Lionel was quite a big boy, and he stood up to Mr Swanepoel. The teacher raced to the corner of the classroom, picked up an assegai that was there for a demonstration, and hurled it at Lionel. It just missed him, the sharp head of the spear thudding into the wooden floor, the staff quivering. We all sat there, absolutely astounded, pale and scared. Within moments, Mr Swanepoel did what he always did when he changed moods. He said, 'Sit down, be quiet, take out the encyclopaedias.' There was a whole set of encyclopaedias at the back of the classroom and we would grab a volume and share it at our desks. We loved this and learnt much from these books, but remained wary of Mr Swanepoel, because we never knew what he was going to do next.

A small group of my friends and I formed a gang. We were fairly harmless, using our catapults to shoot out streetlights, stealing cigarettes and canned food from the local grocer. We were bored and it seemed exciting to band together and get up to mischief. We even had a very elaborate password: '*Ina dina, katkisana, willihaver donker man, elsie kapelsie toof, haba ek sê, moenie metamorphasis, nor pishwish lantan, tabantad shads, hell's bells and buckets of blood.*' Woe betide anyone who couldn't recite this mishmash every time we met! The most serious escapade was when we broke into the junior school and started a fire in one of the classrooms. We were trying to heat up some of the canned goods stolen from Plotkins' Bazaar. One of the cans exploded and we had an anxious time putting out the fire, leaving an awful mess before running like hell to put distance between us and the school.

Junior school was fun. I made many friends and we played marbles in the playground in our breaks. Once a week we walked to the Maitland swimming pool. With my long arms I managed to win the one-length dash on several occasions. I seemed to be perpetually hungry and used to dream of a swimming pool filled with thick soup, into which I would dive with my mouth wide open. We received free milk twice a week at school and, in the summer, grapes from the nearby vineyard. The schoolwork was undemanding, and all in all I enjoyed my first five or six years away from the grim situation that was developing at home.

CHAPTER 2

War at home and abroad

I WAS EIGHT YEARS OLD WHEN GREAT BRITAIN DECLARED WAR against Germany on 3 September 1939. I remember sitting with my parents and my brothers in front of the Pilot radio, listening to Winston Churchill telling his country and the world that 'We are now at war.' This was enormously exciting. We had very little understanding of what it meant, except that we were going to defeat the 'dirty Germans'. We brought out the Union Jack and had it flying from our stoep; we played patriotic songs like 'There'll Always Be an England', 'The White Cliffs of Dover' and 'I'll Be Seeing You'. Gracie Fields and Vera Lynn featured every day.

My mother was thrilled when she heard that Jan Smuts had decided to take South Africa into the war on the side of England. This brought further division in our neighbourhood, because many were angry that South Africa had sided with the hated British.

Growing up during the war, this was the only conflict I experienced. I attended a dual-medium school and there were separate classrooms for English- and Afrikaans-speaking children, each group keeping very much to itself. What stands out for me, however, was a woman (whose name I have forgotten) who taught us Afrikaans literature. She helped us fall in love with Afrikaans poetry and we listened spellbound when she read some of the poems and stories in her warm and impeccable Afrikaans. Our teachers were mainly Afrikaners and very critical of those of us who had fathers and brothers in uniform.

While there was strong division between the two 'white' language groups, I was not conscious of any black/white tension. Ours was a totally white suburb, the staff and pupils at my school were all white and, for almost all of us, the only people of colour with whom we had contact were the garbage collectors, the fishmonger and the fruit and vegetable vendors, who came to our doors with their carts. Occasionally, some whites would talk about the *swart gevaar* and the need to protect 'what is ours', but it went over my head. I do recall, though, some scary nightmares. I kept dreaming that I could hear footsteps outside my bedroom window. It was as if hundreds of black people were crowding past. I used to run to my parents' bed and seek solace under their blankets. Mine was not a political family and we didn't discuss politics until 1948, when the National Party came to power. My mother and I were very upset by the change, but I was never sure what my father's feelings were.

When war was declared in 1939, my father immediately enlisted, even though he was older than most of the young men who were joining up to fight against the tyranny of Adolf Hitler. He was sent to an engineering unit at a place called Zonderwater, north of Pretoria, and my mother went to work in the canteen at Ysterplaat, the air station closest to our home. Soon, many youngsters in their late teens arrived in the Cape from the Royal Air Force in Britain. My mother enjoyed having them around; they pulled her leg, no doubt, and I think she enjoyed flirting with these young men who were all filled with life and hope and excitement and valour. She also started knitting sweaters and socks for 'our boys' – Ouma Smuts' boys, 'up north'. My brothers and I followed the war, but with little awareness of what lay just around the corner. We listened to the news about U-boats off the Cape coast; we rushed to see an aircraft that crashed in Milnerton and gazed at the fuselage and realised that somebody had died. Perhaps the first realisation that war was a costly business entered our youthful understanding.

My eldest brother, Ronnie, couldn't wait to go to war. As soon as he completed matric, he enlisted in the air force. He went to Pretoria for training, so we didn't see much of him after that. Aubrey was champing at the bit and, as soon as he left school, he joined up as well.

Ronnie was only eighteen when he went to North Africa as a rear gunner and wireless operator. In his occasional letters, he told us that up in the air they used to dance to music and that flying was 'as safe as houses'. But, one awful day in 1944, the telegram delivery man, whom we had seen in our streets many times bringing news of boys 'up north' who had been injured or were missing or had been killed, stopped at our gate. I will never forget it. I stood there with my heart in my mouth. I was thirteen years old. I knew immediately that my brother Ronnie was in serious trouble. Sure enough, the telegram told us that he was missing, that his aircraft had been shot down and that we would be kept informed. The shock transformed my mother from a bright, joyful person to someone quite depressed. She no longer sang, and for hours on end she would stand at the window and gaze out, waiting for news. When it came, after months and months of uncertainty, it was even worse: missing believed dead. The strain on my mother was such that she had a mild stroke, which left her face partially paralysed.

Meanwhile, my father had been invalided out of the engineering corps with an illness not defined, but which was a portent of something much, much more serious. He and my mother had a blazing row over Ronnie's enlistment in the air force. The law stated that anyone who was required to go beyond South Africa's borders had to get special permission from both parents if he was under twenty-one. This was to get what was called the 'red tab' that was worn on the shoulders of those in uniform, to indicate that they were available to fight overseas. My brother had pleaded with my parents to give him this permission, to sign the forms. My father had refused. My mother was prevailed upon and she forged my father's signature and then co-signed the form that enabled Ronnie to make the journey that eventually led to his death.

My father blamed my mother and, on top of her own deep personal anguish, this brought about a real crisis in the home and in their marriage. The only thing that comforted me, in a strange way, was that during those pitched battles, no force was used and they continued to call each other by their first names, Mike and Isa. For me, that suggested that the relationship was going to hold firm. On one occasion, my father stormed out of the house. A few hours later he returned, blind drunk. I'd never seen him drunk before – in fact, he was a teetotaller. We didn't know what to do with him, so we called for Mrs O'Leary.

Having seen her husband return home most nights in similar condition, Mrs O'Leary was quite jocular about it, teased him and got him to lie down on the couch. He was very tearful and my mother was struck silent. The next morning he was pale and quiet, but the storm was over. However, I knew that he would always hold Ronnie's fate against my mother, although their relationship continued almost as before.

With my father home again, my mother's time at the canteen was curtailed, and she wasn't happy about that. My father joined those patrolling the streets as part of our civil defence. We had blackouts on the windows and he had to watch for any possible incident, so he used to march around in a very smart uniform 'doing his bit'.

Aubrey had joined the army at the age of seventeen, and in the same year that Ronnie died, 1944, we received the devastating news that he, too, had been killed. It wasn't in combat, but in an army lorry crash in Cape Town, and he had died instantly. This was almost too much for the family; my mother sank further and further down into her own space and my father was distressed beyond words, finding it extraordinarily difficult to cope.

The end of the war was a great relief, but it brought no real celebration in our lives. For my part, I didn't fully understand that the conflict was finally over. It seemed to stutter towards an end – first Germany, then Japan. In 1945, it was announced that Prime Minister Jan Smuts would be visiting Cape Town to lead a victory parade. Owen Morgan and I asked our class teacher for permission to attend. This was bluntly refused. We bunked school and walked to the city centre to join the crowd welcoming Smuts and the troops – very colourful and exciting.

That night, Owen and I forged letters from our mothers to our teachers, excusing us from school because we'd been 'ill'. I handed mine in during the first period, but Owen waited until asked. Our teachers were understandably suspicious, and while we were still at school, one of them visited our homes and the game was up. The next day, we got six cuts each from the principal. I carried the bruises on my behind and legs for days.

I was fourteen when the war ended and I thought that any further schooling would be a sheer waste of time. Unable to comprehend that the fighting was indeed over, my thinking was that perhaps I would be called up and have to go to war and die, so what was the point of going to school? In any event, amid the pressures of home and death and anxiety, high school was grim. I did almost no work. I would go to school early in the morning and crib homework from one of the other boys, who was much more of a do-gooder and did his homework faithfully. I scraped through Standard 8 and received my junior certificate, leaving, as one teacher told me, a great deal of skin behind. Then I decided to leave school, without telling my parents. I read the Jobs Available columns in the newspapers and found a vacancy at the African Clothing Company in Woodstock. They wanted a trainee ledger clerk. I hadn't the slightest idea what this was, but I was very tall, making it easy to bluff my age, so I put on my best clothes, applied for the post, had an interview and got the job.

For the first month, I simply went to work when I was supposed to be going to school. At the end of the month I was paid a very small amount of money and I bought a box of Black Magic chocolates for my mother, put the balance of my salary in an envelope and gave it to her. She didn't know what I was talking about or where I had got the money to buy the chocolates, and was really quite angry and confused. I explained to my parents that there seemed no point in going to school given the current circumstances in our home and country and the world, and that I was not going back. There was nothing they could do about it, but they were desperately unhappy.

I soon became bored working at the clothing company, and after asking for several increases within a year, being granted the first two and having the third declined, I left. I applied for a job with Cable & Wireless in the centre of the city, because I had a hankering to do something that Ronnie had done as a wireless operator. I was the youngest employee, most of the men being quite a bit older then me. I learnt Morse code, which stayed with me throughout my life. In those days, long before faxes and e-mails and text messages, we had cables and telegrams, and I had to sit for hours with ear-phones on, receiving Morse code and translating it into English, pasting strips of text from the teletype machine onto the cables and making sure they went out to the recipients. It wasn't a great job, but I felt it brought me a little closer to my brother.

I also fell into very bad company. My colleagues regularly had beer for lunch and I started drinking, occasionally excessively, with some friends late at night. They did their best to lead me astray. One evening they took me to a brothel in Woodstock. They didn't let on where we were going, but, once there, even I could tell what sort of place it was. It was a small house, quite sordid, and the woman was wearing only a petticoat. We had a couple of beers and my two much older friends tried to persuade me to go into the bedroom. The fact that I refused had nothing to do with morality. I was squeamish, and the place looked grubby and unkempt. My friends were angry and declared me the equivalent of what would come to be known as a wimp many years later. I left them to it and walked to the Woodstock railway station.

Fortunately, I never got into any serious trouble, but I was just drifting, with no purpose in life and no vision for the future. Then, one day, I suppose because deep down I was not happy with what I was doing, I stopped at the headquarters of the Shell Company – which were then in Greenmarket Square – on my way to work, and applied for a job. I didn't have the qualifi-cations – I didn't even have matric – but somehow or other, I managed to secure a job as a trainee manager. I started to study at night school for my matric, reading the textbooks on the train from Goodwood, to which we had moved. That led to a change in my approach. I began to be a little more ambitious about my future, although I still didn't have a clue about how to plan my life.

In 1949, my father became very ill. It was reminiscent of the problem he'd had when he was in the army, but this was far more serious. He was in terrible pain and finally he went to a doctor, who recommended surgery. Ironically, I was in bed waiting for an operation on my knee, having torn a cartilage while playing cricket. I wasn't able to see my father on the night after his surgery. My mother came home from the hospital and said he was peaceful, and that he kept pointing to his lips. She thought that he wanted water, but he wanted her to kiss him, which she did. At about four o'clock in the morning, a policeman arrived at our door. To this day I still don't understand why a policeman came to tell us, but when I limped to the door, he gave me the news that my father had died some time earlier. I went into my mother's room, lay on the bed with her and told her that my father was not coming back. We held each other until dawn and then started telephoning our relatives and friends and made arrangements for the funeral.

I was eighteen when my father died and I never really got to know him. As a typical teenager, I was impatient with him, never understood him and wasn't sympathetic enough to the pain he endured in the last months of his life. In fact, I only really appreciated something of his worth during his funeral.

He was a loyal and devoted member of the Salvation Army; he wore the uniform and over weekends and on some evenings he would go into the pubs in the city and sell *War Cry*, the Salvation Army newspaper. Once a week, he would return the full collection box to the Salvation Army headquarters. His funeral procession wound through the city streets, accompanied by the Salvation Army band. Driving behind the hearse, I was astonished to see barmen, hotel owners and some of their customers spill out of the pubs and stand solemnly to attention. I realised then how much my father was respected. It must have been a tough job going into those pubs and he must have been on the receiving end of many a joke and some abuse. I remember being filled with pride, but also regret that I never really knew him, and now it was too late. The war, his absence from home, my brothers' deaths, and the differences between my mother and father had all taken their toll on our relationship.

CHAPTER 3

Becoming a
man of the cloth

A T THE AGE OF EIGHTEEN, I WAS FINALLY PERSUADED BY MY mother to attend a service of worship at the Metropolitan Methodist Church in Cape Town. She was a deeply committed churchgoer and had urged me to join her on many occasions, but I always found an excuse not to do so. This time, I felt the least I could do was accompany her to an evening service. My father had been dead for a short while, she was on her own and I think she was concerned about the lifestyle I was pursuing at the time.

The church, in Greenmarket Square, is very old and well known. It occupies a prominent space in the city centre and is a beautiful building. That night, I entered with my mother and drank in the tall interior and the lofty pulpit, the organ pipes and the assembled choir. I have to confess that I haven't the slightest idea what the minister said or preached, but during the service he announced that there was going to be a youth camp at a place called Firgrove. Some fifty kilometres from Cape Town, the well-known campsite offered fairly basic accommodation, perfectly adequate for young people, and had a river running through it. Having looked around the church and noticed some fairly attractive young women in the choir and congregation, I decided I would put my name on the list that was available. The camp was planned for the Easter weekend, a fortnight or so hence, and many times during that period I wondered whether I should pull out. But I went and, I must say, I enjoyed it. There were games being played, a lot of fun and banter, but my main objective was to try to get closer to some of the young women. In this, I failed dismally. I was gauche and awkward; I didn't know them, they all seemed to know each other, and I almost gave up the quest. Then something happened that changed the course of my life.

I was sitting on the grass listening to an address by a man called Bert Pfuhl, who was about two metres tall. He was introduced as someone who had been a major in the parachute regiment, and that immediately caught my interest. Here was someone who had fought in the same war as my brothers, so I listened to what he had to say. In a nutshell, he told us: 'You are at the height of your powers. You are young, full-blooded. You are strong, your life is before you. What do you think Jesus meant when he said "Without me you can do nothing"?' I thought about that, and on the surface it sounded quite ridiculous. There were lots of things I could do without him. I was working, I was active, I wasn't too sure about where I was going, but I was alive and well. However, it played on my mind, and that night in the tent I simply couldn't sleep. What it was about for me at that time was *meaning*. I really had no direction, no goals, no vision, no meaning. I had lost two brothers, I had lost a father. My job was interesting but not fulfilling, and suddenly, out of the blue, this large man was telling me, very earnestly, that without Jesus Christ I could achieve nothing. I began to wonder if there was something in all of this speaking to me, urging me to listen and to shape up. So I thought about it, and was troubled.

The other people I listened to didn't impress me very much, but at the end of the camp Bert Pfuhl spoke again, and he started his final address by asking: 'Can any of you remember what I said at the very beginning?' I put up my hand and said, 'Yes, Jesus said "Without me you can do nothing".'

'That's right, that's good,' Pfuhl responded, then quoted the following text from the Bible: 'I can do all things through Christ who strengthens me.' He elaborated to make the point, which was now becoming fairly obvious: on the one hand, without him there is no meaning, you can achieve nothing; with him, your life can be transformed.

'Young men and women,' he said, 'I want you to go and think about it. That's all. I just want you to think about it and make a decision as to whether you want to continue as you are, or whether you want to do an about-turn and change the direction of your life.'

It certainly revolutionised my thinking. I went home as though I was walking on air. I wanted to sing. I hadn't found a pretty girl at the camp, but instead here was something fresh and vital; despite all the negative things that had happened in my life – my lack of formal education, my drifting around, being in bad company, my lack of purpose – there was a way forward. I became a total, absolute convert.

My mother was astonished. She couldn't understand. I started going to church more often than she did – in fact, I went to church morning and evening. I even took a notebook with me and started writing down what the preacher said. I couldn't believe it of myself. Of course, I got caught up in the enthusiasm of all the other young people, attended functions and joined youth groups that met in the evening, listened to visiting speakers and slowly but surely decided that it wasn't enough for me to sit and take notes and listen. I wanted to *do* something. And so, at the age of nineteen, I became a lay preacher in the Methodist Church.

I knew very little about life, but here I was, entering pulpits in churches all over Cape Town and preaching on Sundays. The congregations were mostly small, in suburbs like Goodwood and Thornton and Maitland, and I had the audacity to tell them what they ought to be doing with their lives and what God could do for them. It was extremely presumptuous, but at the time this didn't occur to me for a moment. I was keen and committed to sharing what I thought I had received.

Going through an old notebook to see what subjects I preached on in the early 1950s, I noticed that the first text I accepted was from Acts 16:30: 'And brought them out, and said, Sirs, what must I do to be saved?' I began those early sermons by telling people what had happened to me, then urged them to ask the question about being saved. The language was tough. I made it clear that if people didn't accept Jesus, they were on the road to hell. The second text, used in Parow on 5 February 1950, was from Galatians 6:14: 'But God forbid that I should glory, save in the cross of our Lord Jesus Christ, by whom the world is crucified unto me, and I unto the world.' Again I made the point that Jesus had died for sinners, and if they repented and accepted him, they would be saved. If they didn't, they would go to hell. Repentance, remission and reconciliation were the themes that I focused on.

Strangely enough, although I was so young and so brash, many people seemed to respond, and of course that encouraged me and gave me the strength and impetus to continue. Looking back, I am somewhat ashamed of the absolute certainty I had in an uncertain world, the condemnation to which I consigned those who apparently wouldn't respond to God's message of salvation. It was all very straightforward, very fundamental, very literal – and I needed to do a great deal of growing up.

I also taught in Sunday school and, not yet twenty years of age, even became a superintendent when a vacancy occurred. I loved the children and the teachers and tried to galvanise them into action so as to enlarge the size of the classes and recruit better teachers.

One of the worthwhile things I did was become active in what we called wayside Sunday schools. A group of us, all young, cycled to the nearby coloured townships of Kensington and Elsies River and taught scores of children in the open air. They flocked to hear the simple stories of Jesus, and although what we did probably smacked of white 'superiority', we genuinely loved the children who lived in terribly squalid surroundings. At that stage I never related my spiritual work to the practical and the political. My emphasis was on heaven and hell. I wanted the children to be saved and to go to heaven. I thought little, if at all, of the hell they were experiencing on earth.

When I was approached to become a candidate for the Methodist ministry, it was something I had long thought about. During a visit by a professor from Rhodes University, I had noticed his title on a copy of the paper that he delivered at the church: the Reverend Dr LA Hewson MA, PhD. I wanted that. I wanted the qualifications that he had. With half a matric, I wanted a master's degree and a doctorate. It was an incredible challenge and a vision that came to me early on, but through hard work and a measure of good fortune, I would achieve it in the end.

The first step was to write the local preachers' exams and be assessed by three senior clergymen while I was actually preaching. Having passed those tests, I was asked to serve as a candidate minister. I was twenty years old.

There was a great shortage of ministers and preachers in the church. I thought my first posting would be somewhere in Cape Town, the only city that I knew, but I was sent to Klerksdorp. At the time, Klerksdorp and the neighbouring Western Transvaal towns of Orkney and Stilfontein were raw, rough mining communities. I didn't know what I was getting myself into. I went by train, scared now, nervous, no longer sure of my ground. I was met at the station by the superintendent minister, the Reverend John Wallace, a man of enormous integrity, very strict but very caring. It was a pleasure and a help for me to work with a man like that for a year.

My lodgings were with an Afrikaans family, who hardly spoke a word of English. They had other lodgers, all of whom were also Afrikaans-speaking. At the first meal I was introduced in Afrikaans; I greeted them in my limited Afrikaans and then realised that I was going to have to learn the language quickly, or starve, because I had to ask them to pass the butter or the jam or the salad, and Afrikaans was the lingua franca in that house. It was a strange experience for me. For the first time, I was exposed to the mindset of Afrikaners who harboured a grudge against anyone English-speaking that dated right back to the Anglo-Boer War. I tried to understand their residual rancour, but I'm afraid I never really did. But we were at least civil to one another, and I even made a couple of friends among the other young lodgers.

The work was demanding. I preached two or three times every Sunday, I had to visit the sick and the halt, the blind and the lame. I had to look after the Young People's Guild, as it was called, and arrange programmes once a week. One of the greatest challenges was going to preach in Orkney on Sunday mornings. It was about sixteen kilometres from Klerksdorp and I asked John Wallace how I was going to get there. 'On your bicycle, of course.' So, very early in the morning, I set off.

There was no church building, just a multi-purpose community hall. This played host on Saturday nights to a dance, so my first job on arrival was to clean the hall, which was still full of cigarette butts, smoke, empty bottles and glasses. I opened all the windows to air the place, set out the chairs and hoped that somebody would come. Some always did. I preached there regularly throughout that year, and slowly but surely the congregation grew, but it was extraordinarily difficult.

On one occasion, it was extremely hot and I had cleaned out the hall as best I could, with the help, by that time, of one or two people who came early for this very purpose. During the service, I was in the middle of a sentence when a fly flew into my mouth. I simply couldn't talk. Every time I tried to say something, it got stuck in my throat. The congregants tried hard to keep straight faces until finally, in desperation, I turned to the side, spat the damn thing out and laughed. The congregation joined in heartily, and I resumed my sermon.

This was a time of learning for me. I began to realise that I had an enormous amount to learn from the congregation, rather than the other way round. I was still extremely presumptuous – quite certain and dogmatic about my theological and biblical views – but, slowly and surely, I began to listen to other people. My congregations were all white; there were no blacks in the church, no coloureds. The problems of racism and exclusivity which characterised South Africa left me all but untouched. The only thing that did trouble me was that I had a strong view of God as Creator, and therefore he had created everyone – men and women, boys and girls, black and white.

When the first inkling of the real divisions in South Africa began to prod me, I did little about it. I was so busy evangelising the white community in terms of their relationship with God that I rarely reminded them of their relationships with their neighbours. Not surprisingly, I found my visits to the coloured townships disturbing, in complete contrast to the neat, well-maintained streets and buildings in the white towns. The squalor, the unpaved roads, the tiny houses, the dilapidated school buildings, spoke loudly of poverty and deprivation. My feelings were hopelessly mixed. As I gazed out at a congregation of people who looked depressed and lacking in self-respect, I thought the gospel could bring them comfort and take them out of their misery. But I also wondered if their real need was here and now rather than in some distant heaven. However, such disturbing thoughts didn't last long; I was a preacher, not a social worker, and so I preached!

After my year in Klerksdorp I went back to Cape Town, had a bit of a holiday, celebrated my twenty-first birthday and was then sent to Pondoland East. I had never heard of Pondoland East; I didn't know where it was or what was expected of me. Looking back, I'm astonished that the church would put their trust in so young a person in a somewhat isolated area.

Getting there entailed travelling to Umtata and then a hair-raising bus ride down a winding road to Port St Johns. The rolling hills, the huts, the goats and the red dust were wholly foreign to someone from Cape Town. I hadn't a clue where to go. I had been given one name, that of a layman who worked in the bank, so I said to the bus driver, 'You can't just drop me off at your usual place, you must take me to the bank.' He looked at me strangely, but agreed. And so, at last, this large bus drew up outside the bank, I got off with my luggage, went in and spoke to Mr Floweday. He was embarrassed to see me arriving in this way and asked me to wait a while, before escorting me to a little boarding house.

It was run down and, worst of all, my accommodation was not even in the main building, but in a small rondavel in an overgrown garden. I was dismayed at my first sight of the dark, round hut with no electric light, an abundance of 'wildlife' in the form of a large iguana that emerged from under the sagging bed, huge moths and various creepy-crawly creatures. Coming from urban Cape Town and being somewhat squeamish, it was all a great shock. However, I settled in and then met with some of the local church leaders. They told me that I would be residing in Port St Johns, but would also have to minister to the white communities of Lusikisiki, Flagstaff and Bizana. In addition, I would be involved in the school for the coloured community living outside Lusikisiki: I would be chairman of the school committee and the principal would report to me.

At the age of twenty-one, with six church congregations and a large school to take care of, the real question was: 'How do I get to all these places?' The church leaders answered, 'Well, there's a motorbike in the garage, a 500 cc Matchless.' I had never ridden a motorcycle in my life and no one else seemed able to teach me, but I had to go to Lusikisiki a few days later, which meant crossing the mighty Umzimvubu River by pont and then travelling some forty-eight kilometres on rough, corrugated roads. So I went to the garage and confronted what appeared to be a glowering monster – sitting there, daring me to conquer it. I tentatively took the machine outside and tried to kick-start it. That worked, so I checked the petrol and the oil, then slowly mounted the beast and began to do a few circles. The bike fell several times; I burnt my leg on the hot tailpipe; I came dangerously close to cursing and swearing but, bearing in mind my position, tried my best to exercise patience.

I set off for Lusikisiki as arranged. Since I was to administer holy communion, I strapped a box of small glasses and the bottle of wine securely to the back of the motorbike. When I reached Lusikisiki I was covered with dust and, needless to say, on opening the box, I found that the glasses had shattered and the wine bottle was broken. From then on, I arranged for each congregation to have its own set of glasses and wine, so that I didn't have to risk my suit or the motorbike being bathed in communion wine each time I travelled.

Despite my uneasiness, the discomfort and the dismal living conditions, my two years in Pondoland East were a real experience, though I never came to terms with the dusty, rough roads and the often recalcitrant motorbike. I was a city boy, and felt alienated in the subtropical atmosphere and, despite the many miles we traversed together, that Matchless and I never bonded!

But Port St Johns was a beautiful town, quite small, with stunning scenery and beaches. I used to stand on the rocks overlooking Second Beach and practise preaching. I was a little startled to see the sharks gathering in the blue water below!

I made some friends, in particular a remarkably good artist, Cecil Thornley-Stewart. He and his family kindly invited me for dinner from time to time and introduced me, I think for the first time, to classical music. I experienced the magic of Bach and Mozart, Brahms and Beethoven, and many other great composers. This was the start of a lifelong love and passion for music. Ever since, I have worked to a background of classical music and listened for hours to the wonderful symphonies. Beethoven perhaps became my favourite, but I love all the great composers, and often think that Mozart's Clarinet Symphony would be a good choice to be played at my funeral.

Apart from finding one of the great joys of life in a little town called Port St Johns, a measure of sophistication began to smooth my rough edges. The Thornley-Stewarts' home was gracious, and when we first sat down at the table I felt gauche. Which knife to use first? But I learnt quickly, and being exposed to a number of beautiful homes in Pondoland East stood me in good stead.

The Thornley-Stewarts had a young daughter, Beryl, and I think they hoped we would hit it off. The parents never attended church services, but Beryl was there every Sunday without fail. However, during my time in Klerksdorp I had started a youth club that met once a week. One of those who attended was a sixteen-year-old high school pupil named Patricia McMillan. After matric, she went to Durban to train as a nurse at Addington Hospital. We had become quite close and promised to write to one another. We did so regularly and I visited her in Durban when I could. When she came to visit me in turn, the invitations to the Thornley-Stewarts dried up! Patricia and I became engaged four years after we met, when she was twenty.

I remained presumptuous and arrogant. One Christmas Day, with the church packed for an early morning service, among other remarks I made was: 'Today we receive many gifts from one another and we have great joy in giving and receiving, and God has given us the gift of his son, Jesus. But I wonder what you are giving him today? For some of you it is a hangover, a furry tongue, a late-night party. What else are you going to give him today?' I don't know how I had the nerve and the audacity to say that, or why they tolerated it, but my unforgiving message seemed to get through to people, and the congregations grew. If success is judged by attendance, I was a great success.

I also served the congregations of Lusikisiki, Flagstaff and Bizana. I would leave on a Friday and spend the weekend, preach, visit the sick, bury the dead and do the various other things that a preacher does. There was no money for hotels and no one offered me accommodation in their homes, so I stayed in the vestry, a little back room of the church, where there was a couch and a hand basin. I would cross the street to a hotel to use the bathroom and toilet (although I often went no further than the grass behind the church!), with the permission of the hotel owner, who was a member of the congregation. He never offered me a room either, but I was young and full of energy, and the lifestyle was manageable.

Soon after arriving in Pondoland East, I met the principal of a large coloured school. He was a fine man, much older than me, but my job was to pay the teachers' salaries, receive their reports and chair meetings of the school committee. I was a young white man from Cape Town, in charge of the education of hundreds of children and the welfare of dozens of their teachers. I felt shy and almost ashamed that I was doing this, but it was part

of my job, so do it I did. My church congregations were entirely white –
small, pale islands in a sea of blacks, who were catered for at the nearby
mission station. I visited it from time to time, but only for some company
with the missionaries and staff who worked there. I hardly had contact with
any black people at all, and made very little progress in understanding what
was happening in South Africa.

However, I had a glimpse of the serious issues at play when I met a
remarkable man by the name of Seth Mokotimi. Many years later, he would
become the first black president of the Methodist Church of Southern Africa,
but I met him while attending the Methodist Synod in Umtata, where he gave
one of the major addresses. I was spellbound by his eloquence, his passion,
his love, and I realised that this was the kind of black person that I had never
met in my life. I had grown up with domestic servants and garbage collectors
and sellers of snoek in the street, but I really didn't know anybody who was
not white.

Meeting Seth Mokotimi was an important milestone for me. I talked with
him and told him something of my growing dilemma, caused by a deepening
awareness of race relations in our country. I shared with him my confusion
and feelings of helplessness. In many ways I was fulfilled in my work as
a preacher and pastor, but gnawing at my heart was a concern that I was
working in the margins. Black people seemed so poor and uneducated –
should I become a missionary? Seth was kind and understanding, his response
gentle. He told me never to forget that to love God was to love my neighbour, and if I stayed true to this, I would be given the guidance I needed.
I never forgot this holy man and his sage advice, though it took me a long
time to understand that to love one's neighbour means that one also has a
responsibility towards him or her. Because I was so locked into the white
congregations and had almost no time to do anything else, it was a long while
before I did anything about acknowledging this broader duty. Nevertheless,
I owe a huge debt of gratitude to Seth, a man small in stature but with an
immense capacity for compassion and wisdom.

After he died in 1971, his widow visited us in Durban and presented me
with his Bible. She asked us to name our newborn son after her husband,
and he was duly christened Nicholas Adam Seth.

During my time in Pondoland East, I was also studying for my pro-
bationer exams. Every three or six months, sealed examination papers would
be delivered to my friend at the bank and he would put me in a room on my
own, open the envelope, give me the contents and collect my answers three

hours later. I studied by the light of a hurricane lamp, which in summer was extremely hot and attracted every insect and moth from Pondoland East, or so it seemed to me. To my utter astonishment, when the results were published by the church, my name was at the top of the list, so I must have been doing something right.

What I did find extremely difficult was battling with the motorbike, the backache I suffered on all those rough roads, and the dust and the dirt, which I couldn't stand. I finally told the church leaders that I really could not continue my work using that form of transport, so they decided to buy a second-hand car. 'Surely I should at least have been consulted? I should have seen the car before you bought it,' I said. 'No, no, it doesn't belong to you, it belongs to the church,' was the response. The motorbike was to serve as part payment for the car, so off I went to Umtata – a far greater distance than any I'd previously covered, but on an equally rough road – to pick up the car. On the way, I hit a pig. One might consider a pig quite a small animal, but it is solid. The Matchless went in one direction, I went in another, and the pig ran squealing into the bush. I picked myself up, dusted myself off and continued on my journey.

At the garage in Umtata, I saw what could only be described as a monstrosity. It must have been the oldest car in South Africa; certainly the oldest I had ever seen. I couldn't believe that this was the vehicle I'd been given. I had to drive it to Kokstad, then down to Bizana, where I had some appointments, and all the way back to Port St Johns. I had endless trouble starting the car and keeping the engine running. On the main road between Umtata and Kokstad, as I approached a long bridge over one of the many rivers, I noticed a man on horseback, just starting to cross the bridge. I tapped my hooter to let him know I was coming, although the car's engine made so much noise that he must surely have heard me from a mile away. The hooter jammed and this startled the horse. It bolted, ran the length of the bridge, stopped abruptly and threw the man into the river, my hooter blaring all the while. I was terrified of stopping, because I knew I would battle to restart the car, so I just kept going. I felt terrible. I knew the horseman was all right, but I should have stopped and apologised. It was some distance further before I was able to silence the hooter.

As I approached Kokstad I went down a very steep, winding road, Brooks Nek. There were a number of men working on the road, the usual black team with a white foreman. My hooter blared once again, this cacophony of sound announcing my arrival as people shook their fists at me, thinking

I was being smart or funny. I finally stopped the car close to the foreman, a large and somewhat belligerent Afrikaner, who swore and cursed at me in his language. I explained that the hooter was stuck and he told me to open the bonnet. As he reached in to try to pull the wires out to silence the hooter, the bonnet fell on top of him. The engine was as hot as hell. I have seldom heard such expletives, such absolute rage. He pulled out as many wires as he could, closed the bonnet and told me to get the hell out of there.

I had a number of other adventures in that car. On one occasion, the brakes failed totally and I went right off the road, in the dark, and came to rest against a hut. The poor occupants were terrified and came running out, but they kindly called all the neighbours and helped to move the car to the side of the road. I slept there for the rest of the night and hitched a ride into Flagstaff the next day.

On my first visit to Bizana, I told everyone in advance that I would be travelling by car. A few kilometres from the little town, the car died on me. I didn't know what to do. Providentially, a man driving a team of oxen came along, the car was hitched up and, very, very slowly, I was pulled into Bizana, with half my congregation standing at the side of the road, smiling and jeering at the sight of this poor young pastor with the dreadful car.

During my two years in Pondoland I met some wonderful people, including traders, doctors, bank and postal officials. Many of them were kind to me and, despite my inexperience, put up with me. One of my most bizarre experiences occurred in Bizana. I was called to a home where the husband and father of several children had died of a heart attack. I went into the bedroom and saw a vast figure on the bed. He must have weighed at least two hundred kilograms.

I tried to comfort the family and told them that the local doctor would have to conduct a post-mortem to certify the cause of death. We couldn't find a coffin big enough to accommodate the deceased, so I arranged for the largest coffin available in Kokstad to be delivered. It arrived the next day and a number of us struggled to fit the recently departed man into it, but to no avail. It was searingly hot and the burial had to proceed, so we took some thick rope, wrapped it around the coffin and tied it tight. The lid didn't close properly, but it would have to do.

The coffin was carried into the small lounge and placed on four chairs. I started the funeral service, but was interrupted by a noise coming from below the coffin. My eyes almost popped out of their sockets; there was blood dripping down from the coffin onto the floor, the residue from the postmortem. A member of the family quietly placed a newspaper under the coffin but the spat-spat of dripping fluid was now even louder. I raced through the service and then, with great difficulty, the coffin was placed on the back of a truck, and, with me at the head, muttering verses from scripture, the mourners walked slowly towards the cemetery. The coffin, still secured by the rope, was placed on the supports over the open grave, but they could not take the strain and in a sudden, horrible movement, the coffin lurched sideways, the ropes snapped and the gory corpse fell out. I rapidly pronounced the benediction and left the family and friends to sort out the situation.

I came away from Pondoland East somewhat chastened. Life was much more complicated than I had ever imagined. I had more questions than answers and had developed a sense of disquiet about the political system in my country. When I tried, rather tentatively, to raise these issues with members of my congregation, they told me to steer clear of politics and stick to my job as a preacher and pastor.

CHAPTER 4

Degrees of progress

IN 1953, I WENT TO RHODES UNIVERSITY IN GRAHAMSTOWN TO obtain a BA degree in theology and biblical studies. At twenty-three, I was quite a bit older than most of the students, who had arrived straight from school. Because several of us were studying for the ministry, Livingstone House, where we stayed, was made up of younger and older men. The latter already had a fair amount of practical experience, and I think that assisted us in adjusting quite quickly.

Being at university was incredible. It expanded my thinking and my life and I revelled in every aspect of it. I studied, worked hard, found the Greek quite difficult and philosophy a real challenge. But the theology and history and English seemed to come naturally. I played some sport – a little cricket and then soccer for the university – but couldn't play rugby, as my knee had been smashed a few years before. At Port St Johns, I'd been introduced to tennis by a young woman who was extraordinarily talented. It is a game that still excites me, both as a player and a spectator. Playing at Rhodes developed my game and reinforced my love for a wonderful sport – you need only one other player to have a match, but doubles is also great fun.

In the 1950s, Rhodes was a small institution – about 1 000 students – and it was relatively easy to represent the university in many sports. I managed to get selected as goalkeeper for the water polo team, which played matches all over the Eastern Cape. One encounter in East London didn't finish until early evening. We travelled back to Grahamstown with the swimming team in a covered truck. We were all tired, cold and squashed together. A fellow student was lying next to me, and we shared a blanket. The weariness, the need for warmth and the proximity led us to hugging each other and kissing passionately. As a theology student, I had an overdeveloped conscience, and the next morning I apologised profusely to her. It was a beautiful and in a sense innocent, natural experience, but I felt I had committed a dreadful sin.

More important than sport, however, was the challenge to my own fundamentalism that began during my time at Rhodes. My personal faith remained strong – prayers every morning, I read my Bible every day and went to church regularly. I was passionate about my faith, loved preaching, and used every opportunity to persuade others to embrace Jesus Christ as their personal saviour and God as the Creator and Father of all humankind. But at Rhodes I not only began to listen attentively to some distinguished lecturers, but also had many heated discussions with my fellow students, and in some ways I slowly began to change.

When I arrived, my approach to the Bible was quite literal, almost as if God had dictated it word by word. I based my thinking on that and refused to budge. I felt that the moment you made any kind of compromise as to what was literal and what was poetry, you were on the slippery slope.

There is a verse in the Bible that had influenced my approach and I preached on it often. It is the declaration by Jesus that 'I am the way, the truth and the life, no man cometh to the Father but by me.' This is an extremely exclusive claim. If you didn't come through Jesus, then you were doomed. That was my interpretation. I could consign all Hindus, Buddhists, Muslims and Jews to perdition, because they hadn't come through Jesus. But now I began to consider that perhaps Jesus appears in different forms in various religions. The doubt was there, and I learnt a great deal, becoming perhaps a little more tolerant and a little less arrogant, a lot more speculative in my thinking and certainly more inclusive in my approach, no longer condemning people to hell by the truckload.

I also began to read more widely, and one of the authors who affected me most was Dietrich Bonhoeffer, a Lutheran pastor and German martyr who was killed by the Nazis in 1944 at the age of thirty-nine. He had resisted them, participated in the plot to oust Hitler and stood up for the Jews; he was hanged two weeks before the British liberated Vlossenberg concentration camp.

While at Rhodes, I read some of his works, including the books *The Cost of Discipleship* and *Letters and Papers from Prison*. His courage and life considerably influenced my thinking, particularly in regard to the demand for discipleship. His distinction between cheap and costly grace, as set out in *The Cost of Discipleship*, helped me to shift from a sentimental idea of the Christian faith to a very strong focus on the lordship of Christ. He also advanced the idea of a 'worldly religion'. To be Christian in the modern world was neither easy nor cheap, especially in South Africa.

The second influence on my thinking at Rhodes was the debates and discussions I had with people around me who were training for the ministry, as I was, and also with other students, who were sceptical about those of us studying theology and often made fun of us. I engaged them and discussed with them some of the great, deep certainties I had about God and life and death, and began to be less dogmatic, even though I would never have conceded at that time that I had any real doubts.

A challenge that opened my eyes a little wider to the racist policies of our government was presented by the visits a handful of us made to Fort Hare University, in the nearby hamlet of Alice. We went by truck and met with black students to discuss common interests, naively thinking that they would be pleased by our overture. Not a bit of it. They were, understandably, much more radical than us, and our discussions were decidedly uncomfortable. They gave me an insight into the other side, and for the first time I began to see South Africa through the eyes of black people. I didn't find it easy to cope with this, and our visits to that university didn't continue for very long.

Even as a student, I participated in formalities at the local church and I preached and taught during every vacation. Because I had no money, I had to work. I couldn't afford the price of a bus or train or air ticket, so I hitchhiked everywhere. I had some marvellous experiences. Sometimes it was quite difficult; you could stand at the side of a road for hours, or find yourself sitting on the back of a refuse removal truck, but it was all part of gaining experience. I even slept in a police station one night.

During the holidays I would look after a church, enabling the resident minister to go on leave. One such experience was in Kroonstad, a lovely town with a beautiful river running through it. It was a fairly small church, with a rather sleepy congregation, and I came to know a number of the members. I also played cricket while there. During one match, I bowled a bit, but I was keen to get some runs, and thought being given out leg before wicket after scoring a couple was a bad call.

On a return visit to Kroonstad many, many years later as an older and more senior churchman, I recalled that match right at the start of my sermon. I still felt that the umpire's decision had been a bad one, I said. Almost immediately, a man stood up in the middle of the congregation and said firmly: 'You were absolutely plumb lbw! I was the bowler!'

Because I was young and ambitious and in Kroonstad for only three weeks on my original visit, I could set a different pace from that of the usual minister. By the time I left, the church was packed, but I didn't endear myself to the resident minister, who was upset that so much had happened in his absence.

In addition to the invaluable insights and transformation of my understanding of the Christian faith for which Rhodes was responsible, something happened there which changed my life. I met the woman who was to become my wife, Jennifer Clark. She was from Rhodesia (now Zimbabwe), studying at the teachers' training college and I saw her first at the local cinema, or, as we used to call it, the bughouse. Lots of students used to go there on a Saturday night. I was sitting towards the back when I saw this stunning, very young blonde in the front, talking and gesticulating with a broad, beaming smile. I didn't know who she was, but I said to myself then and there that I was going to marry her.

It was an extraordinary experience to feel so absolutely certain that Jenny was the woman I wanted to share my life with, but first I had to try to get to know her. I discovered she was going out with someone called Don Black and I approached him and said I would really like to meet Jenny. He absolutely refused to introduce me. So I literally accosted the two of them as they were strolling in the nearby botanical gardens, and asked if they would like to join me for tea. Poor Don. What could he say? Jenny blushed furiously and accepted the invitation. We had tea and scones and that gave me an excuse to contact her again. She made it quite clear to me that she did not consider Don a serious suitor, and so we started seeing each other. Our time together was limited. The training college had strict rules and she had to be in quite early every evening, while I was in the middle of my final exams. But even the little time we could share confirmed the feeling I had when I first saw her.

However, there was a complication that had to be dealt with. I had become engaged, about three years earlier, to Patricia McMillan, whom I had met in Klerksdorp. Due to the physical distance created by the different paths we were following, we had seen little of one another, so after meeting Jenny, I wrote to Patricia and told her that, although we were due to be married at the end of the year, I was having some doubts. She said that she, too, was having second thoughts and we agreed to meet in De Aar, where she was attending a special nursing course, to discuss our situation.

As sure as I was about my feelings for Jenny, I obviously felt deeply about this other relationship and my responsibility. That evening, when Patricia gave me back her engagement ring, the reality of the situation hit me. We both wept, said our goodbyes and I went and sat at the deserted, miserable railway station at De Aar – a godforsaken, desperate place – waiting for a train. I sat there for hours, feeling extremely sorry for myself and very much alone. But, with the resilience of youth, I decided to try to put it all behind me, and I have to admit I managed rather well, because as soon as I got back to Grahamstown, the first person I went to see was Jenny, and I told her what had happened.

She was only seventeen when we met, and when I was sent to Pietermaritzburg on completion of my studies that year, she stayed on at the teachers' training college. I returned to Grahamstown for graduation a few months later and she drove back with me to Pietermaritzburg. I was lucky enough to have my mother live with me in Pietermaritzburg for two years, and I know that she enjoyed the fact that we were together again.

My relationship with Jenny deepened and, later in the year, I visited her family's farm in Rhodesia for the first time. This entailed facing their dog named Danny, who was so huge that when he put both his paws on my shoulders he looked straight into my eyes. I knew I had to be brave and show that I was worthy of Jenny, so I just closed my eyes and hoped to God he wouldn't bite me. Happily, I passed the test.

The next morning, I had to go horse riding, which I had never done before. I managed to survive that too, and was generally accepted by Jenny's mother and the rest of the family, but I never did master the art of riding. At first I rode Biscuit, a docile creature and slow of foot, but I then graduated to Mistress Quickly, a former racehorse. We rode along the cotton trail and, when we turned for home, she went berserk and galloped as though we were being chased by demons. I managed to hold on, but that was it for me and the horses.

I had worked hard at Rhodes. I had to, bearing in mind that I had left school at fourteen and had studied for my matric at night school and then by correspondence. I didn't have the background that many of my colleagues did, so I worked twice as hard, staying in the library late into the night and early morning, learning a bit of Hebrew and quite a lot of Greek.

I managed to achieve a very good degree, so much so that Professor Hewson – the very man who had inspired me to study further in the first place – suggested that I should apply for a Rhodes Scholarship. I did, but unfortunately my application was received a few weeks after I turned twenty-five, the cut-off age, so I didn't qualify. I was deeply disappointed, because I wanted to study further. I wanted to get a master's degree. I wanted a PhD. Hewson was most helpful and said he would keep in touch with me and try to solicit funds from people sympathetic to the work of the church, so that, one day, I could get to Oxford.

My time at Rhodes was one of enlightenment, challenge and fun. Many years later, I was proud to be awarded an honorary law doctorate by my alma mater. In fact, I was fortunate enough to be awarded seven honorary doctorates, five of them from America, but the two I prize most are those from Rhodes and the University of Cape Town.

With Oxford out of my reach, at least for the time being, I went to Pietermaritzburg at the end of 1956 as the minister of two churches. As before, my congregations were white, but I did preach to Indian and black communities regularly and served as chaplain to the Pietermaritzburg campus of Natal University, which I found particularly exciting. After six long years of training, I was ordained as a minister, and, in May 1958, Jenny and I were married on the farm in Rhodesia. It was a beautiful place. Later, after we had children, many of our vacations were spent there, walking, climbing, swimming and shooting guinea fowl. Those were glorious times.

After Jenny and I were married, my mother retired to a flat in Cape Town, but until her death at the age of eighty-one in 1985, she spent three months of every year with us. Our eldest son, Andrew Michael, was born nine and a half months after our wedding. His birth was a marvellous experience; I was well known in Pietermaritzburg because of my work at the university and visiting patients in the hospital, so the staff were extra kind to us and seemed to think that this was a great event. It was.

I stayed with Jenny as long as I was allowed to, and half an hour after our son was born, I held him in my arms. I was twenty-eight years old and becoming a father was a deeply moving experience that filled me with a tremendous sense of humility and thankfulness. In the great joy and grati-tude of that moment, there was no hint of the ordeal and suffering that Andrew would be subjected to, twenty years later, in part because he was his father's son, but also because of his own commitment to fight apartheid.

My work with the various congregations in Pietermaritzburg went well, but every now and then I was reminded of the cruel policies of apartheid which were responsible for the inequality of South Africans. An Indian colleague in the church told me the history of his people, who had been brought to South Africa as indentured labourers. I found his account of the discrimination they continued to face so disturbing that I raised the subject with my white fellow ministers in Pietermaritzburg. They played it down, one saying, 'Well, of course he is exaggerating. They do very well, actually, and sometimes the Indian people, you know, can be quite difficult.' I was quite staggered at that, stored it away and continued to think about it – but, as always, I went on with my work.

The last thing that I had time for in Pietermaritzburg was discussion of my growing doubts; it certainly was not for me to destroy, in any way, the faith of people who believed deeply in the traditions of Christianity. I worked in the parish ministry for three years, proclaiming the Christian message day in and day out, working alongside people who found themselves in all kinds of human conditions. Some of them were quite poor, others from the middle class; some were bewildered, others battling with such questions as abortion or their own homosexuality; some were struggling to bring up their children, others facing the challenge of drugs and alcoholism, a serious illness or death.

My work as the university chaplain took up a lot of my time, and I also had to visit many of the old-age homes and the local mental asylum in addition to looking after two fairly large congregations. Visiting the asylum on Sunday afternoons was especially trying. In the middle of a simple homily, one of the inmates would pretend to take a photograph of me, a woman would blow kisses, others would fall asleep and yet others would simply walk about. It was all so sad; although I tried hard, I could never close the gulf between us. They seemed to be in a world of their own and I couldn't help thinking that nothing I said or did made any difference to their existence.

At the end of two years, I was sent to Durban North, a major congregation, with a large number of young people. It served a thriving upmarket community and the church grew and grew until I could barely cope. Meanwhile, I had heard from Professor Hewson that a few wealthy Methodists had collected funds that would assist me to go to Oxford University. I was thrilled and very grateful to Hewson and an anonymous group of benefactors, whose names I never knew. I had applied to further my studies at Mansfield College, and been accepted. One did not seek admission to Oxford as such, but to the college of your choice, and if you were not accepted, you could not study at the university. I was to spend nine months in Durban North before Jenny, Andrew and I would leave for Oxford. It was a very exciting time. I sold everything I could, including my car, cashed in a couple of insurance policies and we prepared to sail on the *Windsor Castle* to a new adventure in England.

PART II

New horizons

CHAPTER 5

On the banks
of the Cherwell

B EFORE OUR DEPARTURE, AN EVENT HAPPENED THAT NEARLY
made me abort our going. On 21 March 1960, the Sharpeville massacre,
in which more than sixty protesters against the pass laws died at the hands
of the police, shocked the nation. I felt that at this momentous time in our
history I should stay at home and be useful in the transition which I thought
was upon us.

There were demonstrations all over the country, including Durban.
Thousands of blacks paraded down West Street, making it impossible for
me to leave my office. I phoned Jenny to see if she was safe. She was alone
with our small son, and was terrified.

'You must come home! There is a group of black people coming towards
our house and they are carrying pangas!' I felt helpless and tried to think
of someone to call. Then Jenny continued, 'Alex, it's all right, they are only
cutting the grass!' That's how edgy we all were.

It was a turning point in the history of South Africa. I sought the advice
of my former superintendent, John Wallace. 'You must go to Oxford,' he
said, 'The struggle for freedom is going to take many, many years. After your
training overseas, you will be better equipped to be useful.' It was with a
heavy heart and mixed feelings that we set off, but it was one of the wisest
decisions we ever made.

This was the first time we had travelled outside Africa and we had an
absolutely marvellous time on the ship, which was on its maiden voyage.
We met a number of other South Africans who were also on their way
to Oxford or Cambridge and we maintained those friendships for many
years. We arrived at Southampton with our luggage, including a baby's bath,
beds, pots and pans and various other household goods. We took a train
to London and then another to Oxford. I didn't know where to go or where
Mansfield College was, and had the cheek to call the bursar and ask him
please to meet us at the station. He very kindly arrived on his bicycle
and showed me where the taxi rank was. We took a taxi to Staunton Road,
followed by the bursar on his bicycle.

Because I was married, we didn't stay in the college itself, but in a tiny

41

house that was made available. It was small and poky, but it was ours. It was very cold and the only source of heat was the fireplace. If the fire went out we had no hot water, so we had to keep it going all the time. Often we failed because we hadn't any experience of living this way, and we had so little money.

I bought a bicycle and pedalled down Headington Hill to Mansfield College. There I met the principal and the tutors and went to the library to start my life as a student. I felt very insecure. Rhodes had been a glorious experience, but the standard at Oxford was much higher and the demands far greater. I had to work like hell just to keep up with some very bright students who had done their A levels, as well as far more Greek, Hebrew and Latin than I had ever seen. They were much younger than me and didn't have families, so they could devote all their time to their studies.

Every student had an individual tutor in each subject. My subjects ranged from biblical studies, Hebrew and Greek to the history of the Christian church, which included readings in Latin. One of my tutors was Professor George Caird. He was a brilliant scholar, but could be intimidating. I would go to his study and, after he had poured two glasses of sherry, he would ask me to read my essay, a completely new experience for me. He would take notes while I read. On the first occasion, I was taken aback when he closed his notebook and was gazing out of the window by the time I reached page three or four. This happened several more times, but it simply made me try harder.

In the rarefied atmosphere of the English-speaking world's oldest university, I had to ask some pretty tough questions relating to my understanding of the Christian faith. It was particularly challenging as I studied in great detail the first three hundred years of the history of the Christian church. I discovered that there had been serious debate on whether Jesus was man or God or man/God, on whether God could become flesh, from the earliest times. These were questions that had first been asked hundreds of years ago, since the death and resurrection of Jesus, and the debate continues to this day.

At Oxford I began to be challenged by some of my fellow students, who were extremely critical of the South African government's apartheid policies. I didn't believe in the policies – I opposed them – but I had done very little about it. I hadn't taken much of a stand. Because it was my country, I had mixed feelings. I felt I had to defend South Africa, though not the apartheid policies, and so I tried to explain the complexity of the situation:

the small white community, beleaguered and fearful, the huge majority of blacks – the usual excuses. Slowly but surely, I realised there was no substance to my argument, that I had no leg to stand on, and at student meetings and the like, I began to be much bolder in my denunciation of apartheid.

Gazing at my country from a distance was a transforming experience. I realised as never before that our racist policies were totally wrong and evil. The feelings I had about loving God and loving one's neighbour had crystallised. Seth Mokotimi's words became my reality: how could you possibly say you loved God, when you were treating the vast majority of people like third-class citizens?

I began to understand the gravity of the repression and to appreciate that there were many, both in South Africa and elsewhere, who were sick and tired of the racism and inequality they had endured and were starting to turn towards the armed struggle. This didn't come easily to me. My understanding of the Christian faith at that point was that one should be a peacemaker and abhor violence, wherever it took place, but I began at least to grasp why people were being driven to the alternative. In a tiny little way, I tried to make a contribution in the midst of my studies. I tried to warn people in England that they should be far tougher on South Africa and its policies rather than simply going along with them. Trade between the two countries was highly developed and many people from Britain went to South Africa on holiday. They didn't see the townships; they didn't see what apartheid was doing to so many people. They simply enjoyed the climate and the people they came in contact with, the fine hotels, good roads and infrastructure.

I learnt an enormous amount at Oxford, and I think Jenny and our son found the experience exciting as well. I played a lot more cricket and tennis – on grass for the first time, a wonderful experience – and represented my college in both sports. My performance wasn't great, but it was of a fairly high standard and I learnt a great deal on those long and enjoyable summer evenings when the sun was shining.

Towards the end of my stay, our second child, Kathryn Louise, was born. It was a grey November day. We went to the hospital and, to my astonishment, I wasn't even allowed to stay with Jenny. At least in South Africa I had been with her until the last possible moment, and held Andrew in my arms half an hour later. In England, however, I was told in no uncertain terms that I should go home and wait for a telephone call. They were tough and rigid, so I went home and waited and waited. Finally the call came, and I rushed back. There was my daughter, crying and crying and crying. Jenny was exhausted, but both of us were thrilled to have a daughter to join our son.

My final exams were extremely difficult and demanding, something of a trial by ordeal. We wrote morning and afternoon for about five days, all dressed up in our gowns and white collars, black suits and shoes, in a hot room with scores of other students. I wrote my final paper – three hours of Greek – on a Friday and emerged, blinking against the sunlight, at about 6 p.m. There was a band playing and friends in the street, and Jenny was there, waiting for me. After she went home, my colleagues whisked me off to go punting down the river. I was exhausted at the end of an arduous period, but they produced a huge leg of fatty pork and cheap wine. I drank a great deal of the wine and ate a lot of the pork and was sick as a dog. I couldn't get home that night and stayed at the college.

The next morning, I awoke to the sound of a spade scraping on cement just outside my window. I thought I was being stabbed. Then I had to face my wife, who was furious that on such an important night I had gone off with my student friends while she was left on her own. She didn't want to talk to me, but I pleaded with her to come and fetch me. She finally relented and I went home and had to do a great deal of penance, but I wouldn't have missed that night. It was part of Oxford life, a long-held tradition and something I would never forget, despite being thoroughly sick in my head and stomach! That was the end of a wonderful period at Mansfield College, and, some years later, I was thrilled to be made a fellow of the college.

I was extremely lucky to have gone to Oxford. Perhaps that was what my mother meant when she said I was born with a silver spoon in my mouth. Serendipity seemed to shape my life on many occasions: being at the right place at the right time, meeting someone out of the blue who would point me in the right direction. I was and am a very lucky person.

But there were also many disappointments. I was devastated when I received my results after working so hard at my studies. There it was in black and white – a third-class pass. I couldn't believe it. I had expected an upper second, at the very least. I sank into a fit of deep depression and told Jenny that I was seriously thinking of throwing myself into the River Cherwell! Reading William Boyd's remarkable book, *Any Human Heart*, many years later, I was comforted to note that his character, Logan Mounstuart, also managed only a third-class degree: 'He was unable to explain how he had performed so badly, and how misconceived his confidence in the result had been.'[1]

At the time, of course, I had to pick myself up and decide what we should do next. The church wanted me to return to South Africa, but I wanted to study further. My choice was to remain at Oxford and proceed with my doctorate, which would require me to move straight into writing a thesis, or go to some other part of the world. I thought Holland would be a good place to be, because it would give me a link with the Afrikaners who were in power in South Africa and equip me to get closer to them, in order to try to make some contribution to change and transformation. We travelled to Amsterdam and I was interviewed by Professor Berkhof, a famous academic. I attended one of his classes and, after an interview, I was accepted.

Back in England, and by pure chance, I went to London and attended a lecture on Dietrich Bonhoeffer. I listened to Professor Frans Hildebrand, a German who had fled his land and gone to London because he was one-quarter Jewish and knew he was destined for the concentration camps. He had known Bonhoeffer well and was now teaching at Drew University in Madison, New Jersey. I talked with him after the lecture about Bonhoeffer and he asked me what I was doing. He suggested I should go and study with him at Drew. I had never thought about going to America and it seemed impossible, but Hildebrand said he was sure that a scholarship could be arranged.

A week or ten days later, I received a cable telling me that I had been granted a scholarship to study at Drew. I would be an assistant to one of the key professors, which would bring in a little bit of money, and they would provide an apartment on campus for the first year. This was astonishing, and yet another example of the good fortune that came my way so many times. So we decided to go to America. Until our departure, I taught at Windsor, a beautiful place where Queen Elizabeth has a residence. I was a tutor to students trying to get into Oxford and Cambridge. We lived in an old coach house and I studied German and French, which I needed for my entrance exams for Drew University.

CHAPTER 6

Theology
and civil rights

W E SAILED FOR AMERICA IN THE OLD *QUEEN MARY*, STEERAGE
class. I could practically hear the water lapping against our cabin
walls. We had to climb hundreds of stairs to get anywhere. With a small baby
and a little boy, it was difficult, but the voyage was relatively short.

I remember with nostalgia arriving in New York harbour early in the
morning, gliding past the Statue of Liberty and being aware of all that it had
meant to so many millions of people who had come to America to seek
a new life. We were met by friends and whisked off to the lovely town of
Madison and Drew University, which was set in a New Jersey forest. Our
apartment was tiny, with one small bedroom, but it was ours, and it had
central heating, which was so different from our sufferings in the house
in Staunton Road, Oxford. We were on campus, which meant that we could
participate in all that the university had to offer.

I soon discovered that the American students all had jobs. Some mowed
the lawn or worked in the library, while others assisted professors, but everybody had a source of income. As assistant to Professor Carl Michalson,
a renowned theologian, I learnt an enormous amount, not so much about
theology, but about how to be a theologian, to think, to form and stand by
opinions, to demonstrate those beliefs and to argue and defend them. Drew
University was another amazing experience.

There were entrance exams and comprehensive exams lasting four to
six hours each before you could even submit the proposal for your thesis,
which had to be accepted by three professors. Then the thesis had to be
written. It was a long, long journey.

In my second year, I was appointed as the part-time pastor at a small
church in a rural, sparsely populated village called Pond Eddy, set on the
banks of the Delaware River. The area was called the Black Forest and many
of the villagers were of German extraction. Pond Eddy was 112 kilometres
from Madison and I spent Monday to Thursday at the university and the rest
of the week in the village. We had a small house alongside the whitewashed
church. Jenny, Andrew and Kathy stayed there on their own for most of the

week. It was a tough, lonely and challenging time for them, especially in the long, dark, snowy winters. But the local people were extraordinarily kind, cared for my family and were always stopping by with homemade breads, cakes, fruit and other treats. It was a close-knit community of unassuming people, few of whom had been to college. It was a helpful exercise for me to try to translate the rarefied theology and philosophy I was immersed in to very ordinary folk on a Sunday morning.

I think it was at Drew that I first began to really struggle with a personal faith. I had to write a major essay on Christology and Professor Michalson rejected my first offering out of hand.

'This is about Christology,' he said. 'You have carefully documented all the views expressed by other people, but you are a theologian in training. What is your theology of Jesus Christ?' This was tough. I had a second stab at the assignment, but he wasn't impressed with that either. My third offering finally seemed to meet with his stringent demands.

I was beginning to ask myself, 'Who is this Jesus, for me and for the world?' I was caught up in exploring systematic theology at an extremely deep level, but at the same time I was a student minister, preaching to a small rural congregation. I certainly didn't want to pass on my doubts to the good people of Pond Eddy and nor did I want to rob them of their faith, which was straightforward and conventional. I tried very hard to be honest in my preaching and teaching, but still clung to the old biblical and theological language, imagery and concepts.

At the same time, my thinking was becoming strongly influenced by the American civil rights movement, which brought me face to face with some huge questions. The very people who in many instances violently opposed leaders like Martin Luther King were often right-wing Christians, who believed that they were the chosen race and that Negroes, as they were called in the 1960s, were subhuman. Dr King, who was a fairly traditional Christian, used Christian imagery in all his public speaking, yet was absolutely passionate about civil rights, particularly for black Americans. Who was right?

As I listened to the conflicting views, it was clear to me that King's was the authentic voice and that I really didn't want to be associated with the right-wing fundamentalists and their prejudice. Just as Seth Mokotimi had done, King reminded me that if you claimed to believe in God, you simply had to believe that all humanity were your brothers and sisters. I began to move quite decisively to becoming a Christian humanist, with far greater emphasis on the need to serve humankind. Jesus was still central to my faith, but he was no longer a prisoner of the written word, no longer confined to Nazareth. I encountered him in my neighbour.

Our third child, Jeremy, was born in the autumn – or fall – of 1964. It was a breech birth, an anxious time, but we had excellent medical care at the nearby Port Jervis Hospital. We now had three small children and not much money; we were far from home, but we were happy. The cosseted life in South Africa seemed a lifetime away.

We had a small black and white television set which, more often than not, was on the blink. I used to climb the hill at the back of our cottage to try to straighten the antenna to improve the picture. It was on this set that we watched, aghast, as Jack Ruby shot and killed Lee Harvey Oswald in November 1963. A few days earlier, I had been sitting in a dentist's chair when I heard with horror and despair of John F Kennedy's assassination. Like millions of other young people, I was attracted by the new style of politics under his administration and believed that the new Camelot was being ushered in. I wasn't American, but I wept that day, along with so many others in the USA and around the world.

One of the highlights of our time in America was a meeting with Martin Luther King. I had been asked to try to persuade him to travel to Cape Town on behalf of the student representative councils at both the universities of Cape Town and Natal. I managed to get an appointment to see him when he visited Drew to deliver a major speech. I listened to him with awe. He was an amazing orator, with a deep understanding of violence and non-violence. I met with him for a brief half-hour and urged him to go to South Africa. His reply was swift and strong: 'I have too much to do in my own country. I cannot leave. But you must go back to your country, because there is much work to be done there.'

The second choice of speaker was JFK's younger brother Bobby, and again I was one of those asked to approach him. Through a contact in the US Democratic Party, I managed to see Kennedy in Washington for all of seven minutes. When I put the request to him, he replied, 'What difference can I make?'

'You can give young South Africans hope and courage,' I responded. When he did visit South Africa in June 1966, he did just that. I was back in the country by then and attended the huge rally at the University of Cape Town. Little did we know that, just two years later, he too would be killed by an assassin.

My time in America was probably the start of the radicalisation of my thinking about race and ethnicity. I participated in the Selma March, I helped to desegregate a barbershop and a small soda fountain where we had ketchup and chairs thrown at us. I was among the 200 000 people in Washington who listened to Martin Luther King deliver his famous 'I have a dream' speech. It affected me deeply and I began to see what was happening in America, through a South African lens. I never doubted that I would return home, and became increasingly determined that my role in South Africa would be to try to do everything possible to rid my country of the blight and curse of racism and apartheid. All my studies became focused in that direction. All the discussions, debates and marches in which I took part pointed towards two questions: What does this say about South Africa? What does this mean for me and my family?

We had intended staying in New York until I had completed my studies and submitted my doctoral thesis. However, Jenny's sister Bridgie informed us that she was getting married on the farm in Rhodesia and was keen for us to be involved in the ceremony. I was to take part in the service, Jenny would be one of the bridal attendants, Andrew the pageboy and Kathy a flower girl. We thought about her request for a long time, and decided that we would advance our departure from America in order to attend the wedding. Afterwards, I would return to New York alone and complete my work as quickly as possible, so that we could be reunited as a family.

The trip was uncomfortable, to say the least. With three small children, we were crammed into economy class on a so-called 'milk run' aircraft that seemed to land at every airport in Africa. It was a long, tedious and boring trip, and travelling hasn't changed a great deal since, except that there are fewer stopovers.

It was intoxicating to be at Gilnockie farm again. The drive from what was then still Salisbury was about thirty-two kilometres on a rough road, but as you turned into the farm road, it wound up a long hill, with a tennis court on the right and the stables on the left. On the plateau at the top of the hill was the sprawling brick farmhouse, with a magnificent view over the fields and the mountains. I felt some of the wear and tear and pressure of the United States fall from me almost immediately and we had a wonderful reunion with Jenny's family.

The wedding was quiet and peaceful. Bridgie married Arie Tresise, who had been managing a farm close to Gilnockie. Now they were going to the far north, where they had purchased a large tract of land for about a dollar an acre. Rhodesian prime minister Ian Smith wanted to open up the country, and of course he wanted young white farmers and their families to settle in the outlying areas. One can only imagine something of the feelings of black Rhodesians when they realised that white farmers were paying so little for large farms. The seeds of discontent and rebellion were sown long before the first shots of the Rhodesian bush war were fired.

After Bridgie's wedding, I stayed at Gilnockie for about ten days before returning to Drew University and a much changed domestic situation. I no longer lived with my family in a little house in the country. Instead, I had a single room in a dormitory and shared a small kitchen with four or five of my fellow doctoral candidates. We cooked together most evenings and, over wine and the occasional glass of whisky, debated the political and social issues facing the United States and the world. The arguments were often heated, but extremely stimulating. I was there for about eight months, working as hard as I could, writing and rewriting my thesis and teaching at Long Island University for a couple of days a week, which brought in some money. I had planned a longer stay, although the separation from my family was hard, both for them and for me. However, I received a letter from the secretary of the Methodist Church of Southern Africa telling me that the post of general secretary of the Youth Department was vacant, and that the church would very much like me to accept it. But I would have to return to South Africa almost at once.

I thought about the offer for a long time. With my clashing theological ideas becoming more radical by the day, it would be all but impossible for me to serve a typical congregation, whereas this was a national post. Despite the fact that I had still not completed my thesis and regretted the feeling that I had come so close but had not reached the end of the race, I accepted the appointment. As it happened, I was able to go back to the United States late in 1968 and completed my doctorate the following year.

As always, returning to Gilnockie was a pleasure, but the reunion with my family was extremely difficult for all of us. The children had been attending the little village school, where Jenny had been teaching, and they had been leading a somewhat idyllic life on the farm, far removed from the world that I had been in. I found it hard to adjust and I know that Jenny had almost dreaded my return, because of the challenges of starting our relationship all over again.

Matters came to a head after we boarded a train in Salisbury to make the long and tedious journey to Durban. It was one thing to be reunited with three boisterous children on a farm; being confined in a small compartment was an entirely different situation. I behaved very badly. I became irritated and found it extremely difficult to cope with the rightful demands of the children. Jenny was really angry with me, and in the end she simply couldn't stand my sullenness and testiness any longer, and suggested that I should try to find an empty compartment so that I could come to terms with, as she termed it, my bad temper. So I did exactly that. I spent the rest of the journey shuttling between two carriages, sometimes taking one of the children back to my compartment with me.

It was a taxing and seemingly endless journey, made much worse when we crossed the border into South Africa. We pulled into a small railway station and I was horrified to see the apartheid signs boldly declaring 'Whites Only'. I had been away for five years, and was not prepared for this reminder of the ugliness of apartheid. Feeling deeply depressed, I wondered if I had made the right decision.

CHAPTER 7

Under surveillance

F OLLOWING MY RETURN TO SOUTH AFRICA IN 1966 AS GENERAL
secretary of the Youth Department, we spent seven years in Durban,
living in a small house in Evans Road, Umbilo. There were thirty-nine steps
up to the front veranda – not very helpful when you have three small children.
The tiny backyard was mostly under cement, but, despite that, the children
and I played cricket there, with a hard ball. The ball would regularly go over
the wall into the neighbouring yard and it was quite difficult to sustain the
playing time, but we enjoyed it. In particular, I think it was Andrew's introduction to cricket in this way that saw him show a lot of prowess in the game
at both junior and senior school in later years. Kathy withdrew very quickly
from our games after the ball hit her toe.

My work was extremely exciting. The Youth Department had a mandate
to be directly involved in and serve churches, Sunday schools, youth groups,
universities and colleges throughout the country. This afforded me a wonderful opportunity for contact with young people and an understanding of the
attitudes and thinking of white and black, coloured and Indian youngsters.
Although I tried to fulfil my responsibilities to the Sunday schools, my primary interest was the high schools and universities. When the first Methodist
missionaries came to South Africa, they very wisely didn't merely build
churches, but set up a chain of mission stations, mainly throughout the
Transkei, Natal and Eastern Cape. At these mission stations they built schools
and hospitals, so their approach was enlightened, to say the least, and the
church thus had a close connection with both the educational and medical
facilities. The Methodist Church also built up a long-standing relationship
with Fort Hare University, and Nelson Mandela stayed in John Wesley
College, named after the church founder, when he was a student there.

Of course, the young people with whom I spent a great deal of time
questioned some of the major theological tenets of the church's beliefs.
Does God exist? Is Jesus divine or human? Why does God allow suffering,
war, drought, earthquakes? Is there life after death? These are typical of the
questions asked by so many in their formative years. I welcomed the probing
and felt that everything was up for grabs, so we argued freely and strongly.

Throughout that seven-year period when I worked with young people of all ages and races, the link between faith and politics inevitably became a central theme. When we talked about the two great commandments – to love God and to love your neighbour – the politics of religion became very real. The fact that my neighbour was oppressed, and that many whites in my own denomination supported the dehumanising policies of apartheid, brought about conflict, not only among young people, but also within me.

My work involved a great deal of travel, but I enjoyed that and got to know many parts of the country I had never visited before. However, it also put a strain on our marriage. I was insensitive to this until I woke up before dawn one morning to find Jenny sobbing. Alarmed, I asked her what was wrong and she said, 'You don't love me, you don't care about the children, you obviously want a divorce.'

I was stunned. I said immediately, 'That's absolute nonsense. It's never entered my head. What are you talking about?' We spent the next few hours talking about our relationship, and my role as husband and father against the background of my regular absences, and I realised that there had to be a change. I tried very hard, although I'm not sure I always succeeded, but spent as much time as possible enjoying a deeper relationship with both Jenny and the children. I suppose this is the challenge of all parents who have busy professional lives and are away from home a great deal. I took solace in the fact that when we were together – sharing quality time – we certainly did have a great time, and the memories of our years in Durban, with the children attending the neighbourhood school, are choice, and we managed somehow to cope.

One of the areas in which I felt there was an enormous need for change was the curriculum used by Sunday schools throughout the country. I started a project that I called 'Breakthrough' which placed the emphasis less on how to teach and more on how people learn. I tried to introduce an experiential approach to teaching and put together a team that swiftly produced a curriculum. But it must have been at least ten years ahead of its time, and the criticism poured in. Those who grasped what we were trying to do welcomed and applied the curriculum, but there were many more who felt this was a departure from straightforward biblical stories and simply jettisoned the material that we made available.

It was around this time that I met John de Gruchy, who would become an eminent Bonhoeffer scholar in later years. He and his wife Isobel, Jenny and I and several others, including Athol and Pat Jennings, worked on the curriculum and were dismayed that we had not been able to sell the idea of starting where the child was, rather than the Bible stories, and helping to bring youngsters to those stories through their own immediate experience. This subsequently became a common approach to teaching, but at the time I was seen as a virtual heretic. John and I taught courses in contemporary theology and biblical studies at Natal University. I think we did this more because we missed teaching than because of the needs of others, but people flocked to the courses and we had a good few years offering adult education on two evenings a week.

Although I was general secretary of the Youth Department, one of my responsibilities was to offer a post-ordination training course for ministers. This brought together black and white clergymen from all over the country. The course was residential and, inevitably, discussions moved beyond theology, pastoral care, biblical studies and preaching practices to politics. I was quite appalled at the lack of political awareness among not only most of the whites, but also some of the blacks. Many of them were quite conservative, believing that religion and politics simply do not mix, as had I, when I was younger. As a result of the courses I devised, I believe a number of ministers changed their approach markedly, which inevitably influenced their ministry and preaching in the townships, suburbs and cities of South Africa. Accused by the church fathers of bringing politics into religion, I tried to demonstrate that politics is to be found on almost every page of the Bible itself, because politics is about people living together in justice and peace.

I worked closely with fellow ministers Enos Sikakane and Ernest Baartman, who was my co-secretary. We made a really good team, travelling the country to speak at youth days and rallies. I finally managed to persuade the church leaders to change the name of the Youth Department to the Christian Education Department, which gave us a wider mandate.

. Perhaps one of my better achievements during this period was establishing what I called the National Youth Leadership Training Programme. It was a simple idea, based on the American Peace Corps but restricted to service on the domestic front. I advertised the concept and battled to get funding, but finally we were ready for the first training course, which would see young people 'give one year of your life' by spending three months in residence and then nine months in different parts of the country.

I was excited by the number of applications from which we selected the first contingent. We were in residence at Botha's Hill near the Valley of a Thousand Hills. It was a fairly rudimentary youth campsite but it afforded accommodation, a kitchen, a small conference room and a sports field to a group of young men and women, black and white, from diverse backgrounds.

I had not realised how tough it was going to be. I had told all of the trainees to bring sports clothes with them, and will never forget the response of a young black man from Germiston. He called me in great distress, because he didn't know what sports clothes meant. The only clothes he had were those in which he was standing. So the first thing I did when he arrived in Durban was buy him a couple of pairs of shorts, khaki shirts and sandals, so that he could join in and relax with everyone else. It was yet another stark reminder of the huge gaps that existed between the different peoples of South Africa.

The training programme was somewhat radical. We covered biblical studies and theology, but also social work, psychology and – inevitably – politics. One of the near disasters involved a young nurse called Jane. I tried to impress on the trainees that they should really make an effort to understand the young people they would be working with – to stand in their shoes, as it were – in order to appreciate their individual circumstances and how best to approach them. Jane took this quite literally and decided that if you wanted to understand what a drug addict was going through, the best way was to take drugs!

I was beside myself when this came to my attention and tried to explain that less drastic and damaging action would suffice. She was adamant, however: if you wanted to understand someone with a drinking problem, you should drink; likewise with drugs. If people were poor, you should live in poverty. She was an absolute literalist. Finally, I asked: 'What are you going to do if you find someone who is serious about committing suicide? Are you going to attempt suicide to identify with that person?' That seemed to get through to her and she stopped her brief experiment with drugs and turned out to be one of our most effective young counsellors.

Athol Jennings and Ernest Baartman assisted me. Athol was a former Springbok miler, dedicated, committed and extremely capable, while Ernest, a black man, was wise and gentle, but also very strong. However, we needed more staff. When I was in the United States in 1969 to complete my doctoral thesis, I appealed to the Methodist Church there to assist us financially, so that we could add young Americans to our team. This resulted in Gus Kious, Tamie Hultman and Reid Kramer coming to South Africa. They were modern, aware of gender issues long before we were, and made an amazing contribution. They had also been politicised by the civil rights movement in their own country.

Inevitably, the fact that our courses were multiracial drew the attention of the security police. They raided our training site many times, often at three o'clock in the morning. They seemed to be more concerned about whether or not black and white students were sleeping with each other than with the political content of the course, but this didn't prevent them from confiscating a lot of our tuition material. They also took down the registration numbers of all the cars parked at the campsite, then contacted the parents of some trainees, especially the whites, saying, 'Are you aware of what is happening on this training course? It's nothing else but communism.' We received a number of agitated letters and phone calls from parents. I tried to reassure them, even inviting them to come and see for themselves what we were doing, but it was a troubled situation.

It wasn't long before the minister of the interior entered the picture and decided that he wasn't going to allow my American staff to stay in the country. He literally threw them out. I was incensed by this and made some tough statements in the press, which aroused concern among the church leaders. They felt that I was going too far and becoming too political, but I was not going to be stopped. We had every right to utilise the services of the young Americans, who were giving up their time and energy to assist us in our training. I knew that the reason behind their deportation was to weaken our efforts, but we persisted, and recruited other people to assist us.

I went to see the minister, Theo Gerdener, to lodge a personal complaint and plead with him to reverse the deportation decision. I will never forget that day. Seated behind the desk in his large office, he reached to pick up a file that obviously contained information about what I was doing. He opened it quickly and the top document fell on the floor, at my feet. I reached down politely to pick it up and, to my astonishment, recognised my own letterhead. It was a letter I had written to the World Council of Churches (WCC). Extremely angry, I demanded: 'How dare you intercept my mail and make copies of personal correspondence?'

The minister was suitably embarrassed and answered, rather lamely, 'Well, it's really not me. I get this from the security police.'

All the way back to my office, I wondered how on earth they had got their hands on my correspondence and decided to question my staff. A young black woman named Jean had been in the Youth Department for many years; she was a loyal and hard worker. In order to save time, she would take the outgoing mail to the main post office every day rather than posting it in an outlying mailbox to await collection. I called her in and asked what procedure she followed on her daily trips. To my dismay, she broke down and told me that every time she went to the post office, she was met by a member of the security police in plain clothes and taken to a room. There, our mail would be opened and copied before being placed back in the envelopes, resealed and handed back to Jean for posting.

I was aghast. She was such a gentle, good soul and I asked her, 'Why did you do this?' She told me that she was a single mother and that her teenage son had fallen into trouble because of housebreaking. The police told her, 'If you are prepared to work for us, we will pay you money and we will not prosecute your son.'

From the late 1960s and early 1970s, this was a pattern of life for many in South Africa. Jean was just another victim. Reluctantly, I had to let her go, but I neither berated nor condemned her. I just said, 'I am very, very sad and I hope this isn't going to have any adverse effect on your son. If we can be of any help to you in the future, please let me know.' It was a grim commentary on the terrible choices made by so many people who were bribed, blackmailed and harassed into abetting the government's implementation of its apartheid policies.

The training courses continued. We assigned a number of really good young people to many parts of the country and, every now and then, we would have a reunion and listen to their stories and the problems they faced. In my role as general secretary I travelled across the country and always made it my business to go and see these youngsters, wherever they were working. It was a small, modest attempt to counter the vicious policies of apartheid.

It was during this period that I had the great privilege of meeting a young medical student called Steve Biko. He was studying to be a doctor and was involved in the Young Christian Movement at the Wentworth Medical School, the only educational institution in South Africa attended by a significant number of coloured, Indian and black students at the time. From our very first meeting, he impressed me enormously. I invited him to go and meet the trainees at Botha's Hill, and he spoke to them. He was rather quiet – there was no fire and brimstone yet. We had long discussions and I remember the two of us travelling to various youth rallies, sleeping at the side of the road, because he was black and I was white, and we could not stay in hotels together. When you camp out in the open with someone, however, you get to know them quite well.

Steve also came to our home, where we would sit on the veranda, have a beer or two and talk about the future. As the months passed, it was clear to me that he was becoming increasingly unhappy as a medical student and wanted to get more deeply involved on the political front. He was fully committed to Black Consciousness and read widely on the subject, but also had a number of original ideas.

One evening, as we sat together talking, Steve said: 'Alex, this is the last time I will be coming to your house.' I was taken aback and asked, 'What's happening? Are you leaving?'

'No,' he said, 'it's not a question of staying or leaving, but relationships between white and black are unequal. We black people need to do some work on our own so that when we do come together, we can debate the future of our country as equals.' I was quiet for several moments, then I said: 'Steve, I hope this does mean that there will come a day when we can talk together as equals about the new South Africa, but I fear it is going to be a very long time.'

He was true to his word, and never came to our home again, but our paths would cross on various occasions before his untimely death in 1977.

My own brushes with the authorities continued. In 1970 I was appointed as the South African delegate for the World Council of Churches' newly instituted Programme to Combat Racism. It was an ill-considered appointment in many ways – the delegate should have been black, but perhaps the South African Council of Churches and the WCC felt it would be easier for me to travel. I went to Geneva and joined twenty people from around the world, including Andrew Young, the prominent American civil rights activist, and other vocal critics of apartheid, most of them black, but including some Scandinavians. Our task was to formulate a programme and ideas that would take a much tougher stand against racism anywhere in the world.

I had to renew my passport in order to attend this meeting but, instead of collecting it from the department of the interior in the usual manner, it was delivered to me by the security police. Two of them, in suits, came to my office in Durban and said they thought it would be unwise for me to go to Geneva, because the WCC had been infiltrated by communists, who wanted to cause chaos in South Africa. For my own sake, they said, I shouldn't go. I replied that I was determined to do so, because I felt that our voice ought to be heard on the subject of a programme against racism, and because I knew and respected many of the leading WCC members.

My uninvited visitors repeated their warning, but handed over the passport and took no further action. Like many South Africans, I suppose, I felt slightly paranoid and was convinced I was being watched, both while I was in my own country and even when I travelled to Geneva. I am quite sure that the security police had informants in the WCC.

In 1971, when the WCC wanted to hold a meeting in South Africa, it fell to me to negotiate with government on behalf of the member churches in the country. John Vorster, the prime minister, was infuriated by the suggestion. I urged him to allow the WCC unrestricted entrance to South Africa and to hold their meeting. He dilly-dallied and finally said they could come, but only as far as what was then Jan Smuts Airport, on the outskirts of Johannesburg. Delegates would not be allowed to enter the country as such. The WCC refused to accept these restrictions and opposition against apartheid escalated from Christian churches throughout the world.

Vorster's intransigence stemmed from the WCC's decision that it was permissible to assist liberation groups. Of course, this included the African National Congress (ANC) and the Pan Africanist Congress (PAC), both banned organisations. Vorster's view was that the assistance took the form of providing these organisations with arms in order to attack South Africa. The WCC's intention was to aid dependants of the liberation forces and offer educational opportunities to political exiles, but this might have been a fairly naive objective. Once you give money to a liberation movement, its leaders understandably make their own decisions as to how that money is used. It was a tough time for anyone who dared to stand up against the likes of John Vorster, the former minister of justice who had become the National Party's leader and premier of South Africa following the assassination of apartheid's chief architect, Hendrik Frensch Verwoerd, in September 1966.

Chapter 8

The highest office

WHILE I WAS ACTIVE IN THE MINISTRY, ELECTIONS WERE HELD annually for the president-elect of the Methodist Church. The highest office in the church was that of president of the Methodist Conference of Southern Africa. This title was subsequently replaced with that of bishop.

The idea of electing the president a year ahead of time was to give him an opportunity to get to grips with the work he would be required to do, so it was really a two-year appointment, followed by a third year as the ex-president of the conference. Traditionally, this office was reserved for men who had served for many years and, in a sense, it was intended to honour that person by entrusting the work of the church to someone who had spent a lifetime in its service.

To my utter astonishment, at the conference held in Johannesburg in October 1970, I was elected as the youngest ever president of the Methodist Church. Not only was I a mere thirty-nine years old, but the position I had taken on the race issue in particular, and my challenge to move the church into the world of politics, was not welcomed by many grassroots members, and certainly not by most of the church leaders. I think the reason I was elected despite this opposition is because it was a secret ballot, and the overwhelming majority of black representatives voted for me. Many of them had indicated that they supported my approach and encouraged me to continue. Nevertheless, I was overwhelmed and struggled to give the customary reply when the outcome of the voting was announced.

Apparently, a number of my senior colleagues were in despair and thought my election would be extremely bad for the image of the church. On the other hand, there seemed to be a number of younger white ministers and even lay people, together with a large black, coloured and Indian contingent, who rejoiced and possibly had too many hopes for what one person could achieve in the short space of two or three years.

The election changed my form of ministry. Athol Jennings took over as the general secretary of what had become the Christian Education Department and I devoted all my time to preparing for leadership of the church.

The most wonderful event that marked this period of our lives was

Jenny's announcement that she was pregnant. Our youngest son Jeremy was seven years old, and the last thing we might have imagined was that we would have a fourth child, especially at an extraordinarily complicated time, when the burden of office was heavy on me and the whole family. But, once we came down to earth, we were thrilled and thought it would be wonderful to have an addition to our already lovely family. Nicholas was born in November 1971. His arrival helped to ground us in the midst of the fuss and attention we were getting from all over the country in the wake of my election as president of the church.

I soon realised that the general secretary, Dr Stanley B Sudbury, was going to be a difficult opponent during my term as head of the church. He was suspicious of me, feeling that I was far too young, didn't have enough background and training, and especially that I was much too political. This made for an uneasy relationship, but I decided that I knew what was right and would have to pursue it, even if it meant taking on the greybeards.

Matters came to a head when I was conducting sessions of the Methodist Conference as president, in Durban in October 1971. It was late in the afternoon and we had a large evening meeting ahead of us. We were discussing a contentious topic and I was summing up the debate. I stated that I didn't think we were ready to put it to a vote, because there was still a lot of uncertainty and perhaps some delegates had not taken part, so we would adjourn and continue the debate the next day. Dr Sudbury was furious. He thought that he had sufficient votes to get the decision he wanted, and virtually accused me of misleading the conference. I was staggered, and when I went to my hotel room and thought about it, I realised the impact of his outburst. I phoned one of my senior colleagues, the Reverend Cyril Wilkens, and told him that I would not be presiding over the conference the next day unless I had an unqualified apology from the general secretary. This really set the cat among the pigeons and church leaders begged and implored me to change my mind. However, I insisted that this was my position.

At 8.45 the next morning, I waited in my room. I received a message that Dr Sudbury would be grateful if I could spare him a few minutes before the conference reconvened. Reluctantly, but without qualification, he offered an apology. I accepted it. We had the debate and he actually got what he wanted in terms of the decision reached. That, I think, helped him to understand that if you want to get the best decision, you should not rush the issue – but our relationship didn't improve.

When I look back and read the addresses that I gave during those two years, I detect my struggle to try to use non-religious language to express some of the deepest dimensions of my faith. It was agonising. I recall sitting in our lounge in Durban, writing and rewriting, and so great was the tension in me that I found I could hardly walk. My legs were almost paralysed, my arms heavy. I had to lie on the carpet to try to relax in between the writing.

It wasn't just the physical strain of a relatively young person in a position of leadership preparing five major addresses; it was also the spiritual struggle to be honest and yet to give people hope. My concern was not to call into question their faith but to try to interpret it in a new way. Clearly, there was within me a strong shift towards humanism, while retaining some of the biblical and traditional imagery. A good example of this was when I was speaking about the role of a minister in the Methodist Church in the modern world. I didn't discuss this using the generally accepted terms of prophet, priest or preacher. I talked about the minister as an interpreter, as a humaniser, a celebrator and an enabler. I urged that the training of the ministry should never be separate along the lines of race, should never be turned in on itself but should be open to every other discipline. I recall quoting HR Niebuhr, who reminds us, 'Theological inquiry is not something that can be added to humanistic and naturalistic studies; it needs to be constantly informed by them and to inform them.'[1]

Apart from presiding at many functions and meeting important people, both from South Africa and abroad, one of the advantages of being president was the opportunity to travel. In addition to South Africa, my responsibilities extended to the neighbouring states of Swaziland, Lesotho, Botswana and Rhodesia. I travelled to these countries, addressed their conferences and tried to understand something of the nature of their specific problems and challenges. The Rhodesian conference, in particular, was quite different from the rather tame South African gathering, and I was struck by the strong political speeches made by black Methodists to the north. Their views reflected both the depth of the divisions between Rhodesians and the inevitability of conflict.

The unfolding political situation in Rhodesia was difficult for Jenny's family, and they always felt that we were taking the side of the blacks and siding with the communists. In fact, my brother-in-law's favourite description of me was, 'You are a bloody communist!' (After independence the same brother-in-law, who could hardly be described as a wide-eyed liberal, said to me on more than one occasion, 'Yes, yes, things are going well, but what happens when Mugabe goes?' In retrospect, this is so bizarre, because two decades later nearly everyone wanted him to go.)

Within South Africa, I had travelled widely as the general secretary of the Christian Education Department, but being head of the church gave me entry to areas where I hadn't been before.

One of the decisions I made was that I would go to as many places as possible where people had been forcibly removed from their homes and dumped in the veld. I was appalled and aghast at the conditions: the lack of water and employment, the rudimentary housing. Each time I visited these areas and listened to the people, I held a press conference, so the forced removals made newspaper headlines week after week. This caused the state to be extremely uncomfortable and angry. It also angered many of our staunch white Methodists, who felt that, yet again, I was straying into the field of politics. I had to remind them that politics is about people and how they live, about their aspirations and hopes and dreams, and that if we consistently claimed that God was the Creator of all mankind, then these were our neighbours; they were God's children, and we had a responsibility towards them.

I began to notice that, wherever I went, the security police would turn up, quite brazenly. In fact, they parked outside our home in Durban every night. I don't know what they expected, but, when I was home, I would walk my dog in the evenings and stop at the small red Volkswagen and rap on the window. The security policeman in the car would reluctantly wind down the window and I would offer him a cup of coffee and ask if he was all right. He was very surly and abrupt and simply closed the window again.

We certainly did have a lot of visitors, some of them active in politics in other countries, and, of course, many of them black, which I suppose was uncommon at that time in a white suburb. The pressure from the authorities was evident, the attention clear, but we simply carried on with our lives as normally as possible.

On a number of occasions, I tried to set out my understanding of the role of politics in religion. It is generally true that most South African churchmen saw no relation whatsoever between their Christian profession and politics. The whole question was so charged with emotion that if any representative of the church dared to remind his institution of its responsibility in the political realm, he was in danger of being publicly vilified and at the receiving end of abusive letters and telephone calls, many of them anonymous, but all in the name of Jesus Christ.

I reminded my audiences that Aristotle defined politics as 'the striving of a community for the good life'. Another way of saying the same thing is that politics always has to do with 'keeping life human in the world'. Essentially, therefore, politics involves people. Politics has to do with housing, education, wages, job opportunities, pollution, old age pensions, hospitalisation and every other social ill or need. The compassion of Jesus for all people is evident on almost every page of the New Testament and I tried to say that the church, which is his body on earth, must surely demonstrate by its word and life the same caring for people.

In all the professional fields of my life, this has been my guiding principle: caring about other people. The Old Testament tells us that the community of Israel was called into being to be responsible for the world, with all its agony and pain, with all its joy and goodness. We hear cries from the depths of personal and collective guilt. We hear the calls of those bound by the intolerable situations of slavery, imprisonment and exile. In the midst of all these intensely deep needs, in these choking repressive structures, there comes a cry: 'O God of my deliverance, hear my voice, come down and deliver me from this oppression.'

What I tried to emphasise was that people of faith must apply, to the situations and structures of society they encounter, that which they time and time again have received from the Lord they profess to serve. It is here that the main difference between the priest and the prophet lies. Instead of focusing on prayer and religious ceremonies, Amos, Hosea, Jeremiah and other prophets emphasised justice and mercy: 'What doth the Lord require of thee, but to do justly, and to love mercy, and to walk humbly with thy God?' (Micah 6:8). It lies within the purposes of God to bring to an end exploitation, hunger and slavish subjection. He aims to make justice stream over the earth as the waters cover the sea, but he has chosen men and women, ordinary people, sometimes weak, sometimes strong, to be his hands and his feet and his lips.

Exactly the same is true of the New Testament. In Luke's account, Mary does not respond to the news that she is to bear a son by crooning sentimental poetry about love and life. Instead, she speaks about God's revolutionary activity in the world. In this strong song/poem, raw political and economic upheaval is depicted. The proud are scattered; the mighty are put down from their thrones; those of low degree are exalted. The hungry are filled with good things and the rich are sent away empty.

It is not surprising that Jesus should have found himself in trouble as soon as he began his ministry. The people who heard him at first became so angry that they tried to throw him off a cliff. Of course, in the end, he paid the ultimate price for his faithfulness to God by being crucified. There is a 2 000-year-old precedent for a preacher going beyond good words to good deeds, and then going beyond those to a direct challenge of both religious and secular authorities. Nor is it surprising that the followers of Jesus should find themselves in trouble because of their revolutionary words and actions. They were called disturbers of the peace, meddlers in business and politics, irreligious disturbers of worship, law-breakers. They were beaten by mobs, arrested, thrown into jail and sometimes put to death.

In short, the message that I tried so hard to deliver during that presidential year was that if you want to separate religion and politics, you have to reach for your scissors and start excising major sections of the Bible.

In his book *Dissenter in a Great Society*, William Stringfellow makes the point that 'The Church and Christians are not simply involved in politics because of the nature of politics as such, by which all are involved and abstinence is a fiction – but because they honour and celebrate God's presence and action in the world. Because they know that the world in all its strife and confusion, brokenness and travail, is the scene of God's work and the subject of God's love.'[2]

William Temple reminds us that 'Social witness is both a preparation for evangelism and the consequence of it.'[3] Dietrich Bonhoeffer powerfully wrote that a Christian is one who is 'there for others', and continued: 'The Church is her true self only when she exists for humanity. She must take her part in the social life of the world, not lording it over men, but helping and serving them. She must tell men, whatever their calling, what it means to live in Christ, to exist for others.'[4]

In his book *A Ringing Call to Mission*, Australian Alan Walker makes the same point: 'I wish I could be sure past mistakes are not being repeated. The servant church, which becomes merely an ambulance church caring for the injured found along the highways of our society and doing nothing about the forces which produce the injury, is only half a church. The chaplaincy church, which sends its representatives into industry or the armed forces to serve the men who are there, but never questions the structure of capitalism or the nature of war, will forfeit basic respect. The counseling church, which pours its man hours into marriage guidance and neurotic case work and is silent on the nature of a society which produces breakdown, is an escapist church.'[5]

Not surprisingly, there were many people within my own and sister churches who felt that this was selling the church short, and that I was simply propagating a social gospel. It was also to be expected that the state would be deeply suspicious of what I was trying to say and do, and did its best sometimes to belittle my words and deeds, and at other times deliberately attempted to impede what I was trying to do. Regrettably, even in the church there were informers.

In one of my sermons, broadcast live on radio from the Greenmarket Square Methodist church in Cape Town, I was talking about the Word of God. I described it as always a gracious Word, secondly a judging Word, thirdly a contemporary Word and, finally, a hopeful Word. That's when I got into trouble. I talked about the problems facing the church and society and added: 'There is one concern which faces the South African church with an urgency unlike any other. I refer to the naked and aggressive sin of racism – racism which is fundamentally a denial of personhood to another human being and is seen in all its monstrous inhumanity of white superiority and black inferiority in South Africa.'

I was no sooner back to Durban than I was contacted by the SABC, which asked for the full notes of my sermon. I said I was quite sure they had recorded it, and therefore I was happy to rely on their transcript rather than my own. They were insistent, so I sent them the full text. I then received word that my services would no longer be required as a radio preacher. In those times, the SABC had a daily morning worship segment, and I was informed that in addition to being barred from further Sunday services for broadcast, my name had been deleted from the list of those who were invited to be on the daily programme.

In the course of my work I met with many church leaders from different denominations. We were often called together by one crisis or another, such as action by the state against individuals, or action by the police against communities. On one occasion I went to Pretoria to meet John Vorster, the prime minister, together with other church leaders. He was flanked by several of his ministers and officials and we sat in front of him, almost like a bunch of schoolboys facing the headmaster. Vorster had an impressive manner – strong, very determined, never smiling, severe. I saw an archbishop reduced to silence when questioned by Vorster about statements that he had allegedly made. Vorster gave the other side and demanded to know why the archbishop had made his statements without having all the facts. I was staggered that tough, good church leaders would succumb so easily to the overt power of the prime minister and his cabinet members.

We made no progress at all, and when I questioned him particularly on detention without trial, his reply was facetious in the extreme: 'We are doing it for their own good. We are trying to protect them from doing anything more serious than they have been doing.' He didn't even smile when he said it. That was the level of the discussions we had so often with the state authorities. When we left that meeting, as was customary, Vorster warned us not to utter political statements while hiding behind our church vestments.

In actual fact, he had a point. We were very much protected. We wore clerical collars, we had preaching gowns, vestments, which seemed to put us in another category and gave us a protection not afforded to ordinary people. It is noticeable that, during protest marches or demonstrations, preachers, priests and pastors generally wear their clerical garb, possibly as an attempt to protect all the marchers, but it didn't always work that way. The religious leaders were rarely attacked, but the people with them were often not so lucky. I think the whole question of political priests can be a problem. We can become simplistic and other-worldly, and this is why I strongly supported Bonhoeffer's theology, which was very much one of being in the marketplace, being present, being aware of what was happening in the streets and in the workplace rather than simply making statements from lofty pulpits. The religion we are called to practise must not be on the periphery of life or in the margins, not only in times of crisis and approaching death, but rather at the centre of life, at the strongest places where people live and celebrate life.

I remember standing on the square in front of the Durban City Hall with Denis Hurley and a number of other leading clergymen and a huge crowd of ordinary people. It was lunchtime and we were protesting against detention without trial. He was as tall as I am and we stood next to one another, holding our placards. There were always comments thrown at us, though very little abuse, but on this occasion a man came towards us, and he was livid. He tried to grab our posters, but we held onto them. Finally, he spat on both Denis and me. I was as close to reacting physically as I'd ever been, but Denis put a restraining hand on my arm and said, 'Just be very still.' The bluster and insults continued, but our silence took the wind out of the man's sails. Hurley was a remarkable man – a man of great faith, an ecumenical person, humble and very strong, one of the finest Catholic leaders in South Africa.

In February 1972 we experienced a tremendous shock. A close friend of ours, a young woman with whom we used to play tennis, went into hospital to have a mole removed from her back. Irritated by her bra strap, the mole had sometimes bled and was inconvenient. Initially, we thought little of what should have been a minor procedure, but then we were informed that she was staying in hospital much longer than we had anticipated. I went to see her and was shocked, because it was clear that she was extremely ill. I spoke with her doctors and they told me that she had lymph gland cancer. They had removed a great deal of the malignancy during surgery, but her survival chances were nevertheless slim. Within three months, she was dead. This was a great blow for us, as she had been a good friend. I had no idea that I was going to face a similar illness.

One evening, Jenny said, 'You really should have that mole on your back looked at. It seems to have changed shape.' I obviously couldn't see my back, but coming so soon after the death of our friend, Jenny's comments scared me. Life was extremely busy and demanding, but I went to see our general practitioner as soon as possible. I was wearing a safari suit and he lifted up the jacket, looked at my back and said, 'You must see a surgeon immediately. This is serious.'

I pointed out that I had a whole series of public meetings, church openings and other engagements lined up and that I simply couldn't afford the time. His reply was, 'Well, it's your life. You make the decision.' This concentrated the mind, and I went immediately to a nearby hospital, where a Dr Barker was doing his rounds. He examined me in a little cubicle and said that he wanted me admitted at once. I was in hospital the next day and he operated within twenty-four hours.

Two days later, he told me that a biopsy had shown my mole to be a malignant melanoma. Since I was a churchman and someone who believed in God, he felt he could tell me quite bluntly that I had possibly three months to live. If I survived beyond that, the next five years would be crucial, but if I made it past that milestone, I would most likely remain cancer-free.

My doctor might have thought that I was tough enough and devout enough to deal with such devastating news, but I was no better prepared than any other human being. I was terrified and close to tears. When Jenny came to see me later, I burst out crying. I was forty years old and had four children; life seemed to be opening up before me, and now this had happened.

The next few months were fraught. The doctor had warned me that a sign of problems would be the swelling of glands anywhere in my body. It is amazing what tricks one's body plays on one's mind. A couple of weeks later, I had a sore throat and the glands in my throat swelled up. Somehow, in sympathy, those in my groin and every other part of my body followed suit. Suspecting the worst, I went back to the doctor. He examined me carefully, then said: 'You know, it's all in the mind. You have an ordinary cold and a sore throat. The swelling in your glands will subside in a day or two. Don't worry.'

It happened exactly as he said, and for the next three months I tried to ignore any symptoms that might suggest the return of the cancer. For the next five years I wasn't allowed to take out any life insurance policies, but I survived. Having been confronted with my own mortality and reminded that no one lives forever, it was time to get on with my life.

CHAPTER 9

In the marketplace

D URING MY TENURE AS PRESIDENT OF THE METHODIST CON-
ference, I visited mining compounds all over the then Transvaal and
Orange Free State on several occasions. Many of our church members
worked in the mines and we had received a number of complaints about
both their living conditions and the dangerous circumstances under which
they worked. I had a cool reception from the people who supervised the
mine hostels. They wanted to accompany me wherever I went, and I finally
had to tell them that I really wanted to talk to church members alone.

I was truly appalled at what I found. The migrant labour system that was
part and parcel of South Africa's economic policy devastated family life.
Many of the men took a second wife, because they were away from home for
the best part of each year. They would return annually to their villages and
towns throughout South Africa, Lesotho, Mozambique and further afield,
and impregnate their 'home' wives. The number of children they sired would
thus multiply, but the fathers would not be around to help care for them.
Further damage to the social fabric was caused by what appeared to be
widespread drug and alcohol abuse by the miners.

Mine compounds accommodated black employees in so-called single
men's hostels, with six to a very small room. They had rudimentary bathroom facilities and a basic kitchen, where they could cook their own food,
particularly over weekends and between shifts. The press inevitably wanted
to talk to me after I had visited the compounds and I pulled no punches,
describing exactly what I had seen. I called on leaders in the mining industry,
as well as government, to listen to the voices of these men and to transform
the working and living conditions under which they suffered.

In 1972, I was most surprised to get a call from Harry Oppenheimer's
office at the Anglo American Corporation, inviting me and Jenny to dinner
at his home in La Lucia, north of Durban. I imagined I was undergoing some
sort of test following my public criticism of the mining industry. When I
arrived there, I was somewhat overwhelmed by the beauty and splendour
of what was, in fact, a holiday home. I surreptitiously observed our fellow
diners closely to determine what cutlery was used for each successive course.

The discussion was lively and I was asked about my comments that had been reported by various newspapers. I said there was huge room for improvement, not only in the system but at the very sites where men mined the gold that was making many people extremely rich. It was not a hostile evening; I was really impressed by the gentleness with which Harry put his questions. Never once did he appear ruffled, although some of his guests certainly were.

Following that dinner, I received a message from Zach de Beer, who had previously been active in Progressive Party politics. He had entered parliament as a young man, but was now working for Anglo American, running their mining and farming interests in Zambia. I had met Zach and Colin Eglin and several party leaders on a number of occasions. I had become a member of the Progressive Party which, though far from perfect in its policies, came closest to my political convictions. I had even been approached to stand as the party's candidate in the Durban constituency of Berea in the 1970 general election. At the time, however, I felt my place was in the church, giving leadership to people by preaching and teaching, so I declined.

Zach asked me to travel to Johannesburg and have lunch with Harry Oppenheimer. We ate in the chairman's dining room at 44 Main Street, Anglo American's head office in the heart of Johannesburg's financial district. There were several Anglo heavyweights in attendance, including Julian Ogilvie-Thompson, who later became chairman of both Anglo American and De Beers, and Gordon Waddell, who first visited South Africa in 1960 as captain of the Scottish rugby side, met and married Harry's daughter Mary and went on to become both a senior Anglo executive and member of parliament for what was then the Progressive Federal Party.

There were many questions for me over lunch. Rather than simply criticising the mining industry, what would I recommend Anglo American should do? I suggested that they could be far more active in bombarding the government to reform the migrant labour system, so that they could build more family housing on mine property. They had done this many times, I was told, but a ceiling had been reached and there was nothing more they could do. I described some of the appalling conditions I had witnessed and said that even though Anglo American seemed to be the most liberal of the mining houses, there was considerable room for improvement, even taking prevailing government restrictions into account. In particular, I emphasised the need for training and the restructuring of wage levels.

That lunch was followed by another call from Zach, and another meeting.

This time, I was given a copy of a document titled *Employment Practices at the Anglo American Corporation* and asked for my comments. I went home, made a number of notes in the margins and sent the document back to Anglo. The document advocated reform, but I didn't think it went far enough and suggested a more radical approach. Yet another lunch in Johannesburg was arranged, and this time I was asked if I would consider going to work for Anglo American and putting into practice the revision and reform of their labour force's working and living conditions. It was an extremely attractive offer, the sort of work that I believed needed to be done, but I was hesitant. I had no background in business. I suggested to Harry that he should engage one of the top people from an American university such as Stanford or Harvard, someone who had expertise in economics and business. His reply was that he could buy any number of such individuals, but he wanted someone he could trust and who was not for sale. This was an enormous compliment. I said I would think about it, but reiterated that I still felt my place was in the church.

That night at home, I told Jenny about both the offer and my response. She replied: 'You were approached to go and work in a marketplace where men and women are in conflict, the very place where you say the church should be active, and you turned it down? And what's more, you never consulted me.' I realised that she was absolutely right. I hadn't talked it over with her or anyone else. I didn't sleep much that night, and the next day we discussed the matter again. Eventually, I said, 'Well, perhaps I should do this.' When I raised the possibility with some church leaders, quite a number of them were pleased that I was thinking in this direction, because I think they were keen to get rid of me! But others were concerned, pointing out that I had started some movement in the church and should stay and see it through. There were also some who felt that this was a great opportunity for the church to be relevant, as it were, in respect of racial conflict and the enormous gap between rich and poor.

At our conference in Port Elizabeth in 1972, I put in a request to be seconded to Anglo American. After a somewhat heated debate, I was given permission to go and work for the corporation.

We moved to Johannesburg at the end of the year. We had never had a house of our own, having always lived in manses belonging to the church, and lacked the capital for even a deposit on a property. My salary from the church was modest and I had four children. But Harry and Bridget Oppenheimer were incredibly generous and let us live in a house called Blue Skies, close to their family home, Brenthurst, for some months, after which, thanks to my increased earnings, we were finally able to buy a small house. At the age of forty-one, I became a first-time property owner, with a large bond!

Thus began an exciting yet challenging phase of our lives. A great fuss was made of us; we were different, so we were invited out most nights. I was totally unaccustomed to black tie dinners, but this was the pattern at the time. We dined often at Brenthurst and Jenny always sat next to Harry, which made her nervous. He was an extremely intelligent man who became easily bored. One of the telltale signs of his waning interest was that he would start playing with his cufflinks. We saw it happen quite often! He never suffered fools gladly and had probably one of the most penetrating minds I ever encountered. But Jenny needn't have been anxious. She could hold her own with Harry, and he took a real shine to her.

Not long after I joined Anglo, there was a particularly interesting test that I had to undergo. Lunch in the chairman's dining room always saw the most wonderful food served, including langoustine. At one lunch, many of the directors seated around the table fired questions at me throughout the meal. I battled to answer them and eat my food at the same time, so as not to keep the rest of the party waiting to be served with the next course. Afterwards, I was told by one of the senior members of staff that this was the 'talk test'. My success at eating and talking simultaneously would count in my favour, he said. I thought this was ludicrous, but he explained that so many decisions and deals were struck over lunch and dinner that it made good sense!

My work at Anglo American was not easy. I began by conducting an audit of some of the major mines owned by the corporation. I looked at the health regulations as published in the *Government Gazette*; I looked at housing standards; I looked at staff dining rooms and their living quarters, their wages and training, before writing a report for the executive committee. The amount of money that we were talking about was huge. The budget that I drew up for immediate improvements was well over R70 million. Most of the executive committee members were aghast and opposed to the proposal I submitted. Harry didn't say a word for most of the discussion, but towards the end he asked: 'This money you are recommending – what timeframe are we talking about?' I replied that it would obviously take quite a long time to make the structural changes and work on a new wage plan involving hundreds of thousands of workers. 'Well,' he said, 'I don't think this is a lot of money. We need to put things right, and we're not going to spend it all in a single month.' I was amused by the fact that the entire executive changed opinion in the blink of an eye and muttered in agreement that this was very sensible, very sensible, and that Harry had put his finger on it. The budget was approved, which, needless to say, gave me great encouragement and I proceeded to identify areas for change.

I was given an office on the same floor as Harry, a highly competent staff, a big car and what seemed like an unlimited travel allowance. I often flew in private aircraft to the various mines in places like South West Africa and Namaqualand, even as far afield as Canada, where I was asked to mediate in a dispute between the Native Americans and the white population over work opportunities and the confiscation of land on which the indigenous people lived and hunted and fished. I managed to resolve the dispute and thought how much easier it would be if our problems in South Africa were confined to similar issues.

There were many at Anglo who were pleased at my appointment and who cooperated at every level. But there were others who were sceptical, felt that I had insufficient experience and would have preferred someone from the business world to do the task assigned to me by the chairman and his executive. There were even some who didn't understand my role and, if not for Harry's backing, would have dismissed me as a 'do-gooder'.

Making the transition from church to corporation was not easy for me, but it was enormously challenging. Some years earlier, if I had gone into the mining compounds I would have tried to preach to the residents, to save their souls and remind them of the comfort of heaven that would assist them to cope with the sordid conditions of their present situation. But now I wanted to change structures. It was the beginning of my understanding of the need for institutional reform. Anglo American itself had to be transformed in order for those who worked with and for the company to have tangible benefits from the wealth that they were digging out of the ground, particularly in the areas of wages, training and housing.

For me, at least, I suppose it was a question of coming to terms with the distinction between the prophet and the priest. I wasn't able to hold the two in tension. In a remarkable way, Desmond Tutu has been able to do just that; he is both prophet and priest. But, for me, the emphasis shifted so strongly towards the prophetic and being an agent for change that I began to slide away from personal prayer and Bible readings. We still attended church services in Parktown North regularly as a family, but it all started to become somewhat unreal for me. I sat in the pew and didn't really understand what

74

the preacher was saying. The language seemed archaic. I didn't seem to have much in common with the people around me.

I really came alive only when my passion was ignited by trying to find ways to improve the lot of black workers, who had no legal recourse to trade union bargaining and were regarded merely as 'replaceable units'. My heart was in the transformation of the institution to pay better, train better, equip employees, improve housing, medical and social benefits. This was the main challenge in my life – a much more prophetic mission.

I had maintained my relationship with the Progressive Party and came to know some of the leaders who were active in the Johannesburg area. One day, I had a visit from Bobby Godsell, a young man whom I had first met while we were both living in Durban, where he was chairman of the Young Progressives while still at high school.

Not only was he passionate about politics, he was also a brilliant student. He had graduated from Natal University and when he came to my office, sporting shoulder-length hair, he criticised me harshly for taking a job with such a capitalist organisation as Anglo. He wanted me to be much more in-volved in politics. I listened to him and then I said, 'Why don't you come and join me and be my personal assistant, and see if we can make a difference here together? If you find it doesn't work and you feel you are selling out or compromising too much, you can always leave.' He thought about it for a while, then decided to take up my offer. He was of invaluable help as we considered the enormity of the challenge, and urged me to be bold in my recommendations. We often travelled together nationally and internationally and talked incessantly, not only about change in the Anglo empire, but also about the need for transformation in South Africa. I wouldn't have thought he would stay on, but he did, and became one of the top executives at Anglo American. Bobby has always been a man of great integrity and I have no doubt that he rose to the pinnacle of his professional life because he was not only an astute businessman, but also a strong moral voice. He retired from Anglo in 2007.

One of our best achievements was changing the tenor of the chairman's annual report, so as to include concrete proposals for change in labour relations. We made it possible for the report to go beyond major deals and balance sheets by also paying attention to employment practices, focusing on the workers, improvements and a way forward. We also persuaded Harry to include a direct commitment to press for change in the labour legislation, so that blacks would be allowed to become members of official trade unions.

This was a particularly brave step for a man whose primary responsibility was to make profits for his shareholders. Negotiations by legally recognised unions would inevitably have a strong impact on wage determinations.

Harry was the most influential business mogul to voice support for this issue, but there were many others who were concerned about the number of wildcat strikes in Durban and elsewhere, and felt that the only way to regulate industrial action was to enable all workers to join a union, if they wanted to. The problem was that, by design, the legislation excluded blacks, so the law would have to be changed. It was not a question of simply saying, 'We will recognise a union.' You could have discussions, you could even take collective decisions, but the law still rendered black workers ineligible to form or join a union. In practice, this meant that any agreement reached between employers and an illegal union would not be binding.

We put together an excellent team which included Bobby Godsell, Hank Slack (an American who would become Harry's son-in-law after Gordon Waddell and Mary divorced) and Clem Sunter, another future Anglo star. I reported directly to Billy Wilson, the deputy chairman. He was a wonderful, gentle man of great integrity, who really believed in the work that I was doing and supported me in every possible way. He travelled with me to many of the mines and manufacturing companies, and I think his presence helped persuade some of the toughest managers that they should toe the line; the reforms we introduced were not the whim of an outsider, but carried the endorsement of the chairman himself.

Some of my experiences at Anglo stand out more than others in my memory. On one occasion, I visited the black staff canteen at our Marshall-town head office. It was a dismal place, dark, gloomy and dirty. After investigating and discovering that the chefs were stealing the best cuts of meat and serving inferior food to the employees, I invited Harry to join me for lunch in the canteen. He did, and was so appalled at the conditions that he ordered an immediate and total renovation. I felt strongly that it wasn't only renovation that was needed, but integration, with staff facilities organised in terms of work rather than racial patterns. This was agreed to in principle.

During my two years at Anglo American, I learnt a great deal from relations between management and labour in other countries. Bobby Godsell and I went on an extended trip to many parts of the world, including Italy, Japan, Germany and Sweden, which all had very different approaches to labour relations. We learnt little from Italy; their trade unions seemed to be as chaotic as the seemingly endless succession of Italian governments. The

Germans, however, were quite different. They had not only acted quickly to recognise labour unions and afford them genuine bargaining power, but had also begun to move beyond that point. In an attempt to improve relationships between management and labour, they had formed working committees on which both were represented. This meant that labour was closely involved with decisions taken by management relating to the work-force generally, investment, new products, expansion and contraction. The system appeared to be working well, although it seemed to me that there was a lot of tension between management and labour and that theirs was a somewhat uncomfortable alliance. This suggested that it might be better for management to do the job that it was expected to do, but in close con-tact with strong labour representation, reaching consensus on important issues.

In Japan, we were startled at the relationship between management and labour. Firstly, it seemed to us that once you joined a major company, that was where you stayed for life. There was an exceptionally low staff turnover and the company was almost like the mother, the workers the children. We wanted to visit a particular large industrial company in Tokyo, but while the Japanese were courtesy itself, they kept putting obstacles in our way as far as this factory was concerned. They finally admitted that they were deeply ashamed, because the workers at the plant were on strike. My response was that I would nevertheless like to see the layout and conditions at the factory. Most reluctantly, our hosts agreed, and we were taken to the plant in ques-tion. To my utter astonishment, the place was a hive of industry; everyone seemed to be working flat out. I turned to the general manager and said, 'I must be under some misapprehension. I was told that your workers were on strike.' He replied: 'Yes, they are on strike. They are very unhappy with management. You will notice that they are all wearing white armbands.' How much easier it would be, I thought, if relationships between labour and management could always take this form! But of course this was some-thing not likely to occur in other parts of the world and, indeed, things changed rapidly in Japan after that as well.

It wasn't easy to learn much from Sweden, other than an appreciation that the trade unions not only exerted labour power but also influenced politics considerably. Strongly opposed to apartheid, the Swedish unions refused to meet two white executives from a powerful company in South Africa, so we were unable to hold discussions with them. We met with management, who explained to us that the labour movement had a strong influence on legislation, and part of this legislation was to have nothing to do with white South African businessmen. It was yet another imbalanced relationship, with management and labour working together, but with labour seeming to have the upper hand.

Despite some of the setbacks, we were generally well received and, on our return to Johannesburg, drafted a report recommending certain significant and far-reaching changes. We emphasised that labour had to have a genuine voice if we were to enjoy industrial peace. Since legislation made it impossible for black trade unions in South Africa to be recognised, we urged management to start talking to unofficial black unions and take matters as far as existing legislation would allow, in the hope that – one day – the laws would change. We also strongly recommended that, instead of waiting for black unions to be legalised, Anglo American should focus on overhauling the wage structure; increase the emphasis on training and map out clear routes for promotion; improve staff housing and put pressure on the state to allow more family housing in mine compounds; improve the health services and general living conditions of miners who risked their lives every day to maximise the profits of the mining industry. The point we underlined was that it was in the corporation's own best interest to do as much as possible, as soon as possible, hoping that this approach would be well received.

In large measure, it was. Many of these recommendations came to fruition only after I had left Anglo, but some of them were implemented while I was still there.

PART III

Progressive politics

CHAPTER 10

To parliament

A S CHALLENGING, EVEN EXHILARATING, AS MY WORK AT ANGLO American was, I was a fish out of water in some ways. When the Progressive Party began casting around in April 1974 for a suitable candidate to fight a parliamentary by-election in the Cape Town constituency of Pinelands, a new opportunity arose.

During the run-up to the general election in that month the incumbent member of parliament, Ossie Newton-Thompson of the United Party (UP), had been killed in an air crash. Election of the provincial council representative (MPC) would go ahead as planned, but voting for a new MP would be deferred until 12 June.

Zach de Beer, both a former member of parliament and a seasoned political campaigner, was the Progressive Party's first choice as a candidate, but his work and heavy responsibilities for Anglo in Zambia made him unavailable. The constituency then put forward a charming and sincere man, Eric Oettle. However, the party leadership felt that, with the UP in some disarray, Pinelands would be a marvellous opportunity to put another 'Prog' in parliament and decided that, since I already had something of a national image, I would have a better chance of winning.

My immediate reaction was to resist any request to fight the election, for a number of reasons. Firstly, I had been seconded by the Methodist Church to a specific company with specific concerns regarding black workers. I wasn't at all sure whether the church would agree to a further secondment, and a party-political one at that. Secondly, the scope for real change at Anglo was immense. Thirdly, we were settled as a family; the children were attending good schools; we owned our own home for the first time in our lives and for me to rush down to Cape Town could be quite upsetting. Fourthly, it was unlikely that we would win the seat, since the UP's man had been elected as MPC with a huge majority.

Despite all these doubts and very real problems, I felt something stirring deep inside me that attracted me to politics – the prime underlying problem confronting South Africa – and trying in some modest way to make a difference.

Of course, going into politics was a far cry from improving the working and living conditions of black employees in a major corporation, and I could make no decision without consulting the Methodist Church. I had begun to feel that parliament was a place where I could put my beliefs and energy to good use, and, to my surprise, when I raised this possibility with the leading Methodist officials, they agreed that I should go ahead if that was my wish; they would re-examine the situation year by year. This is exactly what happened.

My colleagues at Anglo American were equally enthusiastic, with Bobby Godsell in particular being determined to spend at least some of his time assisting my campaign.

Harry Oppenheimer, however, was sober and cautious. 'You haven't a hope of winning this seat,' he told me candidly. 'We lost by nearly 3 000 votes mere weeks ago.' Nevertheless, he said, if this was something I really wanted to do, I could take a leave of absence for the duration of my campaign, 'and know that your job will be waiting for you afterwards'. I couldn't ask for anything more generous than that.

Needless to say, the most important people I had to consult were my wife and children. Andrew, who was in high school, was beside himself with excitement at the prospect of a father in politics. Kathy and Jeremy didn't fully understand what the fuss was about, but were thrilled all the same at the thought of me doing battle against the National Party. Nicky was too young to grasp the situation, while Jenny was in two minds. One of the most remarkable things about our relationship is that she has always given my endeavours 100 per cent support. Without her, I would never have achieved anything. When we left the safety of the church, she threw her full weight behind my job at Anglo, but now, having barely settled into the first house that we had ever owned, I was asking her to face my long absence from home, fighting a battle that almost no one expected me to win. And if, by some chance, I did manage to take the seat, she would have to deal with yet another upheaval in our lives. No wonder she was torn – but in the end, as always, she gave me her blessing: 'If this is what you want to do and you believe it is right, then I will back you all the way.'

I went to Cape Town and met with the Pinelands constituency leaders before being interviewed by party leaders Colin Eglin and Frederik Van Zyl Slabbert. I accepted the nomination on condition that Eric Oettle would be agreeable. He stepped aside and made a public statement to that effect.

The Progressive Party's announcement of my candidacy had a mixed reception. The NP's mouthpiece in the Cape, *Die Burger*, gave me a hard time from the very first day, describing me as a carpetbagger and ultra-liberalist who was in Harry Oppenheimer's pocket. But the English press were fair. They didn't think I could win the seat, but acknowledged that I had at least some of the qualifications required. After all, I had been born in Cape Town, so I certainly couldn't be regarded as a carpetbagger.

My political debut marked the beginning of a deep and warm friendship with Van Zyl Slabbert, who had won the Rondebosch seat in April, against all odds. He was charismatic, intelligent, attractive and an enormous plus for the Progressive Party. He made it clear that he would do everything he could to support my campaign. The party was still elated beyond words at their success in the general election, which had seen five excellent candidates join Helen Suzman in parliament. For the first time in the party's history, the redoubtable MP for Houghton was no longer the sole voice of progressive opposition against the Nats. Admittedly, six seats made up a tiny bloc in relation to the overwhelming power and control of the NP, but it was a great improvement on the single seat that Helen had occupied for some thirteen years.

Unfortunately, in the same election, Roger Hulley had lost the Progressive Party's battle for a provincial council seat to the UP by 2 554 votes. We had to reverse that in a matter of six to eight weeks. We planned public and house meetings, bumper stickers, letters and interviews. It was a whirlwind campaign, crammed into less than two months. I was assisted by teams from several neighbouring constituencies and, in particular, Marlene Silbert from the Sea Point Progressive Party office. She was an absolute gem and headed up the by-election operation, playing a major role in planning our strategy. True to her word, Jenny soon joined me, worked at the office, attended house and public meetings, did special canvassing, posed for photographs and led by example.

The weather was changing and winter was upon us. I found it tough work walking the streets, knocking on doors and, as it were, selling myself. It is one thing to sell an ideal, a set of principles, but now I was asking people to vote for Alex Boraine. I didn't find that easy, and the reception I got from many of the people I visited was extremely negative and sometimes hostile. The old guard of the UP, many of whom lived in retirement homes, found it hard to accept the tragic death of their former MP. Newton-Thompson was a well-known Capetonian and an excellent parliamentarian and had the best-organised constituency in the Western Cape. My response to voters who lamented his passing was, 'Unfortunately, he is no longer here, so you can't vote for him and you are now confronted with a choice. This is who I am, this is what I stand for, and I hope you will vote for me.' Attitudes seemed to soften as the campaign progressed and people started getting to know me, read what I was trying to say, and heard me at public meetings and at what seemed like hundreds of house meetings. The latter were extraordinarily effective – small groups of people who could put question after question to the candidate.

I was driven all over the constituency by a young man named Barry Streek. He was employed by the Progressive Party and had been very active in Colin Eglin's successful election campaign in Sea Point in April 1974. He later became a distinguished journalist with the *Cape Times* and an outstanding parliamentary correspondent. Sadly, he died of a brain tumour in the first half of 2007.

During that first campaign, it was Barry's job to make sure that I stayed on the campaign trail and canvassed as many voters as possible, no matter how awful the weather. He always waited for me in the car, and when I complained bitterly about the rain and the cold and the dark and the dogs, some of which were the size of small ponies, his standard response was: 'Get on with it. The sooner you finish, the sooner we can get out of here and have a beer.' He was tough, but always supportive.

I remember visiting one home where a man with an overly large stomach, his pants held up by braces, invited me in and said, 'Listen, I'm going to vote for you, but I am sure you agree that you can bring the black out of the jungle, but you can't get the jungle out of the black.' I was appalled at this racism and replied: 'Frankly, if that is your attitude, I don't want your vote. That is not what I stand for. I think I'll leave.' He was astonished and said, 'No wait, wait. Come and sit down. I've never heard a politician being honest before. Tell me about your campaign.' In the end, he did vote for me, I think with a somewhat modified view of things, and so did his wife. On another occasion, I was greeted by a youngish man, perhaps in his early thirties, who was delighted to see me. He said he was dead keen on the Progressive Party, but he had one problem. I asked if I could try to help him sort it out and he said: 'I'm a bit worried that the Progressive Party is going to be taken over by the Jews.' Once again, I simply had to say that I didn't share his views, that who controlled the party was not the issue, that it was a party of principle and that all supporters were welcome. In light of his attitude, however, it might be better for him to cast his vote for some other party. He immediately changed his mind and declared that he didn't really mean it, and would certainly support me on election day.

When I told my campaign manager, Neil Ross, about these encounters, he was furious. 'Don't you ever do that again! We could have lost votes. Just shut up and let them say what they want to say. If they vote for you, we can change their attitudes afterwards.' I replied that I did not see the situation that way, and wasn't going to change my approach. I believed in what the Progressive Party stood for, namely non-racialism, and I wasn't going to remain silent when people used abusive language about any section of the population. Neil and I agreed to differ and I continued as before.

To this day, I truly believe that being honest and not playing to people's prejudices actually won me votes. Throughout the campaign, whether visiting homes or at a public meeting, I spelt out what I believed was essential for a peaceful and just society in my country. I emphasised not only non-racialism, but also the need for full participation by all South Africans at every level of government; that there ought to be a national convention where a new constitution could be negotiated that would meet the aspirations of all our people. This was not an easy message to get across to white voters, but I didn't want to play games and be in politics without stating fairly bluntly that transformation was needed from top to bottom in our political system and social order.

Public meetings presented their own challenge. There was a group of people that followed me from one venue to another, asking the same stock questions every time. They were well organised, young and old, English and Afrikaans, and deliberately set out to try to influence the audience. The questions were always put politely. 'Dr Boraine, if you are elected as our MP, will you open the schools to all races?' Obviously, all schools in the constituency were for whites only. My reply was, 'Everybody has the right to a decent education and people should be able to find that education wherever they can.'

Inevitably, the second question was: 'Dr Boraine, will you allow blacks from Langa to live in Pinelands if you are elected?' Once again my reply was to the point: 'People should have the right to live wherever they can afford to live. The tragedy in our country is that so many people are poor and confined to overcrowded, isolated areas. I think that Pinelands, like every other place in South Africa, should be available for all to live in.' This was greeted with jeers and cheers and many of my more timid supporters wished that I would try to put a bit of spin on my message, but I thought it far better to state the truth exactly as I saw it.

The final question was usually: 'Dr Boraine, once you have opened the schools and housing to everyone in this beautiful suburb of Pinelands, are you also going to allow blacks and coloureds to take over our old-age homes?' This was a blatant sop to the many, many old people who – understandably – were nervous of change and wondered if their future was secure. My answer was: 'The people who live in old-age homes are someone's mother, somebody's father; they deserve our love and our respect, and I think, no matter what colour a person is, he or she should have the right to the same care and attention at all the amenities which are currently available only to whites.' My inquisitors doubtless thought they had won the battle, but somehow even conservative people were not put off by such questions and listened to my responses. I always tried to end by saying: 'I want to challenge those of you who have been asking me these tough questions, and they are tough. You have two choices. Do you want your sons and fathers and brothers to go on dying on the border to defend a racist, unfair society? Or do you want to open up society and enable us to live proudly and without fear from anyone outside our borders?' This seemed to make some impact. South Africa *did* have a choice; it was not pre-ordained that we were going to end up in bloody chaos or continued oppression of the vast majority of people. Maybe it was this realisation that changed a lot of views. The irony is that, from 1994, Pinelands saw many blacks taking up residence, the schools were all integrated and no one seemed to object.

The day of the election dawned warm, but soon the clouds gathered, the heavens opened and we had a violent storm. De Waal Drive was closed to traffic, people splashed through pools of water on foot, the tents at voting stations collapsed under a deluge. In fact, 12 June was one of the wettest days of the winter of 1974. The previous day I had received many phone calls, but two in particular were important. First, Colin Eglin called to say that the *Cape Argus* had conducted a final poll which showed that we would lose by about 10 per cent, or approximately 1500 votes. Colin was reassuring, saying he didn't believe that the poll was accurate, but that, even if it was, we would have done well to slash the majority in the general election, when our provincial candidate had lost by 2800 votes. I was extremely depressed at this news and my mood was not helped when Colin's call was followed by one from Harry Oppenheimer, who said much the same thing. 'You have done very well. You have come close, but you are not going to make it. Just remember that your job is waiting for you,' he said.

But, as I watched the stream of people who turned out to vote despite the cold and the pouring rain, I felt in my bones that perhaps we still had a fighting chance. Perhaps there could be a miracle. When the polling stations closed at 9 p.m., I rushed to a house that had been placed at my disposal for the day and changed into dry clothes before joining the count. Jenny was with me, along with Neil Ross as my official agent. My opponents, one from the NP and the other from the UP, were there as well. The NP candidate was characteristically well prepared, with flasks of coffee and tasty sandwiches. We had no refreshments.

My chief opponent was the UP's Annette Reineke. She sat quietly and we kept our distance from each other as the count got under way. It seemed to take forever, and when the presiding officer finally read out the result, I was shocked to hear him giving me a 33-vote victory. Only moments before, I had approached Annette and said, 'My agent tells me that we have probably lost by about 500 votes. I want to congratulate you and say that it has been a tough fight, but I think a fair one, so well done.' She was thrilled by my concession and asked permission from the officials to go to the cloakroom to comb her hair and fix her make-up before facing the crowd and the press outside. Understandably, she was stunned to hear, five minutes later, that she had not won after all. Her agent, André Fourie, who would later become a National Party MP, immediately demanded a recount. I found myself saying, 'Absolutely. This is very close. I think we should have a recount.' Neil Ross was livid with me – again – but the UP had every right to challenge the outcome, and so the votes were counted a second time.

The result was that I picked up a vote, and won by 34 ballots. In a moment of elation, I promptly blurted out: 'Let's have another recount! Perhaps I'll win by even more!' However, both the UP and the NP conceded that I had, indeed, won the seat, and thus began my political career.

We walked out of the hall at 2 a.m., to be met by a huge crowd of Progressive Party supporters, including Colin Eglin and Van Zyl Slabbert. They hoisted me onto a car and demanded a speech. Because the UP's David Graaff had accused me early in the campaign of not replying to a question of his in Afrikaans, I started my acceptance speech, 'Dames en Here ...', but got no further, because the crowd simply erupted into loud cheers. I clambered off the car, my clothes plastered to me by the driving rain, but filled with excitement. I have never been small of stature, but Van Zyl wrapped his arms around me and lifted me clear off the ground, saying delightedly, 'Now we are both in the shit together!' I think that even at this early stage he had real reservations about whether or not he should be in parliament, but at least he now had someone who was as new to the idea of being an MP and with similar reservations. Colin Eglin was beside himself and described it as a historic win. The next morning, the newspapers were filled with news of our victory and forecast the demise of the deeply divided UP. Annette Reineke actually said, 'The United Party is sick in its soul.'

At about 4 a.m., as Jenny and I lay in bed, she nudged me and said, 'Alex, do we have to accept this? Can you say that you don't want to be the MP for Pinelands?' I looked at her in astonishment and replied: 'After all we've been through, with all the work that these people have done, are you crazy? Of course we have to!'

Later that morning, I received a message from Harry Oppenheimer, acknowledging that he had been wrong in his forecast and that this was a remarkable win. When I returned to Johannesburg, he said, I should see him before meeting anyone else. When I presented myself at 44 Main Street a couple of days later, he wanted to hear all about the election. Then he gave me a most magnificent set of gold cufflinks and said he wanted to talk about my future at Anglo American. He suggested that I should stay on in exactly the same capacity, as a senior member of staff, receiving the same salary and benefits. I sincerely appreciated his more than generous offer, but explained that it would be extremely difficult for me to do justice to my position in parliament if I remained on the Anglo payroll. Many of the debates would focus on mining, manufacturing and the economy and I would have to be free to follow the dictates of my own heart and mind, as well as the policies of my party. Reluctantly, I would have to resign as a member of his staff. He immediately saw my point and didn't press me, saying only that he hoped we could keep in touch.

A few days later, I was told that Anglo American would nevertheless welcome my services as a consultant from time to time. Since I would no longer be a full-time employee, I would have to surrender my share options, my large Mercedes and obviously my salary and excellent fringe benefits. Somewhat dismayed and disappointed, I suddenly realised, for the first time, that a political career would demand sacrifices. I couldn't have my cake and eat it.

When I took my seat in parliament soon afterwards, I was the proud owner of a new Volkswagen Beetle, which could almost have fitted into the boot of the Mercedes! But I had paid for it and it was mine, with no encumbrances. I had made a campaign promise to live in my constituency, so we also had to look for a house, which meant taking another bond. But, despite the material changes in our family life, I felt I was in the place I needed to be at that particular time – a place where I could confront and look the beast in the eye, as it were. On my first day at parliament, having forgotten where the entrance was, I got a little lost, but once inside, sitting on those green benches and looking across at the phalanx of cabinet ministers and National Party MPs – who were extremely hostile from the start – I was ready to join the battle.

In 1974, parliament was overwhelmingly dominated by the NP, which, as a result of its large numbers, was extremely smug and arrogant. John Vorster, a tough man and former minister of justice, was the prime minister. His defence minister was PW Botha. Vorster had a presence that made most of us feel quite nervous when he entered the House of Assembly. He was ponderous, leaning forward in his bench and gazing at those opposite him. We were few in number and new to parliamentary politics, and he took full advantage of both factors.

The history of what became the Progressive Federal Party and the official opposition for many years began in 1959, when a number of liberal UP members broke away to form the Progressive Party. The split was the result of the UP's inability to find a clear-cut alternative to the NP's apartheid policy. From the outset, the Progressive Party advocated constitutional reform, calling for a Bill of Rights, an independent judiciary and a federal dispensation. It also stood for an economy based on free enterprise.

Since 1961, Helen Suzman had been the Progressive Party's lone voice in parliament, tirelessly fighting against such iniquities as detention without trial, the pass laws, influx control, job reservation on grounds of race, separate amenities and forced removals. I was the last of the six 'reinforcements' to join the parliamentary team in 1974, the other newly elected MPs being Slabbert, Eglin, Rupert Lorimer, Gordon Waddell and René de Villiers. The official opposition at the time was the UP, led by Sir De Villiers Graaff. Clearly, after their losses in the general election and the Pinelands by-election, the party was making a last-ditch stand. The opposition members bickered among themselves incessantly and, if his party were to survive, Graaff would have to launch some new initiative. He did this by calling for a united opposition under the 'Save South Africa' banner.

Key members of the UP resigned, namely Harry Schwarz, David Dalling, Brian Bamford, Horace van Rensburg and Dick Enthoven, who was, in fact, expelled for openly criticising the party. They formed the Reform Party, which merged with the Progressive Party in 1975 to form the Progressive Reform Party (PRP).

I fully appreciated the need for the opposition to grow and present a united front against the NP rather than fighting one another, but I have to say that right from the start I felt that some of the great strengths of the existing group of seven Progressive Party MPs would be somewhat diluted by the addition of more members. There was a different approach, a different culture, among some of the dissident UP members. I think this was particularly true of Schwarz and Van Rensburg, and it came as no surprise that Schwarz was later appointed by the NP government as ambassador to the USA, or that Van Rensburg resigned from our party, declaring us soft on security and communism, and joined the NP. Enthoven was a very different kettle of fish, as were Bamford and Dalling. They were far closer to the Progressive Party's unambiguous opposition to the NP.

Led by Colin Eglin and former judge Kowie Marais, who later became an MP, the Progressive Party entered into discussion with Graaff and his chief lieutenants. I think that he was willing to meet us halfway, but, regrettably, he was stymied at each turn by two formidable characters on the right wing of the UP: Radcliffe Cadman and Vause Raw. The talks finally broke down and the UP decided to disband. Ironically, its final meeting took place at the Johannesburg Ice Rink, resulting in many jokes about the UP being ice cold, dead and buried, skating on thin ice and so on. From the remnants of the party formed as the result of a 1934 coalition between generals Jan Smuts and JBM Hertzog, and which governed South Africa for thirty-eight years before its shock defeat by the NP in 1948, emerged the New Republic Party (NRP), which assumed the role of official opposition by virtue of its numbers, though several of the old UP members chose instead to join us. While I think that some of our cutting edge was lost in the process, we undoubtedly benefited from the experience, wisdom and knowledge of many who joined our ranks.

Other splinter groups continued to emerge, such as one formed by expelled NP member Japie Basson, and, having absorbed several of them, we became the Progressive Federal Party (PFP) in 1977. More importantly, by the end of that year, when Sir De Villiers Graaff announced his retirement, we had the numbers for the first time to become the official opposition in parliament, rendering the struggling New Republic Party all but inconsequential.

Throughout my twelve years as an MP, the dilemma of serving in an all-white parliament, while standing very much for an inclusive, non-racial democracy, was a major challenge. The situation was somewhat ameliorated by the fact that I was asked to head a small commission to look at interracial policies, which gave me wide scope for direct contact with black, coloured and Indian leaders and members of their communities. This helped me enormously to understand better what they were enduring and how they saw the future. Discussions and conversations throughout that period were pointers to the direction that I think we ought to have taken.

For a period, one of the PFP's key policies was a qualified franchise. This was an attempt to encourage white voters to support the party without the threat of being overwhelmed by the black majority. Black, coloured and Indian people were very critical of this policy, which they saw as a sop to white voters. I was not alone in being unhappy about this. There were many in the party who, while understanding the need to move gradually, found it extremely difficult to defend a qualified franchise. It was easy to defend it to white voters, but impossible to justify to black South Africans. It was my belief that we needed to move courageously and swiftly towards acceptance of a universal franchise. Fortunately, over the next few years this is exactly what happened, and the official policy was changed to make it clear that every person had the same voting rights, irrespective of colour, race, social or economic standing.

I also held the firm conviction – shared by many within the party – that there ought to be a coming together of all South Africans to debate a future programme and, in particular, work towards a new constitution that would guarantee the rights of all South Africans. It took far longer than we had imagined for this to become a political reality, but many of those who had struggled throughout the 1970s and 1980s to put this message across rejoiced in 1994, when at long last we reached the point where all South Africans had equal access not only to voting rights but also to the law courts.

The tension between principle and strategy was at the heart of my service as an elected member of the South African parliament. On the one hand, I firmly believed that the institution was fatally flawed, in that it excluded people of colour and therefore was illegitimate and unrepresentative. It flouted the principles of justice and equality, which were non-negotiable. On the other hand, it was unthinkable that the ruling party should go unchallenged in its determination to maintain white power and privilege at all cost. Helen Suzman had ceaselessly condemned racial injustice and reminded not only the government but also the country of the dangerous consequences inherent in the policies of apartheid. For far too long, hers was the sole voice of reason and compassion that gave many people hope. When the opportunity arose, it seemed to me strategically sound and morally defensible to add my voice to hers.

Those of us elected in 1974 took up the challenge with vigour and passion. Several of us had no prior experience of local or provincial government. We didn't see politics as a career; we were driven by a necessity to take on the NP in its own backyard, and not only condemn and criticise existing policies but also try to put forward alternative policies for a new South Africa. It was a great privilege to be part of an excellent team. We brought to parliament considerable experience from various fields and an idealism not generally characteristic of political parties. The period during which we were the only seven elected members of the party was the happiest of my parliamentary life and, in some ways, I think the most effective.

I went to parliament with the fundamental aim of transformation, so that – one day – there would be a new democratic and non-racial institution serving all South Africa, but I was always conscious of the system's imperfections. This was a discussion that I had many times with friends and colleagues outside parliament, who felt that by becoming part of the existing dispensation we had somehow betrayed the cause. This was particularly true of black and coloured friends. They often charged me with compromising my principles by entering an establishment from which they were barred.

On the other hand, throughout my time in parliament, many black South Africans would approach me, either by telephone, in person or when I went into the townships, and ask me to raise a specific issue or try to make representation to the government about a particular incident – a forced removal, the disappearance of a family member, someone detained without trial. So here was another contradiction. Publicly, blacks condemned parliament, and rightly so, by implication indicting those of us who served as the official opposition. Yet privately, and many times, the same people sought our help. I was comfortable with this. I knew the desperate need that the voiceless majority had for any kind of assistance when things went badly wrong.

Soon after entering parliament, I was appointed chairman of the Progressive Party's Western Cape region. This gave me the opportunity to interact with both the organisation and machinery of the party, which I found exciting. Not only was I in touch with my own constituency of Pinelands, but also with a much wider support base in the Western Cape.

Between the demands of being an MP and party caucus member, as well as running the Western Cape region, I needed some assistance, and was given permission to appoint a part-time secretary. Aged just twenty-two, Paddy Clark came for an interview, and a working partnership that has lasted more than three decades was born. She was enthusiastic, politically committed to what the Progressive Party stood for and had impeccable credentials, as well as all the necessary secretarial skills. But, from the start, Paddy was so much more than that – she was a member of a team. Her good sense of humour has doubtless helped her deal with my impatience and demand for quick action while heaping huge amounts of work on her, but I think the fact that she was named Secretary of the Year in the Western Cape in 1981 testifies to her many abilities. As the party grew and our caucus expanded, we were given more funding for a typing pool, which Paddy joined on a full-time basis. This meant that I had to share her with several other caucus members, which I didn't like at all and found quite difficult to adjust to, because we worked so well together.

Because there were so few of us opposing so many Nats, we were under enormous pressure in terms of preparation, research and actual participation in debates. However, we worked as a team, relied on and assisted each other and were never idle spectators, as were so many in the NP benches. Many of the ruling party MPs spoke only once or twice during a full session of parliament, and we suspected, I think rightly, that in the main even those rare speeches were prepared for them by the relevant government departments. Because several of our members took part in key debates every day, we received excellent press coverage.

I recall with enormous gratitude and respect the work done by journalists such as Bruce Cameron, Frans Esterhuyse, Barry Streek, *Cape Times* editor Tony Heard and his deputy, Gerald Shaw, brilliant columnist John Scott, cartoonist Tony Grogan, Helen Zille – perhaps the hardest worker in the parliamentary press gallery – Tos Wentzel, Michael Acott, Peter Sullivan, Percy Qoboza, editor of *The World* until it was banned in 1981, and many others who reported the parliamentary proceedings day after day, thus allowing the message we were trying to convey to be read throughout the country and beyond our borders. We were not as fortunate with television and radio coverage, the SABC being the state broadcaster and, as such, controlled with an iron fist.

Despite being under tough strictures, the newspapers somehow managed to publicise the most important issues. In many ways, I think this prepared the ground for the eventual transformation that took place in South Africa. Had our questions and comments been confined to parliament, the effect would have been tantamount to a quarrel between two brothers behind closed doors. Thanks to *Hansard*, the verbatim record of parliamentary debates, and because the press gallery did its job, even the most robust exchanges were accessible to all.

When I went to parliament in 1974, each of the Progressive Party's seven MPs had several portfolios. Mine were labour, health and Bantu education. I was also the second spokesman on foreign affairs. All of us took part in the major legislative debates and the no-confidence debate, a long-established, week-long feature of Britain's Westminster system, on which South Africa's pre-1994 political dispensation was modelled. Traditionally held soon after the annual ceremonial opening of parliament, this debate allowed the prime minister to deliver a state of the nation address, and the opposition to both respond and raise matters of particular concern.

In addition to debates, we served on select parliamentary committees and had many extra-parliamentary demands on our time: visits to party branches, work within our respective constituencies, speeches, interviews, conferences and the like. We were all extremely busy, but we preferred it that way.

CHAPTER II

This turbulent priest

Q UITE EARLY IN MY PARLIAMENTARY CAREER, JOHN VORSTER – a formidable character, strong, security conscious and 'Minister of Injustice', as I used to call him before he became prime minister – glared at me across the floor and muttered: 'Who will deliver me from this turbulent priest?'

On another occasion, defence minister PW Botha called for my blood, telling parliament: 'I am after some people's blood, including the Honourable Member for Pinelands.' This prompted a marvellous newspaper cartoon by the well-known Bob Connolly. It showed a building, emblazoned with the name 'Botha's Blood Bank', PW Botha in full military gear, brandishing a long, sharp knife, and me, walking past, under the caption, 'potential blood donor'.

I think the main reason for Botha's ire was that while campaigning for my parliamentary seat during the 1974 by-election I had stated at a public meeting that, under the National Party government with its race classification laws, 'to be born black is to be born with the kiss of death'. Extravagant language, to be sure, but I wanted to make the point that under apartheid black people had no viable alternative, from birth to death, other than subservience and oppression by a minority government. Such was the attitude of the National Party that several newspaper columnists declared me 'The Prime Minister's Enemy No. 1'.

I think there were other reasons for the NP's vitriol. Even though I had vacated my Methodist Church pulpit and become a labour consultant with Anglo American before entering politics, I was probably best known for statements I had made as a church leader. In many respects, religious conviction was the NP's Achilles heel. A large number of the cabinet members and ordinary MPs firmly believed that God was on their side, and frequently invoked his blessing on the iniquitous laws they constantly imposed.

When I took my seat in parliament as a Progressive Party member, I decided that, however difficult it might prove, I would adopt a strong moral and religious line in my arguments against the government's racist policies. At every opportunity, I tried to show the contradictions of the NP's claim

– supported by the policies and practices of the Dutch Reformed Church, which was really the party at prayer – to be a godly people. A strong moral line, backed up with religious arguments, must inevitably focus on concern for people rather than on policies, so wherever possible I tried to highlight the impact of apartheid on individuals or families as well as on institutions. This drove the Nats to distraction.

When the NP attacked journalists, students and clergymen, as they often did, my response was to defend those who bravely opposed the government. By far the most vulnerable were the students, who continued to march, wave placards and attack the government at every opportunity, but the most bitter pill for the NP to swallow was that church leaders – albeit a minority of them – dared to take a stand against the immorality of apartheid, some openly denouncing the policy as a sin against God and his Creation.

When the government attacked the Christian Institute and its founder, Dutch Reformed Church minister Beyers Naudé, I went out of my way to defend him. Naudé had refused to give evidence to the Schlebusch Commission (which later became the Le Grange Commission), appointed by Vorster in 1973 to probe 'radical' organisations such as the CI, the Institute of Race Relations, the University Christian Movement and the National Union of South African Students (NUSAS). During the parliamentary debate on the justice department's budget, I stated: 'Beyers Naudé has dared to test the apartheid ideology by his Christian faith. As a consequence, he has opposed discrimination on the grounds of race and colour with every fibre of his being. Beyers Naudé's real sin in the eyes of the Schlebusch/Le Grange Commission was that his ultimate allegiance was not to a political party, to a language, to skin colour or even to the state, but to God. History will judge Dr Naudé not as a danger to the state, but as an urgent warning to South Africa.'

I also attacked the government's intention to exclude blacks in the Western Cape from its ninety-nine-year leasehold plan which applied to the rest of the country. Describing the policy as 'inhuman, immoral and un-Christian', I put a number of questions to Connie Mulder, the minister of plural relations and development, including: 'Does he believe that God has placed us in families, and how does he reconcile this with the break-up of family life which is the direct outcome of the policy he is now advocating?'

In response, JT Albertyn, the NP's representative for False Bay, said he was convinced that my speech would be 'used' in black homelands and elsewhere to attract even more blacks to the Western Cape.

During the same session of parliament, I was thrown out of the chamber for refusing to apologise for my response to a remark made by the United Party's Radcliffe Cadman. Attacking the Progressive Party's attitude towards the Schlebusch Commission, he had said the party 'is soft on communism and soft on those who are attempting to break down the free enterprise economy, and is soft on all those things which are outlined in these reports and which are inimical to the interests of South Africa'. I couldn't resist interjecting, 'And you are soft in the head.' I was ordered by the Speaker to apologise for this remark and, when I refused, he immediately said, 'Then the Honourable Member must leave the chamber forthwith.'

I went to my office, thinking that, since I could not return to the chamber for the rest of the day, I would get a fair amount of work done at my desk. However, no sooner was I in my office than the Sergeant-at-Arms, his sword at his side, came to escort me out of the precincts of parliament. So I packed my bag and left. I went home, picked up Jenny and we went to Rhodes Memorial for tea and scones. I gazed at the view from the tearoom, reflecting on the stupidity and childishness of debates that so often took centre stage in a forum that was supposed to determine the future of a country and all its citizens.

I must concede that the line is thin between a strong moral and religious approach and a pompous, self-righteous one. Although I tried to include my party colleagues in demands for a just and fair approach to the challenges facing South Africa, my focus on moral issues caused some of them to cringe, and I know that at times Van Zyl Slabbert stared into the distance and hoped that my 'preaching' would not boomerang on all of us.

As time went on, my relationship with organised religion became more tenuous. I had been in parliament for several years when I received a delegation from the Methodist Church, wanting to clarify my position as an ordained minister and MP. What they really wanted was for me to make myself available for an appointment by the church. I tried to advance what I thought were sound theological and biblical reasons for taking a stand in keeping with the church's teachings regarding the sanctity of human life, and therefore raising a strong voice against the policies of apartheid. Eventually, however, without any further consultation, I received a letter informing me that I was no longer 'a minister in good standing'. Frankly, it didn't worry me, because I didn't feel I needed to be an ordained minister, or use the title of 'reverend' in order to do the work that I felt was important and urgent. From then on, my links with the church that I had embraced with so much fervour at the age of nineteen became virtually non-existent.

After my election to parliament, we had joined the Pinelands Methodist Church, but I felt extremely uncomfortable among the congregation. I felt that people would imagine I was there only in order to solicit votes and support, and I really couldn't handle that. At the same time, my children had lost interest in religion, some of them becoming active in politics, and could not see the relevance of spending Sunday mornings in church. When we moved to Rondebosch, I started going to the Congregational Church there, but I didn't last very long. I simply didn't feel any resonance with what was being said and preached. The words and phrases of religious language had lost their meaning, and in my mind I challenged claims that I once adhered to. I came to believe that we don't have to persuade God by fervent prayer to care for his world. I could no longer handle the idea of a God in heaven who is masculine, who is Father. But it didn't help to start talking about God as 'her' and 'she'; it was a shifting away from the concept of a God and heaven and hell. For me, heaven and hell were present in the world, and I saw my role as fighting for justice and against oppression.

During those early years in parliament, certain events took place that stand out more than others. Among those never to be forgotten is 16 June 1976, the fateful date on which schoolchildren in the Johannesburg township of Soweto marched against apartheid. It was a day that changed the nature of resistance in South Africa and very nearly saw a group of MPs come to blows in the parliamentary dining room.

Andries Treurnicht, the ultra-conservative, deeply Calvinist newly appointed deputy minister of Bantu education, had insisted that Afrikaans be used as a medium of instruction in black schools. As an opposition party, we repeatedly warned the government against the recklessness and stupidity of this decision, but to no avail. One of my colleagues, the beloved René de Villiers, a former newspaper editor, warned on several occasions of a growing antipathy towards the new regulations, but even he – an Afrikaner – was labelled by National Party MPs as someone who hated his country and was trying to cause trouble. When the violence finally erupted, and in a classic case of the messenger being damned rather than the message itself being heeded, government members immediately blamed those of us occupying the opposition benches. Such was the depth of feeling that a heated altercation took place during the lunch break.

Within days, the uprising began to spread. In the months that followed there were strikes, rioting and arson across the country. The state's response was an unprecedented crackdown on protesters. The stern measures adopted led to a period of calm for a while, but it was the proverbial lull before the storm. Black schoolchildren had ushered in a new period of intense opposition to apartheid, and it could not be contained. Children marching in the streets were shot and killed; mayhem erupted; Soweto went on the rampage; violence was the order of the day; cars were stoned and burnt; property was destroyed. Thousands were jailed, strong-arm tactics were liberally used by the police, and public protest was banned.

While the ostensible cause of the uprising was the use of Afrikaans in black schools, this was merely the spark that ignited deep and long-standing grievances against the shameful standard of black education, the lack of facilities and overcrowded classrooms. What 16 June actually did was unleash a long-suppressed anger and a new generation's loathing of the dehumanising apartheid policies. In the years that followed, it would become evident that the brave march of a few thousand schoolchildren would coalesce into demands way beyond the use of Afrikaans, or even a decent education. Nothing less than equal rights and an end to racial discrimination at every level would suffice.

Another major event, and one that touched me at a deep personal level, was the death in detention of Steve Biko. I had seen Steve several times after his final visit to our home in Evans Road, Umbilo. In 1969 we had both attended a conference of the University Christian Movement. He was a delegate and I was what they termed a 'theological adviser'. The conference was held in the small Eastern Cape town of Stutterheim, and it was there that Steve, together with a number of his colleagues, founded the South African Students' Organisation (SASO), an all-black movement, distinct from NUSAS, which, in large part, was run by whites.

The conference was memorable, not only because it saw the birth of this extraordinary breakaway movement, but also because we staged demonstrations and marches, carrying branches high above our heads and declaring that we, not 'they', were 'the special branch'. In later years, it became clear to me that genuine security police informers had also attended the conference. Subpoenaed to appear before the Schlebusch Commission, I was questioned about my involvement with various organisations, including the Institute of Race Relations, the Christian Institute, the South African Council of Churches, NUSAS and SASO, though I was never part of the latter.

Even though I had just become an MP, it was extremely intimidating to be grilled by a hostile minister of police, Louis le Grange, and other cabinet ministers and officials. They questioned my every movement and public statement in past years, finally getting to the Stutterheim conference. One question in particular intrigued me: 'Dr Boraine, I understand that during the two or three days that you were there, the local store in Stutterheim ran out of liquor. Do you want to comment on this?' I didn't know whether to laugh or cry at the absurdity of it. I said I had no idea who had ordered what; drinks had been served, as at most student conferences, but I neither understood nor appreciated the correlation between running out of liquor and what took place at the University Christian Movement conference. They left it at that.

My relationship with Steve Biko was a strange one: I was white, privileged and a member of the official opposition in parliament, while he was banned, cut off from society. His every movement was watched, his telephone tapped and he was constantly harassed by the security police. I would write to him on parliamentary letterheads and post the letters in envelopes bearing parliament's crest, signed by me to indicate that no postage stamps were required. He never replied, but we both knew that the letters were read by the security police. I wrote, as it were, to them as well! In my letters I argued against banning orders and called for a national convention leading to a new constitution that would usher in a new South Africa. Steve and I spoke regularly on the phone, always aware that we had uninvited guests listening in.

The only time I ever saw Steve Biko agitated was when he telephoned me at parliament to tell me that Mamphela Ramphele had been roughly and crudely arrested and detained. The co-founder of SASO and the Black Consciousness movement, she and Steve had met as medical students at the University of Natal in 1968. His marriage to another woman and a son notwithstanding, Steve and Mamphela fell deeply in love and had a passionate, albeit often stormy relationship. In post-apartheid South Africa, she became one of the earliest and most prominent black businesswomen, serving on the boards of several major corporations – including Anglo American – and parastatals. In 2000, Mamphela was appointed as one of four managing directors of the World Bank, the first South African to hold this position. She also served as vice-chancellor of the University of Cape Town from 1996 to 2000.

As a young woman, however, she was a prime target of the security police. In 1974, she was arrested and charged under the Suppression of

Communism Act. Two years later, she was detained in terms of the Terrorism Act, and from 1977 to 1984 she was banished to the Northern Transvaal town of Tzaneen. At the time of Steve's death in 1977, she was pregnant with his second son, Hlumelo.

It was her detention in 1976 that prompted Steve to call me. He clearly loved Mamphela deeply, and while he never showed anxiety about his own safety, he certainly cared about what would happen to her. He asked me to make her arrest public as a means of ensuring her safety. I made a strong statement to the media, calling for her release. Steve had also asked if there was anything I could do for her. I told him it was unlikely and, indeed, when I approached Le Grange, he said, 'The law must take its course.'

The last time I saw Steve was after he had been banished to the King William's Town area, where he was born. I went to see him and we walked in the fields, because the buildings were obviously bugged. We talked about many things. He was extraordinarily eloquent; his eyes shone with his commitment, not only to Black Consciousness but also to a new South Africa. When we parted, he said: 'You and I are in very different places. You are in parliament with the Progressive Party, and I am here working, banned, but I would welcome an opportunity for you and your party and me and my group to come together to discuss what our scenario is for a new South Africa. What would it mean in concrete terms?' I said I was quite sure there were many of us who would welcome such a discussion and undertook to talk to Colin Eglin. I did, and Colin later travelled to the Eastern Cape to see Steve.

As I turned to leave that day, I looked back and said: 'Steve, for God's sake be careful; they hate you and they're going to get you if you break your banning order. Please, please be safe.' He smiled and waved and turned away. I think he really believed that he was almost invincible.

In the aftermath of the Soweto uprising in 1976, the Black Consciousness movement that he led found greater support than ever among young black South Africans who had lost patience with moderate resistance. On 18 August 1977, having defied his banning order, Steve was arrested while travelling home from a political meeting and detained in Port Elizabeth under the Terrorism Act.

On 12 September, the news broke that Steve Biko was dead, and the press asked me for a comment. I said, 'Steve didn't die in prison. He was killed, of that I am absolutely sure.' I was proved right: he was severely assaulted by the security police in the Eastern Cape and then, naked and unconscious, flung into the back of a police van, driven 1 200 kilometres to Pretoria Central Prison and thrown into a cell, where this remarkable man died in the most shameful and undignified way. South Africa lost one of its greatest sons, who would have made a rich contribution to the consolidation of democracy and the development of a true human rights culture.

His funeral service, held on a rugby field in King William's Town, was attended by some 20 000 people. There were very few whites, but Helen Suzman, Donald Woods and I travelled together from East London where Woods, one of Steve's greatest champions, was the editor of the *Daily Dispatch*. The one other white person I remember seeing at the funeral was Francis Wilson, a professor of economics at the University of Cape Town, who was a friend of both Steve and Mamphela.

The mood was angry and the mourners were sullen. There were many speakers from different parts of the world. Some of those who had wanted to attend were prevented from doing so when buses were turned back at roadblocks. More than coming to pay their last respects, those who made it came to protest against the murder of this young black leader.

With typical African courtesy, the organisers invited Helen, Donald and me to sit on the platform on which the casket rested. Helen and Donald agreed, wisely, I think, but I felt awkward, that I had no right to be there, so I stood with the crowd below and waited for the funeral to start. I felt the people immediately in front of me, young black men, pushing me back, while those behind were pushing me forward, so I was squeezed between the two groups. Then I felt some of them take hold of my arms and pull me down. I probably panicked and was perhaps overly concerned, but I really did believe that they had mistaken me for a security policeman. I was white, blond, tall, and I suppose I looked the part to them. I thought this was one hell of a way to go. Then an older man immediately to my left turned to the young men, who by that time were pulling me to the ground, and said, 'Do you know who this man is?' He told them my name and some of the work I was involved in and my captors immediately released me, patted me on the back and welcomed me. I was sweating profusely, as for a brief moment I thought I was going to be trampled to death.

Amid the shifting currents within opposition politics and radical protest against government policy during the second half of the 1970s, South Africa was confronted with what became known as the Information Scandal. Also known as 'Infogate' or 'Muldergate' (after the central figure, John Vorster's information minister Dr Connie Mulder), the scandal cost several prominent

Nats their political careers. They included Mulder, who had been tipped to succeed Vorster as premier, General Hendrik van den Bergh, head of the dreaded Bureau of State Security (BOSS), Dr Eschel Rhoodie, a senior official in the government's information department, finance minister Dr Nic Diederichs and, ultimately, Vorster himself.

Through excellent work by investigative journalists from the *Rand Daily Mail* and other English-language newspapers, the country learnt that the government had channelled taxpayers' funds towards financing a daily tabloid newspaper, the *Citizen*. Solidly pro-government and vociferously anti-PFP, the newspaper was merely the tip of the iceberg, but formed part of a concerted effort by the government to sway both national and international opinion in favour of its apartheid policies. The propaganda war saw some R64 million in secret defence funds squandered on bribes for influential lobbyists abroad, the purchase of a newspaper in Washington, DC, and numerous secret projects aimed at gaining support for the NP government. When the unauthorised use and laundering of funds was exposed, parliament set up a special committee to probe the information department's finances, and the consequences forced Vorster to resign as prime minister in 1978. Connie Mulder, the NP's crown prince, fell from grace after he was found to have lied to parliament about the relationship between the government and the *Citizen*.

While the Info Scandal revelations rid South Africa of Vorster, they also opened the door to the PW Botha era, one of the darkest in the country's history. I have no doubt that he leaked details of the scandal to his own caucus, resulting in a shift of support from Mulder to Botha in the last few days before the election of a new NP leader. Mulder was subsequently dismissed from the cabinet and resigned his seat in September 1977.

During my twelve years as an MP before resigning in 1986, I fought three elections: the 1974 by-election that won me a seat, and the 1977 and 1981 general elections. The 1977 poll sprung on us by Vorster was, I believe, an attempt to divert attention from or to cover up the Info Scandal, as well as to disrupt the opposition. My opponent in Pinelands was David Graaff and I was in for a tough fight. The son of well-known and deeply respected former United Party leader Sir De Villiers Graaff, David bore a name familiar throughout the country, but especially in Cape Town. Die-hard UP supporters revered his father and were keen to support the son. David had earned his political spurs in the 1974 general election, when he stood for the UP against Colin Eglin in Sea Point.

Eglin won, despite the fact that PW Botha, the NP's leader in the Cape, publicly urged Nationalists to support Graaff. Three years later, I put it to David (now standing for the NRP) that he was actively courting the support of the NP in Pinelands. He denied it, but a marvellous cartoon by Tony Grogan captured the information we were getting from our many volunteer workers in my constituency, namely that the Nats were going to vote for Graaff. Grogan depicted a very tall Alex Boraine and, next to him, a stunted David Graaff, on stilts. He had a poster around his neck saying, 'Walk tall with the NRP', which was the party's campaign slogan, but on the stilts Grogan had written: 'Nat supporters'.

The NP candidate had garnered more than 1 600 ballots in the by-election which I won by a mere 34 votes. Since then, I had diligently nursed the constituency, responding to every request for assistance and visiting schools and old-age homes regularly. However, there was a possibility that some of my constituents were uncomfortable with my parliamentary speeches, particularly my strong emphasis on the fact that the problem in South Africa was not black power, but white power, which inevitably spawned black power and was leading to serious conflict. If some of my former supporters and all the Nats in Pinelands sided with the NRP in supporting Graaff, I would be in serious trouble.

My position was not helped by the fact that, following Steve Biko's death mere weeks before voters went to the polls, I had come out with some strong statements against Jimmy Kruger, the minister of justice, and NP policies. During a public meeting in the Rondebosch Town Hall, which was packed to the rafters, someone released a teargas canister, causing total mayhem as people struggled to get out, breaking windows and cutting themselves on the glass as tears poured down everyone's cheeks. The next day, the incident was reported on the front pages of newspapers, and on the radio and television news. Conservative Pinelanders and others in my constituency didn't like this kind of public controversy, and I was concerned that all the publicity would work against me. Indeed, a National Party MP drew me aside soon afterwards and told me I was foolhardy to raise the question of Biko's death on the eve of an election. 'If you wanted to do it, you should have waited until after the election. Now you are going to lose,' he warned.

In the end, what might have helped was that the venom spewed by the NP got under the skin of people who had voted for me previously, resulting in many deciding to join my campaign and ensure that I was re-elected.

John Scott put it succinctly in the *Cape Times*, calling me 'the man the Nats love to hate'.

After a tough and bruising struggle that went down to the wire, with most pundits forecasting that the Progs would lose the seat, we managed not only to hold it but also to increase our majority from 34 to 337. In 1981, David Graaff and I faced one another yet again, in a fiercely fought battle that saw an incredible turnout by the voters – 82.2 per cent, the highest in the country. This time, our majority jumped to 1555, the largest yet.

Throughout my time in parliament, the major focus of opposition debates was race relations. Whatever the subject – water affairs or health or education – we invariably brought it back to race relations – the nub of the conflict in South Africa. Over and over again, we hammered the point that all South Africans should experience and enjoy full citizenship in their own country. Both as a team and individually, we repeatedly emphasised the danger of deteriorating race relations due to the effect on black South Africans of the apartheid policies. It was clear that resentment and impatience among black people were escalating, yet the government seemed both blind and deaf to this fact. As the official opposition, we felt it was part of our responsibility to highlight the situation and suggest alternatives, so that we could have some hope of sustainable peace in South Africa.

One incident that sparked a fiery debate concerned Dixon Kohlakala, a resident of Langa and the father of a sick child, who had been fined R50 (or fifty days) for harbouring his wife, Alice, illegally. She had joined her husband in the Cape township to seek help for their child, and the magistrate had stated that the mother's presence was not essential while the child was in hospital. I couldn't believe that something like this could happen, especially since Dr Piet Koornhof, the minister of cooperation and development, had argued not long before in the United States that apartheid was dead. I made the point that the punishment of a father was obscene. 'This must rank among the most despicable incidents which have occurred in South Africa's very bad history in race relations,' I told the assembly. 'The magistrate's remarks are breathtaking in their lack of sensitivity and common humanity. When, for God's sake, will we come to our senses? What kind of people are we to allow this sort of thing to happen? It makes me deeply ashamed to be part of a system that allows this kind of law and this kind of inhuman treatment. So long as this sort of thing continues, so long will South Africa's name be a swear word in the world, and so long will the seeds of revolution be sown and hope for a peaceful resolution of our racial conflict be diminished.'

Unlike Dr Koornhof, it was clear to me that, far from being dead, apartheid was alive and kicking.

Another matter which demanded our attention and vigilance was the government's increasingly harsh approach to any form of opposition to apartheid. We were particularly deeply concerned about detention without trial. Pik Botha, the minister of foreign affairs, was a formidable debater, who had a powerful way of attacking our approach with telling remarks. On one occasion he said, 'Show me one single instance of a person being detained and later brought to trial where the state was proved wrong. These powers will not be used to put anyone in jail just because they tell a joke.'

In my reply, both in parliament and an article in the *Financial Mail*, I said:

> This statement is untrue, highly misleading and frighteningly callous. There are a number of cases where people have been detained in terms of the Terrorism Act, charged under that Act and acquitted. Advocate Botha should read up the law reports of so many of these cases. The statement is highly misleading, for many people detained under the Terrorism Act are never charged and never appear in court. It is impossible to say how many, for the Minister of Justice has consistently refused to disclose how many people are being detained under the Terrorism Act. But press reports give us the following information: detained: at least 236; released without ever being charged: at least 100; died awaiting trial: 7; acquitted: 43; found guilty: 63. Thus fewer than one-third of the total known detained have been found guilty. The statement is also frighteningly callous. 'These powers will not be used to put anyone in jail because they tell a joke.' How can he expect the United Nations and the US or even his own countrymen to believe him when literally hundreds of people have been put not in jail, but in solitary confinement for extended periods, without ever being told what crime they have committed?

And then I gave just one example:

> In June 1969, Mr Peter Magubane was detained with a number of others and held in solitary confinement under the 180 day clause of the General Laws Amendment Act. On October 28 he was charged with others with offences under the Suppression of Communism Act. On April 16 1970, the state withdrew its charges and Magubane was released. On the same day he was rearrested and charged with offences under the Terrorism Act. On 14 September 1970, he was acquitted and again released. During March 1971 he was re-detained under the Terrorism Act and held in

solitary confinement for a further 98 days. On release, he was served with a five-year banning order. In September 1974, he served a six-month jail sentence for breaking his banning order. On 30 September 1975, his banning order was lifted. In other words, in the six years from June 1969 to September 1975, Peter Magubane served a total of 586 days in solitary confinement, a further 90 days in jail and a further 1 642 days under a banning order. During all this time, the single proven crime Magubane had committed was a breach of his banning order regulations – a ban imposed by the state after the courts had twice found him innocent of crimes threatening security.

The labour portfolio assigned to me held implications for the hundreds of thousands of black workers who were still denied the right to form legal trade unions. Over and over again, I tried to emphasise that legislation had to be amended and that blacks should be included in the definition of workers. Illegal strikes were starting to take place because black workers were excluded from union membership. Instead, the government had introduced so-called works and liaison committees, but they were totally inadequate. They were not compulsory, which meant that a bad employer and a leaderless labour force, without regulation or provision, often equalled an unstable labour force within a particular company. Secondly, the powers of the committees were purely advisory and most of the committee systems had powers that could not be enforced by law. In no other country in the world were works committees offered as an alternative to trade unions. In each case that I looked at, they complemented trade unions already in existence. I tried to stress that as long as South Africa distinguished between workers on the grounds of race or colour, the country would not enjoy the labour stability that it sought. I quoted facts and figures which revealed that South Africa had the second-worst strike record in Africa. The only country that was worse off was Morocco. I urged the government to appoint a commission that would look into the question of workers' rights, and to accept the reality that all workers should be allowed to organise and join trade unions, if that was their wish.

This happened with the appointment of the Wiehahn Commission in 1977. The recommendations of both this body and its companion, the Riekert Commission, charged with reviewing influx control measures, were tabled two years later and were very much along the lines that I and others had argued for: legalisation of black trade unions, elimination of statutory job reservation, and recognition, for the first time, of blacks as workers in terms of the law. The government gave in, somewhat reluctantly, and the Industrial Conciliation Act was amended accordingly.

The Riekert Commission of Inquiry into Legislation Affecting the Utilisation of Manpower accepted the fact that poverty in the homelands would continue to push tens of thousands of black migrant workers to the cities. Instead of using the pass laws to punish those who entered urban areas illegally, Riekert proposed the prosecution of employers and landlords who gave jobs or housing to blacks who lacked documentary proof of their right to be there. PW Botha accepted this recommendation, but it was not until eight years and more than one million arrests later that he introduced legislation abolishing the pass laws.

I thought that allowing blacks to form and join trade unions was a huge step forward. It gave the unions a power base they had never had, which I believe accelerated the shift from oppression to democracy.

My stint with Anglo American had given me the opportunity to debate labour problems with management, workers, academics and experts in the field. As the Progressive Party's labour spokesman, I believed it was strategically advantageous, until blacks had a platform and took their place in local, provincial and national government, to introduce measures that would allow them to work towards enhancing their opportunities and personal situations. The 1973 strike by black workers in Durban, and those that followed, had served as indications that we had seen the end of passivity and docility among the black labour force. 'They want a meaningful say in determining the basic conditions of their employment,' I told parliament. 'Black workers are displaying not only a new set of needs, but also demonstrating a new powerful set of demands.'

Interestingly enough, one of the key members of the government who spoke strongly against allowing registered black trade unions was the MP for Vereeniging, FW de Klerk. He argued that the legalisation of black unions could lead to one man, one vote. Official recognition of black trade unions would bring far-reaching changes in the economic field and be a great risk politically, he said. 'Should the government yield to opposition demands for black trade union rights, certain elements would use black trade unionism to change the existing order in South Africa,' he warned, referring to NUSAS leaders and, of course, some of us in the opposition benches. Clearly, De Klerk realised better than most of his colleagues in government that once black workers had gained fundamental rights in the workplace, they would not rest until they had fundamental rights in the country. Mercifully, his arguments did not win the day, and blacks were finally granted the same collective bargaining power as all other workers in 1979.

There were two other major labour issues that I felt strongly about. The first was the exploitation of children. When the *Sunday Times* published reports about children being taken from rural to urban areas and made to work under dreadful conditions, I made the point that child labour was an anachronism that could be equated only with slave labour. I argued that a child had no ability or standing to bargain and that child labour 'is particularly evil because it perpetuates the cycle of poverty which already has so many of our people in its grip'. I urged the department of labour to crack down hard on those who exploited children. Unfortunately, and as a matter of course, the authorities brushed aside as unsubstantiated allegations the frequent reports about recruitment of children for work in the cities.

The second issue that concerned me deeply was migrant labour. There were many incidents of violence in the Cape townships of Nyanga and Guguletu and other parts of South Africa. I denounced the migrant labour system – which even the Dutch Reformed Church described as 'a cancer' – as one of the root causes of the clashes between contract workers from the Transkei and township residents. 'The heart of the matter,' I told parliament, 'is that you have migrants living in communities to which they have no commitment. They have been transplanted from a rural setting into urban areas, where values are different. Their interests do not lie in the townships but with their families in the homelands. Thus they have become social misfits living in ghastly bachelor barracks without wives, preying on local women to whom they feel no responsibility, turning to homosexuality and drinking excessively for want of something better to do.' When people were deprived of their families by law, the one place where they could find some sort of community life was the shebeen.

I made many, many speeches during my time in parliament, but the one that sums up what I was trying to achieve, what message I hoped to convey, dealt with white versus black power. During the third reading of the Appropriation Bill in 1977, I urged the government and all MPs to pledge support for the eradication of every piece of legislation that robbed men and women of their basic humanity, and attempt to see South Africa through the eyes of those for whom discrimination and degradation were daily experiences:

> Let us, once and for all, accept that the black man living in the cities of our land is there to stay and that he has the same hopes and fears, aspirations

and needs as we do. As a specific symbol of that recognition, let him have the security of freehold tenure now – and more than that, let us make it clear that all South Africans need to be equal before the law and enjoy equal citizenship.

The seeds of black consciousness and black power are to be found in the history of South Africa and were planted at a prodigious rate by the wielders of white power. The thesis is white power, the antithesis is black power, and what we need to struggle for is a synthesis which will resolve the basic conflict between white and black power. A change of heart which leads towards a fundamental change in direction and will result in justice and security for black and white South Africans alike, should be the aim of all of us.

I want to quote from a man by the name of Thema, who wrote in September 1922: 'Today the African is being rendered landless and homeless, taxed heavily and cruelly exploited because he has no voice in the making of laws. Daily he is coming more and more to look upon the laws of the country not as protecting safeguards, but as sources of humiliation and oppression. There can be no doubt that the perpetuation of this system will only serve to aggravate the race prejudice which now exists. What is wanted is a policy which will permit mutual understanding and cooperation between the races. The policy of "White South Africa" has naturally given rise on this side of the colour line to a cry of "Africa for the Africans", and as a result the two races are drifting apart. Unless a change is made now, the coming generation will be separated by active hatred and hostility.'

How true that prophecy has come since 1922. This is the major point that I want to make. It did not start in 1948, the 1960s or the early 70s. This is the conflict which is inherent in the South African situation and with which we have to come to terms if we are going to have any kind of development in the future at all. White power results in black power. This we have seen in the rising of the ANC, PAC, SASO and BPC. It is a long, long story.

There must be in this country among every one of us a change of heart, which will issue forth in a change of legislation and practices, which will ensure a movement towards justice and security for black and white in South Africa. Let there be no mistake: Unless there can be a desirable future for any of us, there can be no future for all of us.

When Mr Jimmy Kruger responded to my impassioned speech, it was with remarkable venom. He warned me that he was going to Pretoria that night and would return with information in reply to what I had advocated.

Sure enough, when he spoke the next afternoon, he had in front of him a bulky file and he kept turning the pages and referring to documents and reports in it. It became very clear that this was a dossier on me, put together by the security police, which spanned a twelve-year period from 1965 to 1977.

Kruger accused me of advocating black power and said that this had resulted in the riots taking place in Soweto and elsewhere. He was clearly looking for scapegoats. Referring to the file, he mentioned that I belonged to a wide range of organisations, including the University Christian Movement, the National Youth Leadership Training Programme – which I had founded when I was still in the Methodist Church – the Christian Institute, the South African Council of Churches and the World Council of Churches. He gave detailed information as to where I was on what date and with whom. Clearly, I was the bogeyman who was stimulating and encouraging black power.

During this tirade, there were a number of interjections from my own colleagues, but also some from the National Party benches. JC Greyling, the NP's MP for Carletonville, shouted across the chamber, '*Jy hoort agter tralies*' (you belong behind bars). PTC du Plessis, who was the NP member for Lydenburg, went even further: '*Daar is bloed op jou hande, Boraine*' (there is blood on your hands, Boraine). Tempers in the house were running high. Kruger's posture suggested that he was a prosecutor and I was in the dock, being cross-examined on a number of charges.

What troubled me was the blindness and stupidity of the NP leadership, which didn't seem to understand that black power, the fruit of Black Consciousness, was a direct and inevitable result of the white power that was being used to dominate black, coloured and Indian South Africans. This debate sparked discussions far beyond parliament, and many individuals were interviewed about their views on Black Consciousness and black power. On 11 September 1977, Kruger had told Juliet Bell of the *Argus*: 'The black consciousness movement is infiltrated by communists. They want something completely separate from the government. Blacks will never put this government down. We cannot give them our country or our white institutions.' A brigadier in the security police said: 'Black consciousness has a long and chequered history and there are many, many organisations which are supporting it.'

In the same article, I had said: 'Black consciousness emerges whenever a black person refuses to accept that black is inferior, negative or even evil. It is a throwing off of the slave mentality imposed on him and a standing-up for common human rights. It brings the black man into direct confrontation with the white power structures, and this is why the government harasses and intimidates those who subscribe to the black consciousness movement. To try and stop the growth of black consciousness in South Africa is like trying to stop the sea from breaking on the shore. You will find the emergence of black consciousness everywhere in South Africa, in small villages and big cities alike. It could be God's gift to South Africa, but we are making it into a whip.'

Also interviewed was Professor Nick Olivier, one of my PFP colleagues, who said: 'I can't understand how Mr Kruger will not grasp the concept of black consciousness. This is the road the Afrikaner himself travelled. When consciousness evolves, you cannot eliminate it, you have to accommodate it.' He pressed for consultation with Black Consciousness leaders, not black stooges.

After Steve Biko's death, I was viciously attacked by Minister Kruger for supporting him and the black power movement. I responded with an article in the *Sunday Express*, which read as follows:

No amount of name calling, insinuation or character assassination by the Minister of Justice can minimise the desperately serious breakdown in race relations in South Africa. Against the onslaught by the Minister, I want to state as clearly as I can that my whole life's work has been to prevent the growing polarisation between black and white and to work for reconciliation and justice within South Africa, and I have constantly maintained this stand in and through every organisation I have been associated with. The Minister reveals his basic ignorance of the black power movement when he suggests that I and other whites have any kind of influence at all. The truth is that black power is exclusively black, and even if I might have sought to influence this movement, my approaches would have been dismissed in no uncertain manner.

I want to reiterate that I am as opposed to black power, insofar as it is racially exclusive and strives for total domination, as I am to those manifestations of white power which seek to maintain its privilege at the expense of others.

If we were to consider the history of South Africa, it is clear that black power is no new phenomenon. There are innumerable documents which illustrate the growing resentment among blacks at the treatment which they received immediately prior to the Act of Union and subsequent to that date. It is important to note that in those early days, black men used every constitutional means at their disposal, limited as these were, in seeking their aspirations in the country of their birth.

Today the races continue to be separated by 'active hatred and hostility'. Tragically, the hallmarks of South African society are not peace and security, but anger and fear. Its fundamental policies have caused blacks to feel rejected and thus isolated. To that extent it must take a large measure of the blame for the emergence of black consciousness and black power. In every avenue of life, at home, in the workplace, in society, in education, the stress has been on separatism, which has at no time been equitable and fair, but always at the expense of the black community.

If whites want to live in peace and security, and surely we all want this, then we have to come to terms with the fact that until such time as blacks believe that they are getting a fair deal and have access to the 'making of laws' which influence their lives, black power will remain and will grow, feeding on the general discontent.

No amount of bluster and smear tactics should be allowed to obscure the fundamental and urgent need for negotiation between white and black and practical cooperation, which will ensure a just society and therefore a peaceful and secure future for black and white alike.

We are sitting on a time bomb. The defusing lies in our own hands, but we have no time left except for positive action.

This was a major theme in many of the speeches by PFP members of parliament during the 1970s and 1980s. We warned repeatedly of the dangers of isolationism, of the dangers of separatism, of the dangers of injustice. But we didn't stop there. We urged some form of national convention, a bringing together of all the parties, so that a new constitution could be drawn up that would bring about equality, freedom and justice for all. Despite our best intentions, we were not heard. Instead, we were largely blamed for encouraging blacks to oppose the status quo. It took the National Party many, many years to appreciate that the only way towards a united country was to scrap the pernicious laws that denied full citizenship to all South Africans.

Tragically, the vicious forms of oppression the state imposed in order to perpetuate its exclusive access to power would deepen the divide, exacerbate suspicion, hurt and anger, and the scars remain deeply embedded on the public face of contemporary South Africa. Many of the major problems that post-apartheid South Africa faces are in large measure due to the legacy of years of shameful abuse of power by a minority government.

At every opportunity, the PFP emphasised that the way forward lay in negotiation politics. We were viciously attacked whenever we called for some kind of national convention that would bring together representatives from all sections of our community, in order to work out an equitable plan for the future that would give every person the vote and protect minorities. How ironic that in the end, many years later and after so much hatred and hardship, death and conflict, the National Party agreed to exactly what we had called for so long ago.

It may be that we, the official opposition, sowed the seeds of negotiation politics and the resolution of conflict over the years we were in parliament, but the journey to the negotiations that started in 1990 and finally led to the first democratic election in our history in April 1994 was a slow and grinding process. There were many times when we were in utter despair and wondered whether it was worthwhile continuing to urge the government to change laws and introduce reforms. But we persisted, in spite of the jeers and catcalls from the National Party benches and the government's stubborn refusal to move in any meaningful way towards an inclusive democracy.

CHAPTER 12

Pressure on the family

FROM THE VERY BEGINNING OF OUR MARRIED LIFE, JENNY AND
I were under considerable pressure arising from my work in the
Methodist Church. It involved travelling and a number of meetings in the
evenings, which meant that I was away from home for a large part of the day
and most nights. This placed a burden on Jenny, who had to cope with the
bulk of the normal domestic issues, particularly once the children started to
arrive. She had to look after them on her own far more than was desirable.
However, both of us felt that the work we were doing was important and
worthwhile. It wasn't even a sacrifice; it was something that we needed
to do.

When I went to work for Anglo American, I thought it would be a lot
easier. But I hadn't realised that so much business was conducted at dinner
parties, breakfasts and business lunches, which meant that I was still not
home a great deal of the time. If anything, I was travelling even more, both
within southern Africa and abroad. Anglo American's empire was huge,
and my responsibilities extended to wherever people were employed. For
several years, and a great deal of the time, therefore, Jenny had to be both
father and mother to our four children.

When I entered politics, the pressures on our home life intensified considerably. We moved to Cape Town and lived within my constituency of
Pinelands, which meant – quite rightly – that we were accessible to about
15 000 voters and their families. I wanted it that way, because I felt that if you
were an elected representative, you ought to be concerned about the people
whose votes put you in parliament. I was also fully aware that the brand of
politics I was advocating was not popular, and that service to my constituents
would probably gain me more votes than my advocacy of negotiation for a
democratic state.

In order to run a constituency, one has to have a reliable support staff.
I was extremely fortunate to have Derek Ashley, a venerable and wonderful
man, running our office in Claremont, which covered the Rondebosch/
Claremont area, and equally good people running the office in Pinelands.
But in addition to my work at parliament there were regular meetings,

especially in times of crisis, preparing for a by-election or a general election, dealing with often extremely contentious issues that came up in parliament. Party committee workers also wanted to meet with their public representative, so constituency meetings took up a great deal of time as well.

In 1974, there were so few opposition MPs that, besides the enormous amount of research and preparation we had to do as part of our daily routine, we were also very much in demand among the diplomatic corps. Foreign representatives were encouraged that we had finally made some sort of breakthrough in the election and I think they were keen to have politicians other than National Party members at their functions. Equally, we thought it was important to attend in order to get our message across to governments across the globe.

Our home was always open to all. In addition to constituents, committee members and fellow parliamentarians, we had people of all races coming and going in a constant stream. There were huge advantages to our 'open house' policy, but it came at quite a heavy price. We lacked the privacy that most families enjoy and the children were certainly affected by the lack of time and attention we could give them. Jenny accompanied me to many of my meetings at night, and in later years our daughter, Kathy, said: 'The worst thing of all was both of you being out almost every night of the week.' Fortunately, all my children subsequently indicated, in adult discussions, that they believed it had all been worthwhile. The cause was just and it was inevitable that the demands were great.

I think the anonymous and obscene telephone calls, and the death threats, were the worst of all. Obviously, the children sometimes answered the phone and such calls really frightened and disgusted them. But there was nothing we could do – it went with the territory. When security police cars were parked outside our home, when strange people came to our door at all hours, it was a precarious existence. Because I was in public life, my children were known as Alex Boraine's sons or daughter. Many of their schoolmates did not agree with our politics, and Nick in particular had a hard time at school. He wasn't merely teased, he was effectively abused, in a mild sort of way, simply because he was my son.

Many other families experienced a similar impact of the parents' lifestyle on their children and, as I have always pointed out, it was far worse for black people, who often had their loved ones wrenched from them. Some had to go underground and hardly ever saw their families; many were in prison, thousands fled into exile and others disappeared without trace.

But every family, white or black, which took some kind of stand against apartheid had to pay a price. Our children certainly did.

This was the time when thousands of young white men were conscripted for national service. Compulsory military service is not uncommon in various parts of the world, but in South Africa it was limited to white males, some of whom believed that by serving in the defence force they were actually aiding and abetting apartheid. For example, many young white men were sent into townships to quell riots or arrest and detain – sometimes even shoot – young black men and women. They were fellow South Africans, but they were lined up against each other. This in itself must have been distressing for many of those young white men, but they were also called to fight on the borders of South Africa, notably in South West Africa, and beyond, in Angola. Some were killed, some were injured, some participated in horrifying killings. This, too, left a terrifying legacy, and their families suffered along with them.

Many young white men left the country, some never to return, and we lost so much of their skills, enthusiasm and commitment forever. Some stayed, but refused to be conscripted.

Our middle son, Jeremy, decided that he would do one year of military service in the navy and then attend the University of Cape Town. Unfortunately, he was still required to attend month-long camps, once a year for two decades.

As he grew older and became even more aware of the stand-off in South Africa, he felt more and more uncomfortable about serving in the military, and decided that he would not attend camps, but he refused to leave the country. This meant that he virtually became a fugitive. I recall the telephone calls we used to get at home from people saying they were friends of his, while they were actually naval authorities. Because we had been alerted by Jeremy, we simply said he was no longer living at home, which was true. When asked for a forwarding address, we said we didn't have one. 'You know what young people are like,' we would say, 'they just move out and we haven't a clue where he is at the moment.' Did we have a phone number for him? No, we didn't. This went on for a while, and eventually they arrived at our front door. They asked the same questions and we gave the same answers. It was almost like a game, but a frightening one, because, like so many other young men who had made a similar decision, Jeremy was perpetually on the run. To this day he has an uncomfortable relationship with the telephone! Often, when it rings, he is reminded of that time, when he refused to answer the phone so as to evade those who were trying to find him.

Inevitably, they caught up with him and he was duly charged with refusing to attend camps. He appeared in court and was given a suspended sentence on condition that he reported for his next camp. He was adamant that he wasn't going to do so, and for the next few years he had no real permanent address and moved from place to place. Fortunately, he was president of the South African Student Press Union and had to travel all over South Africa, visiting universities for training sessions of future writers and editors.

He was finally picked up in Johannesburg, strangely enough, not by the military authorities, but by the security police, and not because he was avoiding military service, but because of his involvement in student politics. He was taken to John Vorster Square, police headquarters in Johannesburg, interrogated for about six hours and then released. Much to Jeremy's relief, there was clearly a lack of coordination between the military and security police, but now that both had their eyes on him, he had to go deeper underground for about two years, until 1985.

Our daughter, Kathy, was on the receiving end of many of the abusive telephone calls and threats that came our way. One evening, she returned from a school function to find a wreath hanging on our front door. The message, addressed to Jenny, read: 'You will receive many more wreaths when we kill your husband.' Undeterred, when she left school and went to the University of Cape Town, Kathy was elected to the Student Representative Council in her first year and participated in many marches and demonstrations against the apartheid government.

I was called out of parliament one day by Louis le Grange, the minister of police. He told me my daughter had been arrested and was being held at the Paarl police station. He said she had been taking part in an illegal march but that no charges would be brought against her or the others involved, adding: 'Please try and control your children.' I replied: 'My daughter has every right to express her opposition to government policies and doesn't need my permission to do so. I am very proud of her.' The minister retorted: 'Then you people must face the consequences.'

More serious was the fate of our oldest son, Andrew, who was elected to the Student Representative Council in his first year at the University of Cape Town in 1978. Three groups contested the election: the young liberal Progressive Party group (which Andrew had been involved in at first, mainly as a result of my being a member of the party and representing it in parliament), a conservative group and an emerging left-wing group. Andrew opted to stand on the latter's ticket, and won. In his second year he was re-elected, this time as vice-president of the SRC, and he became more involved in politics, not only on campus but in the country.

At the end of 1979, aged nineteen, he was elected the youngest-ever president of NUSAS. From that moment on, he worked virtually full time for NUSAS.

On 16 June 1980, he was on the University of Natal's Durban campus when he was detained by the security police under Section 6 of the Terrorism Act. They took his glasses (later returned) so he could hardly see; they removed his belt and shoelaces, threw him in a car and drove him through the night to Cape Town. That morning, he was taken from a police cell at Caledon Square to Parow, where he was held in a cell at the police station for fifty-eight days. He was interrogated for six weeks. One of his interrogators was the notorious Craig Williamson, who betrayed many young opponents of apartheid while posing as a campus activist and infiltrating student organisations. Initially on the security police payroll and later that of Military Intelligence, Williamson would eventually be granted amnesty by the Truth and Reconciliation Commission for a string of offences, including the letter bombs that killed Ruth First, Jeanette Schoon and her little daughter, Katryn. Although not a member of the Amnesty Committee, I often attended amnesty hearings, including Williamson's. I watched him perform before the committee with great confidence and arrogance. Remembering that he had told Andrew, while interrogating him, that they were 'both working towards the same thing ... we just use different methods', I felt revulsion as I listened to Williamson admitting to human rights violations over a long period.

Andrew's cell was small and cold. There was no natural light, so it never warmed up. There was a toilet without a seat and a small tin mug of water, which was filled from time to time. His abiding memory of that experience was a sense of utter hopelessness and loneliness.

'There is a difference between feeling lonely and being completely and utterly on your own. They are so different,' he later recalled. 'When you are lonely, you can always call someone on the phone, you can look up a friend, but when you have absolutely no choice in the matter, and this was the first time in my life that it had happened to me, twenty years old, there was no choice but to be on my own – no contact. This was a shattering feeling. There was no one I could turn to, no one I could call, no one I could talk to, no one I could tell.'

This was the experience of so many who were detained without trial and without knowing how long they were going to be held, because Section 6 of the Terrorism Act allowed for indefinite incarceration. Jenny and I were simply informed by the security police, the day after he was picked up, that he was in detention.

Andrew was allowed no visitors. After a few weeks, we were told that we could leave parcels for him at Caledon Square and that they would be delivered to him, wherever he was being held. We brought clothing and food parcels three times a week. The police there assured us that he was well and was getting everything that we took him, but this was an outright lie. Andrew told us after he was released that he had seldom received food parcels from us.

Thanks to Jenny's ingenuity, we managed to smuggle a ballpoint pen refill to him, hidden in a tube of toothpaste. He told us afterwards how he had brushed his teeth three or four times before the slim cartridge suddenly popped out. It was an absolute godsend, allowing him to write in the one book that he was allowed, a Bible. The policemen at Caledon Square had agreed that I could give him a Bible, but said they would need to examine it carefully first. I wrote a message as though it was for his twenty-first birthday, as well as a text from Deuteronomy 31:6: 'Be strong and of good courage.' He read the Bible, which reached him only two weeks later, several times because he had nothing else, and used the blank pages at the back to tick off the days and write down his feelings in some kind of code.

For two and a half months, there I was, an elected member of parliament, with no knowledge of where our son was being detained. I sat in the opposition benches, gazing at the minister of police and the minister of justice, knowing that they had done this to my son – and there was nothing I could do about it. I tried to meet with them, I tried to reason with them, but they didn't want to discuss the matter at all. Andrew was behind bars, and that was that. The long tentacles of the apartheid state reached not only hundreds and thousands of people in the townships and suburbs, but even the families of those who were part of the government's 'loyal opposition'. It was impossible to be loyal to a gang of thugs who could do this to so many young people. So much for Pik Botha's statements about detention without trial.

One night Jenny and I discussed the possibility of chaining ourselves to the gates of parliament so as to alert the press and prompt them to focus not only on Andrew's situation, but also on the policy of detention without trial which was so prevalent in South Africa at that time. Remarkably, the security police released him the next day! We always believed that our telephones were tapped, but hadn't realised that the authorities could actually eavesdrop on private conversations in our own home.

Andrew immediately returned to work with NUSAS, so I suppose it wasn't surprising that he was soon detained again. He was picked up at the NUSAS offices in Cape Town and held under the General Laws Amendment Act. In a strange way, he was grateful for this, because you could be detained under this Act for only two weeks before being charged or released. Unfortunately, at the end of the prescribed period, he was fetched from his cell and told, 'Bring your blankets, you're going to need them. You're on your way to Pretoria.' This time, he was held under the Internal Security Act, which allowed for indefinite detention.

Once again he was driven through the night, wrapped in blankets because it was freezing, with three chain-smoking policemen as his escort. About noon the following day they arrived at the old Pretoria Central Prison, which Andrew recognised from *Cold Stone Jug* by Herman Charles Bosman. He was taken to B Section, which was the isolation wing, and put in a tiny cell. There was a bed and a bucket, and that was it.

The routine was strict. 'You were woken at 5 a.m. for breakfast,' Andrew recalled later. 'Lunch was served at 10 a.m., supper at 3 p.m., and then all the lights were switched off for the night. You sat in the dark, not sleeping, wondering how long you were going to be there. You were almost out of your mind. You had no natural light, you couldn't walk around in the pitch darkness, it was freezing cold, you lay on your bed trying to get warm.'

But during this period of detention, he was allowed some literature and occasional visitors. My good friend Charles Villa-Vicencio gained access to him because he was still an ordained minister, although he was teaching at the University of South Africa at the time. We all really appreciated the visits Charles made.

We went to Pretoria to see Andrew, and every time we did so or spoke to the press, we tried to keep it in context: our son was only one of thousands of people in a similar situation; many were far worse off, many badly tortured.

On one trip to Pretoria, I went to see the minister of justice, Kobie Coetsee. I walked into his office and even before sitting down I said to him, 'Minister, I can only assume that my son has been seriously involved in violence, that he must have been making home-made bombs in his backyard for you to do this to him.' He was genuinely shocked and replied, '*O my God! Wie het so gesê?*' (Oh my God! Who said so?)

'Well,' I said, 'what on earth could he have done for you to have him detained yet again without trial?' Coetsee tried to explain that they had acted against Andrew for his own good – the usual story – that he was detained so that he wouldn't get involved in any further political activities. I dismissed this as absolute rubbish and urged him to charge Andrew or release him. He then confided in me that Andrew was, indeed, to be released within the next week or so, but that the police were going to slap a banning order on him.

I hated doing it, but I asked one favour: I told Coetsee that my son had been terrified by the way he was driven through the night at 180 kilometres an hour, and that I would willingly pay the airfare so that Andrew and I could fly back to Cape Town together. I would also pay the fare of the security policeman who would accompany us. The minister refused point blank, saying that it would be a security risk, but said he would make arrangements for Andrew to be transported on a routine military flight. A week later, I returned to Pretoria, Andrew was released and we embraced for the first time in ages, because we hadn't been allowed any contact when we visited him; we had communicated on a telephone through a glass panel. It was wonderful to be with him again, but the flight was awful. The aircraft was an old Dakota, which chugged along for four hours. A security policeman sat between my son and me and the noise was such that we couldn't speak, even if we wanted to.

The police were waiting for us at Cape Town airport and they drove us to our home in Rondebosch. There, in my study, they had the temerity to serve a banning order on my son, which I had to sign.

We spent the rest of that day and the night together, but I knew he would want to be on his own again, so that other people could visit him, one at a time. He was confined to the magisterial area of Cape Town; he was not allowed onto any campus; his passport was confiscated; he was not allowed to visit any place of business, factory or airport. It was a kind of self-imprisonment. Although he was supposed to be with only one person at a time, we made it very clear – publicly – that we would not obey that restriction in our own home. The authorities never took action against us on this score, but from time to time there was the usual police car parked outside our house and Andrew was tailed wherever he went.

He couldn't go back to university and had no means of earning a living. He was already fiercely independent and thought the best thing would be to become part-owner of an extremely small bookshop, called Open Books, in Observatory. However, he needed money to buy a share in the business.

Dick Enthoven, a friend and a parliamentary colleague, came to see me in my office and said he wanted to help Andrew, but felt helpless; he wondered if Andrew needed money to set himself up? We borrowed R10 000, and in later years, when I tried to repay the money, Dick declined. 'I never intended it to be a loan, but I knew you wouldn't accept it as a gift. It's gone, it's forgotten,' he said. It was a very generous act by a very generous man. Cruelly, the security police set fire to the bookshop in the early hours of one morning. Neighbours saw the police cars come and go and the place going up in flames, but no one was charged.

For the next few years, Andrew kept a low profile in public, but began to work much more closely in the underground movement with the ANC, helped to set up the United Democratic Front in 1983 and became its treasurer in the Western Cape. It is remarkable that, having been through so much, he later became city manager of Cape Town and then executive director of the Cape Town Partnership.

Our story is but a single example of what happened to so many hundreds and thousands of families throughout South Africa, but it certainly left its mark. Andrew suffered post-traumatic stress for several years after his experience, but counts himself – as we do – lucky. In evidence before the TRC, Ferdi Barnard, an operative with the SADF's Civil Cooperation Bureau, testified that one Peaches Gordon had been paid R1 000 to kill various people in the 1980s, including future cabinet minister Dullah Omar, journalist Gavin Evans and Andrew. So he is lucky to still be alive, when so many more are not.

Foolishly, Jenny and I tried to protect our youngest son, Nicky, from the reality of what was going on in our lives at the time. He was just a little boy, who had one brother being hunted by the military police and another brother in jail. Meanwhile, people were constantly moving in and out of our house or seeking refuge there. I came home one day to find a number of black babies in bathtubs or being fed at the table. Crossroads was in crisis and Jenny and many other women were fetching the babies from their homes and bathing and feeding them, then returning them to their mothers. Sometimes they also stayed overnight. There was also a regular flow of people – strangers – knocking on our door, passing on messages. I didn't know who they were, nor did my family, but, inevitably, some who were on the run from the police sought shelter in our home.

Nick was aware of all this activity, but didn't understand it. It was a tough time for him and we tried to shield him, to surround him with our love and protection. We were troubled that he didn't want to go to school and would complain every morning that he had a terrible tummy ache. We didn't believe him, and we didn't understand, so we would take him to school as usual, but finally Jenny took him to our family doctor, George Dommisse, to have the persistent tummy ache checked out. He gave her hell. I should have been there as well, because we were both responsible. 'What you are doing is forcing your young son to internalise all his emotions and fears and confusion, and that's what is causing his stomach pain,' George said. He sent Jenny and Nick to see a psychologist, who confirmed George's diagnosis and said that we, the parents, were far more in need of treatment than Nick.

That evening, we sat down with Nick and talked quietly to him about what was happening and why; we explained as best we could what we were trying to do and reassured him that as long as we could love and be close to one another, it would be all right. In particular, we explained to him why his oldest brother was in prison. He told us then that he thought 'only crooks go to prison, so my brother is a crook'. How we could have allowed this to happen, I will never know, but it was stupid beyond words. The marvellous thing was that the next morning there was no tummy ache, and off he went to school without a problem. There was never a recurrence, because we took him into our confidence from that moment on.

CHAPTER 13

Moving on

IN THE 1980S, SOUTH AFRICA WAS IN THE HANDS OF PW BOTHA, who had succeeded Vorster in 1978. In many ways, Botha was a self-made man. Originally an NP organiser, he used both fair means and foul to disrupt and break up public meetings of the then UP. He was a tough man and a cruel one. My first encounter with him was soon after I was elected to parliament in 1974. During my first parliamentary session, I began to observe him and tried to decide whether or not the accounts I had of him were accurate. I soon discovered that he was indeed powerful, often irritable and rude, and that most people seemed to be terrified of him. I gathered that within his caucus he ruled with a rod of iron, and he certainly gave that impression in parliament. He loved to see people squirm.

In his book *The Last Trek: A New Beginning*, FW de Klerk recorded how he very nearly resigned from parliament because of PW Botha's 'surliness, aggression and poor human relations [which] were doing serious harm to the National Party and the country'. I heard from people within the NP of powerful cabinet ministers going into Botha's office and often coming out in tears. He was a formidable opponent, ideologically hidebound, and yet with a certain pragmatism that led to his fiddling with the apartheid policies without any serious intention of transforming or abandoning them.

In September 1983, following a multi-party commission chaired by cabinet minister Chris Heunis, parliament voted by 119 to 35 to approve a new constitution, in terms of which a tricameral assembly would be established. This was Botha's response to the growing resistance against apartheid within and outside South Africa. In addition to the parliament for whites, there would be separate houses for coloureds and Indians. Not surprisingly, there was a built-in majority of white parliamentarians whenever issues of common interest were debated. Blacks were totally excluded, and Botha made it clear that he had no future plans to include them. They could have representation in their own institutions in the so-called independent homelands. Botha was very smug and satisfied with the result and immediately called a referendum on the new proposals. However, only whites would be asked to respond to the stark and simple question: 'Do you approve of the Republic of South Africa Constitution Act of 1983?'

The Progressive Federal Party, which held twenty-six parliamentary seats at the time, had argued long and hard while this constitutional change was debated. We opposed the proposal on two major grounds. Firstly, we were opposed to the built-in white majority which meant, in effect, that this was a mere sop to coloured and Indian South Africans, who would never be able to outvote the whites on any key or critical issue. Secondly, and more importantly, we argued against the exclusion of black South Africans. We warned that this would only exacerbate a situation that had already provoked major conflict within the country, and that blacks would become even angrier and more determined to oppose the apartheid policies.

In this, we were strongly supported by Mangosuthu Buthelezi, and we often appeared on the same platform with him and other members of the Inkatha Freedom Party in opposing this measure. We travelled the length and breadth of the country, held public and house meetings, published pamphlets and did everything a small opposition party could do. We believed – and stated unambiguously – that if the constitution was to be amended, it should do so meaningfully and include all South Africans. But we were on a hiding to nothing.

Adding to our problems in persuading voters to reject the new constitution was the fact that the Labour Party, which had the support of the majority of coloureds, belatedly and surprisingly decided to support the proposed change. I recall the Reverend Allan Hendrickse and several of his co-leaders calling for a meeting with the PFP. We met at my home and talked for several hours. When they left, I was convinced that they were going to have nothing to do with Botha's plan. Unfortunately, other influences were brought to bear, notably Heunis using all his persuasive powers and skills and generous hospitality to win the day. There was division among the Indian population too, but Amichand Rajbansi's South African Indian Council followed suit and decided to support Botha's move. The government could claim that this was progress – gradual and slow, to be sure, but, nevertheless, at long last coloured and Indian people would have a say in how the country was governed.

The National Party campaign was built around the catch phrase that the new constitution would be 'A step in the right direction'. Relieved and confused white voters bought the argument and gave Botha a two-thirds majority. The Nats were understandably cock-a-hoop. Both as a party and

as individuals, we were deeply depressed. We knew beyond a shadow of
doubt that the exclusion of blacks would only pour fuel on an already
smouldering and resentful mood.

Ironically, as a direct consequence of this new constitution, 1983 saw
the birth of the United Democratic Front, in which Allan Boesak played a
prominent role. More than 300 organisations from around the country
joined together under the banner of the UDF and stepped up the pressure
on the government's policies considerably. It wasn't long before the government decided that it couldn't tolerate this new opposition, and the UDF,
together with many other organisations, was banned.

Following the overwhelming support for government from the electorate,
I felt it was time for the PFP to take a stand by refusing to take our seats
when the next session of parliament convened. I discussed this with several
colleagues at our annual congress, but the only one who was enthusiastic
in his support was Harry Pitman, the mercurial member of parliament
from Natal. Tragically, he collapsed and died from a heart attack at the
congress.

I had fully intended raising the idea of a strong protest for open discussion. However, when I mentioned this to Van Zyl Slabbert, he argued that,
having spoken to Helen Suzman in particular, we should at least give the
new dispensation a chance, and urged me not to raise the option of refusing
to take up our seats. We could consider such action at another time, he urged.
Out of respect for him and Helen, I agreed not to bring up the issue, but
from that moment on I was restless and unhappy in parliament. So, too, was
Van Zyl. He and I often had long debates about new strategies and what we
could do to halt the government colossus that was moving towards inevitable
dire conflict in our country.

With the advent of Botha's national security plan to counteract the 'total
onslaught' against apartheid, the military became more and more involved
at every level of South African society, while parliament became even more
irrelevant. By the mid-1980s, the key decisions were no longer being taken
by elected representatives of the ruling National Party. They were being made
by the military high command, the State Security Council and PW Botha.

Towards the end of 1985, Van Zyl and I had a long discussion about the
forthcoming parliamentary session. We agreed that, unless Botha used his
state of the nation address to introduce some major reforms, we would have
to reconsider our continued presence at parliament. We rarely discussed the
possibility of leaving parliament with anyone else, but Van Zyl did try to raise

the matter with Harry Oppenheimer, the most generous donor of PFP funds, and with Helen Suzman, who pooh-poohed the idea. As Colin Eglin acknowledges in his book, *Crossing the Borders of Power*, Van Zyl also specifically raised the possibility of his resignation while they were on a trip to Australia.[1]

In January 1986, immediately before the no-confidence debate, Eglin, as chairman of the caucus, Van Zyl as party leader and I, as federal council chairman, met to discuss our strategy. Van Zyl made it quite clear that he had become increasingly impatient at the lack of progress and our own apparent inability to make a significant impact on government policy. He even recommended that we should all resign our seats, fight them again in by-elections, and then refuse to take our places in parliament until certain conditions were met. Eglin, a pragmatic politician who believed strongly in the role of parliamentary opposition, was aghast at the suggestion. He indicated that he had discussed this with Helen Suzman, who was equally dismissive. Clearly, this was a plan that was not going to fly.

At the end of our discussion, I said that regardless of what anyone else was going to do, I would really have to reconsider my position at the end of the no-confidence debate. Eglin was furious and Van Zyl was silent. I had no sooner arrived home that evening than the phone rang. It was Van Zyl, asking me to come and see him immediately. I did, and he told me that he had made up his mind to leave parliament at the end of the following week, and would announce this in his speech at the conclusion of the no-confidence debate. I was thrilled, and said I would do the same. Van Zyl said he would prefer to make the announcement on his own, as leader of the party, and that as chairman of the federal council I should hold the party together and leave a week or so later. Looking back, that made absolutely no sense at all, but it seemed reasonable at the time. Obviously, the impact of the leader of the opposition ending a no-confidence debate in a packed house with a crowded gallery, the press poised to hear what Van Zyl would argue as far as the future was concerned, would be enormous. I supported Van Zyl wholeheartedly and wanted to resign at the same time, but agreed to defer my departure. As events clearly showed, however, this made my own position untenable.

Van Zyl shocked the caucus by revealing, immediately before going into the house, that he was going to resign. He delivered his speech as leader of the opposition, then made his announcement, and all hell broke loose. The National Party was furious, because he was effectively impugning parliament – their parliament. The media were all over the story and the

PFP was stunned and extremely depressed. Most of my colleagues were very angry at Van Zyl's move.

I was put in an extremely awkward position. Inevitably, the media approached me and others for our views on this dramatic turn of events. I knew that I would soon follow Van Zyl; I could hardly condemn him as many of my colleagues did – but at the same time, and at his urging, I was still chairman of the federal council. In my public statements, I encouraged people to listen closely to what Van Zyl was saying, to try to understand why he had made his decision and to learn from it.

In private, however, matters were rapidly going from bad to worse and I felt extremely awkward. A delegation led by Roger Hulley (who later died of a heart attack on the squash court) urged me to seek leadership of the party in place of Van Zyl. They came to my home and we had a long discussion, to which I listened carefully. Throughout that weekend, the media constantly asked if I was available to take Van Zyl's place. My response was that I would have to think about it carefully and consult my colleagues. I had called an emergency executive meeting for the Monday after Van Zyl quit, and various members of the party leadership flew to Cape Town. I was attacked for not being tough enough on Van Zyl and unclear in my statements. Douglas Gibson, who can be a nasty character – I have often thought that Tony Leon borrowed some of his abrasiveness from Gibson – delivered a scathing attack on me. 'If you think you are going to be the new leader of this party, think again,' he said. 'Colin Eglin has been hurt enough and he is the man I am going to support.' Bound by my agreement with Van Zyl not to reveal my own intention to resign my parliamentary seat, I couldn't admit that I had no interest in becoming the party leader, and had to take the criticism on the chin – but I cursed Van Zyl several times a day for landing me in that particular predicament.

The situation was not helped by the fact that, at this critical time, I had to travel to Johannesburg for an important report-back meeting with the CEO of the pharmaceutical company Johnson & Johnson, for whom I had been acting as a consultant. The trip was interpreted by some of my colleagues as a mission to test the waters to see what support I would have if I stood as leader of the party. In truth, I saw no one from the PFP while I was in Johannesburg. I presented my report to Johnson & Johnson and flew back to Cape Town the next day.

The atmosphere at parliament was extremely tense. People were glum and clearly puzzled by my position, wondering what on earth I was up to.

I know that Colin Eglin felt particularly unsettled, and there was great tension between us. Because I had enormous respect and regard for him, I went to see him late on the Wednesday afternoon and told him that I was not available as party leader and hoped speculation in this regard would not come between us. His quite brusque reply was that this was not a matter for us to decide, but that it would be up to the party. I felt that I had to come clean and tell him that I was leaving parliament and would announce this at the caucus meeting the next day. He was deeply shocked and urged me to sleep on my decision, and meet him again at 8 a.m. the following day. I reluctantly agreed, although my mind was already made up. I knew beyond all doubt that I wanted out. The next morning we met as arranged and I told him that I was going ahead with my resignation.

The word spread quickly. Clearly, Eglin had confided in some of the senior members, including Harry Schwarz. He came to see me and told me bluntly that although he was not happy I was leaving parliament, I should know that had I become the party leader, he would have had to resign, because he could never serve under me. I appreciated his honesty. I had never been comfortable with Schwarz as a member of our caucus. I knew him as some-one who was extremely bright and able, but I didn't find it easy to trust him. I knew that he had deep feelings about the fact that his family, fleeing Nazi Germany, had found asylum in South Africa at a time when many other countries were turning Jews away, and that he felt a tremendous debt of gratitude towards the state. But I think that sometimes he could not distin-guish between the state and the government of the day. I always wondered if he was having discussions with senior members of the National Party to which his PFP colleagues were not privy. Whatever the case, Schwarz and I certainly didn't get on. I was way to the left of him in my political approach and we often clashed.

One particularly memorable caucus meeting had been specially called by Schwarz following a 'Release Mandela' rally at the University of Cape Town in 1984. Along with Nelson Mandela's daughter Zinzi, I had been asked to speak at the gathering. It was a huge event, attended by about 2000 people. Naturally, I called for Mandela to be released from prison, then raced back to parliament for the afternoon debate.

Unbeknown to me, Vause Raw, leader of the New Republic Party at the time, and a National Party member whose name I can't recall, had brought posters advertising the rally into parliament. At the appropriate time they held up the posters, which showed a black and white sketch of me and Zinzi.

In the background was a hazy portrait of Mandela – who had not been seen for decades by anyone except immediate family members, lawyers, prison warders and fellow inmates – as the artist thought he might look. The headline on the poster was, 'Release Mandela Now'. Raw and his NP cohort rose to their feet and slated me for daring to demand the release of this communist terrorist.

They were playing politics, of course, and they knew there were people in my party who would be unhappy that I had addressed the rally. I hadn't consulted anyone in advance over what I thought was a perfectly natural thing to do. But, in caucus, Schwarz accused me of deciding for blacks who their leaders should be, by calling for Mandela's release.

His argument was quite ludicrous. It was obvious that, regardless of who black South Africans chose to follow, Mandela was going to play a major role in any new political dispensation.

Nevertheless, my participation in the rally prompted a lengthy debate by the caucus, which had not been resolved by the time we had to return to the house. Later that day, I had gone to see Van Zyl in his office and told him: 'Listen, I don't make idle threats about resigning – it's not my style. But if you decide to come down against me on this issue, then there is no place for me here.' To his credit, Van Zyl thought about the situation overnight and, at another caucus meeting the next day, he pointed out to the members that pardon was often offered to prisoners who had been in jail for a long time, and that it would make political sense for Mandela to be released. So I won that battle, but I don't think Harry Schwarz was happy about some of the positions I continued to take.

Exactly six days after Van Zyl had resigned from parliament in February 1986, I entered the caucus room at 9 a.m. and asked if I could make an announcement. I said I thought the time had come for alternative strategies. While there might well be a case for opposition members to stay in parliament, I saw no point in doing so. I then tendered my formal resignation, not only from the caucus but also from the party. There was a deflated atmosphere. I think my colleagues were still trying to deal with Van Zyl's resignation, and my departure, not only as a senior member of the party but also as chairman of the federal council, caused an even deeper gloom.

I didn't feel at all comfortable. In fact, I suddenly felt very alone and wished fervently that Van Zyl and I had done this together. What I hadn't anticipated was the antagonism that followed my announcement. Caucus members had been denied the opportunity to react to Van Zyl's resignation, because he had packed his bags and left immediately, but now they had an opportunity to vent their collective spleen, and the rest of the meeting was most unpleasant. The party closed ranks, understandably, and I felt ostracised. I asked Harry Schwarz if I could have five or ten minutes during the afternoon debate on finance, which was his portfolio. He agreed with alacrity.

Early that Thursday afternoon, I rose in parliament and told the Speaker and the house that I was resigning my seat. There were immediate cries of derision from the National Party benches, and complete silence from my colleagues. After a while, however, the members settled down and listened as I gave my reasons for leaving. I emphasised the unrepresentivity of the current parliament, the deliberate exclusion of blacks from the new constitution and the need for alternative strategies that would include consultation with all South Africans in the search for a negotiated settlement. I concluded my speech and left the chamber, never to return. Immediately afterwards there was a press conference, and one of the key questions put to me was: 'Would you consider returning to parliament at some future time?' I replied, 'In a transformed parliament which is accessible to all South Africans and fully representative, I might well think about it – but right now, my decision and desire is to look for other ways of trying to continue the fight against apartheid and work towards negotiation politics.'

As soon as the news was made public, I received a call from Van Zyl, who came to our home with a large bottle of whisky. Thus ended an extremely unsettled, uncertain and unhappy week of my life. There was a huge sense of relief, but it had not been an easy decision to make. From the moment I left parliament, my salary and benefits ceased. I had four children, no job, and no plan. But I believed I had done the right thing.

Van Zyl and I discussed our next steps at some length and decided that the first thing we should do was consult black leaders, both in and outside South Africa, as to whether they thought two middle-aged white males had any contribution to make. Should we simply sit on the sidelines? Should we consider leaving the country? Should we seek university teaching posts? Should we try to make money for the first time in our lives? What were the options?

There is one statement in Colin Eglin's book – an excellent account of fifty years of politics in South Africa – that warrants a response. At one point he writes: 'There was much conjecture about what Alex Boraine was going to do. He was a close confidant of Slabbert and had been chairman of the party's federal executive throughout the period of Slabbert's leadership.

His immediate response did not help anyone to understand the rationale behind the precipitate resignation, for without supporting or criticising Slabbert, Boraine told the media that he would decide that week both on his candidacy for party leadership – and on whether he too would resign.'[2]

While I can well understand why Colin and my other colleagues were puzzled by my position, I think what I have written above explains the dilemma that I faced. I had made an agreement with Van Zyl that, before resigning, I would preside at the next federal council meeting, at which his resignation and its implications, as well as the party leadership, would be discussed. As it happened, I could not last that long.

Some other members of parliament, notably Marius Barnard and Errol Moorcroft, had confided in Van Zyl and me that they too were fed up with the way things were going and were prepared to follow us. As Moorcroft put it, 'If you hold a handkerchief in your hand and you let it go, I will be behind you before it hits the ground.' When we did make the move, we looked behind us and there was no one there! In fact, Moorcroft and Barnard were two of the strongest critics of our decision to resign our seats. Not only did nothing come of their earlier assurances, but I had barely made my announcement to the caucus before Barnard said: 'Mr Chairman, I want to assure you that I am not going to be a rat deserting a sinking ship.' Moorcroft said it was beyond his understanding that we would make this decision without having any other strategy in mind. He said it reminded him of someone deciding to dump one girlfriend without having another waiting in the wings! Graham McIntosh chided me, saying I might have the moral high ground, but that the remaining MPs would continue to do what they believed was right.

Strong though our convictions were, I don't think that Van Zyl and I fully anticipated the fallout. The consequences of walking out of parliament were really quite severe. Firstly, the National Party and its press did everything possible to play down our decision, which called into question the very institution of parliament, not so much as a place of policy-making, but rather as illegitimate and unrepresentative. This was anathema to a government that was trying to portray South Africa to the outside world as a democracy in which provision was made for representation of all sections of the population. The NP and its media supporters were quite vicious in their sustained attacks on us.

Secondly, we had not realised how strong the criticism was going to be from our own colleagues. There were a number of reasons for this. Perhaps

Van Zyl could have taken them into his confidence a little earlier, though in his book, *Tough Choices: Reflections of an Afrikaner African*, he does record that he told Andrew Savage, Errol Moorcroft, Pierre Cronje and Peter Gastrow – 'the members of my caucus I trusted most' – prior to going public.[3] Many of our colleagues had great faith in him, looked to him for leadership, respected him, and felt that the plug was being pulled on them when he left so abruptly. I believe there might also have been a sense of guilt among some of the remaining MPs, who possibly felt that they should have joined us. Whatever the reasons, they really let us have it, with both barrels.

I felt most sorry for the party supporters and volunteer workers – people who had walked the streets, knocked on doors, defended us and struggled for many years to put us in parliament as their representatives. In a sense, we had let them down, and I didn't feel good about that or the fact that I would no longer be part of my constituency.

What I didn't anticipate was the loss of so many people I considered friends. We had made some wonderful friends through our political struggle, but after we had left parliament, people would sometimes cross the street in order to avoid talking to us, a number wrote scathing letters to the newspapers, while some told me quite bluntly and to my face that they wanted nothing to do with me in future.

Helen Suzman was vehemently opposed to our departure. She had been in parliament for a long time, most of it as the sole voice of Progressive opposition, under constant attack from the government benches, and felt that we had given up because we couldn't take the heat. Actually, I think she liked the institution of parliament; she was very much part of the formality and traditions, and when Van Zyl and I turned our backs on it, I think she felt that we had abandoned the fight for constitutional or peaceful change.

This was absolute nonsense, of course. We were leaving a specific battle-field, but we had no intention of giving up the war. We had no idea what we were going to do, but we did know, with absolute certainty, that we could no longer be the political equivalent of spectators at Wimbledon, heads turning in unison as we tracked the lobs and volleys on centre court, but playing no significant role in the outcome of the match. In our view, the way that PW Botha and his cohorts – particularly the military – were running the country presented a serious danger to our future, and we felt the time had come to make the strongest statement that we could. And the way to do so, we believed, was to exit the hallowed halls of parliament and move on.

PART IV

A democratic alternative

CHAPTER 14

Towards
negotiation politics

L EAVING PARLIAMENT WAS ONE THING; FINDING AN ALTER-
native platform for opposition to apartheid was another. Neither Van
Zyl nor I had any clear idea what we would be doing. We didn't even know
if we would be doing something on our own, together or entirely different.
The only way we could make that decision was by consulting with as many
people as possible and, in particular, talking to extra-parliamentary organisations and especially black leaders throughout the country. We also realised
that we would need to consult beyond our borders.

We had known for some time that the ANC, although banned, enjoyed
wide support. We had also talked with many people in the townships who
could not openly admit to membership of the ANC, but were quite clearly
supportive of the movement. In time, we were able to meet a number of
the leaders who were operating underground, as well as those in various
African states and other foreign countries. We needed to hear their views on
the future of South Africa and whether they thought we could play some
modest role in bringing about the transformation that was needed.

Many of the struggle leaders were still in prison, including Nelson
Mandela. We were denied access to him while we were in parliament and
were hardly likely to be given permission to see him now.

One of the first people I spoke to about what we ought to consider for
the future was the Reverend Allan Boesak. We got on well and Jenny and I
had become friendly with him and Dorothy, his wife at the time, and their
children. We visited each other's homes and had good-natured arguments as
to who made the best curry. Allan cooked a mean curry, but my concoctions
more than matched his!

Even though he was – understandably – opposed to a whites-only or
tricameral parliament, Boesak had been quietly supportive of what a few
of us were trying to accomplish. After I left parliament, he, Charles Villa-
Vicencio and I had lunch one day and, to my astonishment, they both stated
categorically that I shouldn't get involved in anything at all. I was a white
liberal, and I should take an ordinary job rather than becoming directly

involved in working for possible change in South Africa. In reply to my question, 'What sort of work should I do?' one of them said quite facetiously, 'Well, perhaps a petrol pump attendant or something like that.' They were joking, but they were really quite dismissive of the thought that either Van Zyl or I could play any meaningful role now that we had left parliament.

Two sources of income helped to sustain us as a family during this time. Firstly, Johnson & Johnson had engaged me as a part-time human resources and labour consultant. The job didn't pay a great deal, and came to an end when we started IDASA, but it was hugely helpful to an unemployed man! Returning to the church was never an option. I was deeply immersed in politics and felt I could contribute much more in this field.

Secondly, Jakes Gerwel was at that time the vice-chancellor of the University of the Western Cape and a good friend. After the general election in 1994 he was appointed director-general in President Mandela's office. In 1986, Gerwel and a few other people were approached by the Coca-Cola Corporation to serve on the board of a new entity called the Equal Opportunity Foundation. He told me that he had no experience in setting up a non-governmental organisation and asked me to become the executive director. I agreed, on condition that it was a short-term appointment and that Paddy Clark could assist me.

We threw our energies into starting the new organisation from scratch. We found premises, bought furniture and arranged the first board meeting, There were some very important people on that board, including Boesak, Archbishop Desmond Tutu and Gerwel, as chairman. David Schneider, a former South African lawyer, visited frequently from Atlanta to assist with the writing of the foundation's constitution, while some of the board members and I travelled to the US for meetings with the president of Coca-Cola. Our main task was to get the foundation up and running. It wasn't easy getting a group of luminaries together to take important decisions, but we managed several productive board meetings. We were still at the stage of defining basic philosophy and the finalising of the constitution. At the same time Van and I continued to listen to advice regarding our long-term initiatives. After six months of rewarding work, it looked as if clarity was emerging from discussions between Van, me and a large number of organisations and leaders in the field of human rights. Paddy and I left the foundation and they appointed a permanent executive director.

In the very week that I had quit parliament, Bjarne Lindström arrived in South Africa as Norway's consul general. He invited me to lunch to explain why I had taken action that was unheard of in his country. I explained that Van Zyl and I had resigned our parliamentary seats because we were impatient with the lack of progress towards a free and fair South Africa. We were alarmed at the deep divisions within the country and the need for dialogue between all South Africans that would hopefully lead to a negotiated settlement.

I told the Norwegian diplomat that we had no intention of sitting on the sidelines and that our first step would be to consult with as many of South Africa's black leaders as possible. 'How on earth are you going to manage that?' Lindström exclaimed. 'You are out of a job, you have a family to look after and you don't have any funding.'

I acknowledged all his concerns, but assured him that we would find a way. He then offered me R10 000 to assist with airfares and expenses. I told him I couldn't accept his offer, because we didn't have an organisation or a bank account. He was quite sanguine about that and said I should take the money and deposit it into my own account, as he was sure I would use it wisely and for the purpose intended. Again I declined, wanting to talk to Van Zyl first. Van Zyl agreed that we couldn't simply accept money and pay it into a personal bank account. I went to see a bank manager in Cape Town and explained that we didn't have an organisation yet, but needed a bank account and a chequebook. We stipulated that all cheques would have to be signed by both Van Zyl and me. The banker understood our dilemma and agreed to make the necessary arrangements, so we were able to bank the donation and use it to fund our immediate expenses.

Van and I set about meeting black trade union leaders, including Cyril Ramaphosa, general secretary of the National Union of Mineworkers. He was most encouraging and put me in touch with various other people in the trade union movement. We spoke to a wide range of Indian, coloured and black people, as well as whites, and each time we asked: 'How do you see our options? Should we simply forget about moving forward, accept that we have done what we could and go back to teaching, get jobs that will see us earn good money for a change, or simply sit back and watch the disaster unfold? Or should we take the last resort and leave the country?'

The overwhelming majority of those we approached were adamant that we should try to find a way to set up an organisation that would enable us to do what parliament could not, in conjunction with both white and black South Africans. Van Zyl and I had in mind some kind of institute or foundation. Initially, we thought it should be linked to a university, but there were already similar academic centres. Because we intended being politic-ally active and hands-on, independence would be preferable. We decided, separately, that our emphasis should be on democracy. I suggested we name our proposed entity the Institute for Democracy in South Africa, but Van Zyl came up with a much better idea: the Institute for a Democratic Alternative for South Africa, or IDASA. He commented wryly, 'It even sounds African!'

There were some people who were sceptical, and told us so. They didn't think our plan would come to anything and wondered what on earth we were playing at. There were even those who suggested that we were opposed to peaceful change and were seeking other options. We lost a lot of friends, a lot of colleagues. It was quite a tough period in our lives, but we were inspired by the idea that we could make a real difference, and greatly en-couraged by the response that we had received from inside and outside the country. Bjarne Lindström gave us air tickets to Scandinavia and arranged for us to talk to top people in Denmark, Sweden, Norway and Finland. We visited all four countries in a week. Our reception was mixed. Most of the people we met were suspicious and somewhat purist in their approach. How on earth could whites make a difference? This was a black struggle, they pointed out. Their support was clearly for the ANC and they said, in so many words, that they would have to check with the ANC before they could consider giving us any assistance. We weren't confident that the ANC would give the green light, but obviously the organisation's leadership decided that we could, indeed, make a contribution, and we received remarkable and regular financial support from the Scandinavian countries. It was only in later years that I realised how fortunate we had been.

Allan Boesak, who had his own extra-parliamentary organisation, felt strongly that blacks should control any attempts to effect change in South Africa. He had become the absolute darling of the Scandinavians, dining with kings and queens and prime ministers, who all thought very highly of him. Unfortunately, according to what the Scandinavians later conveyed to me, he had apparently felt that they should not support any work that I did, and that, if I wanted anything, I should go to his organisation and ask for financial assistance on a project basis. Of course, this would mean that all grants from Scandinavia would be directed to Boesak's organisation rather than any group in which I was involved. I would not have been prepared to accept such an arrangement, and thankfully the donors were of like mind.

The Nordic support enabled us to make a small start in a little house at 1 Penzance Road in Mowbray, Cape Town. Paddy was with us from the beginning, which was an enormous help, while Beverley February, a lovely person who had worked for the company that occupied the house before we took over, joined us as a receptionist. However, our first professional appointments were made only several months after the official launch of IDASA. Van Zyl and I were co-directors; I took no salary for the first nine months and he never took one at all, claiming only for expenses incurred when he undertook work on IDASA's behalf. Indeed, without the proactive support of Bjarne Lindström and the regular generous donations by the Scandinavian countries, IDASA would have remained a great idea in our heads but would never have seen the light of day.

We had decided that the formal launch should take place in Port Elizabeth, where the unrest was possibly the highest in the country at the time. The Eastern Cape also seemed to have the largest concentration of activists who strenuously opposed the government; many people had been arrested, detained and killed by the security forces. For precisely the same reasons, perhaps it was a little unwise to open our campaign in the heart of the inferno; we could easily have been burnt, but we felt it was worth the risk to make the point that we were not simply another study group or yet another pair of analysts trying to work out where South Africa was going and how it would get there. First, however, we felt the need to establish communication with the 'comrades' – extremely angry, mostly young blacks who were making life difficult for the security forces in townships around Port Elizabeth and elsewhere. Brutalised by the apartheid state's policies and police, they were ready to risk their lives in order to get rid of the government and work towards a truly democratic state. Most of the media had written them off as a 'lost generation' or dangerous thugs. Certainly there were those among the comrades who resorted to violence, and we found them tough, yet often naive and vulnerable. In most cases, they were disciplined and totally committed to a new South Africa in which they could enjoy freedom and justice. Through various contacts, we arranged to meet some of them. They insisted that this should happen in one of the townships. They knew us by reputation as white parliamentarians and weren't keen to meet. Indeed, they were apparently quite nervous about doing so, but if they were worried, I was doubly so.

The first meeting was a remarkable experience. I was told to park my car one evening at a particular petrol station on the outskirts of Port Elizabeth. I sat in the vehicle for quite a while before another car finally drew up alongside. The three young men in it said they were taking me to Little Soweto. I got into their car and we drove for some distance, my companions hardly saying a word, before stopping at a deserted spot. Another car drew up and the four of us switched vehicles, then drove off in a completely different direction, hopefully still heading for Little Soweto. Somewhere along the way, we transferred to a third vehicle and my escorts eventually explained that this was one of the methods they used to evade the security police, who constantly shadowed them. It gave me a brief glimpse into how they had to live in order to survive.

My meeting had been planned for midnight. It was late when we finally reached a little house in a deserted, dark and dismal area. The street was untarred, the houses were small and there was no electricity. I was led into a tiny kitchen, where a woman was waiting. The three youths who had accompanied me sat around for a while and then left, telling me to wait. I waited and waited until long after midnight, but no one else arrived. Long afterwards, I heard that the comrades had been watching the house from a distance, thinking that they were being led into a trap, and were testing me to see if I would stick it out: was I committed enough to go through all the subterfuge, or part of a plan to lead the security police to them?

As the night dragged on, I became quite angry and increasingly nervous, wondering what on earth was going to happen next. At about 12.30 a.m. I spoke to the woman who had been sitting in the kitchen in total silence with me. She had no English and my Xhosa was limited to a couple of sentences. I kept asking her what was happening, but I think she was even more bewildered than I was, probably wondering who this large white man sitting in her home could be. Eventually, at about 1.30 a.m., one of the young comrades returned and said I had to go with him. I climbed into a car again with all three of my original companions and they drove me back to the petrol station where we had first met. I got into my car and returned to my hotel, pretty fed up with the whole situation.

About two hours later, my phone rang. It was one of the comrades, who explained that the events earlier had been designed to test me and make sure that the security police were not involved. They were now satisfied that I was not a spy, and the meeting would take place that night. I was not at all impressed. I didn't know if I had the guts to go through it all again. But I agreed and said I would be at the petrol station as arranged. I couldn't help wondering if all this cloak and dagger stuff was necessary, but I reserved my judgement in silence.

The morning newspaper carried the gruesome account of a necklacing that had taken place in Little Soweto, the township I had visited the night before. Later, one of the comrades told me a suspected informer (or *impimpi*) had been burnt to death, one street away from the house where I sat waiting in vain. I was beginning to get a glimpse of what township life was like, and I was certainly a long, long way from the sedate environs of parliament.

Nevertheless, I did go back and had a successful meeting with about twelve comrades, mostly young men. Later in the week, Van Zyl and I met with a similar group and tried to explain to them what we were attempting to do. I don't think they fully understood, but they agreed to give us their support and put the word out in the townships that we could be trusted.

Sure enough, the launch of IDASA was an enormous success. The Feather-market Hall was packed with a strident and noisy, overwhelmingly black audience asking questions, making comments. I think a number of our white colleagues, and even some of the media, were a little alarmed. This was very different from the normal, well-controlled political meetings that we had held in the past. Some of our friends felt we were treading on dangerous ground, and I suppose we were. But we thought the only way to make some kind of breakthrough was to do it this way. From that day on, we had regular access to the black leadership in the Eastern Cape. The speakers we attracted to the launch were a remarkable group. They included Advocate Arthur Chaskalson, national director of the Legal Resources Centre and later president of the Constitutional Court; Joe Latakgomo, editor of the *Sowetan*; Mvuyo Ralawe of the National Education Union of South Africa; and my eldest son, Andrew, in his capacity as the first treasurer of the United Democratic Front, who read a paper on democracy and government.

Papers were also presented by Professor John de Gruchy on democracy and religion; Leon Louw, director of the Free Market Foundation on democracy and business; and Dr Charles Simpkins of the Southern Africa Labour Development and Research Unit at the University of Cape Town, also on democracy and government. Among the respondents were a good friend, Professor Heribert Adam, the brilliant sociologist and author from Simon Fraser University in Canada, and Dr André Odendaal, who was a professor of history at the University of the Western Cape. White delegates included Dr Christo Nel, an Afrikaner, and English-speakers such as the Watson brothers, Cheeky and Valence, from Port Elizabeth. But it was the participation from the floor, primarily from the black delegates, which added unusual zest and sparkle to the discussions.

Van Zyl and I chaired the conference jointly and tried to sum up at the end where we would be going in the future. We pledged that we would dedicate our efforts to working towards an inclusive democracy in South Africa. In order to do this we would appoint professional staff and hold similar conferences and workshops throughout the country. Following the launch, we met with the leaders of the ANC underground in Port Elizabeth and sought their advice about appointing staff to open an office in the city. Among the names they gave us were those of Wayne Mitchell and Max Mamase. They were our first professional appointees and they duly set up our Eastern Cape office. Wayne later left IDASA and was killed in a motor accident. After the ANC came to power, Max became a provincial minister in the Eastern Cape.

Van Zyl and I went back to Cape Town, glad to be alive, but with many questions about what to do next. Van Zyl decided that, although we had accumulated some funding and IDASA was a going concern, he would not become a staff member. Instead, he suggested that we should appoint a board, which he would serve as chairman, to start with. I was to be the full-time executive director, and he would make a living through teaching or being a consultant. For the next seven years, I gave my full attention and time to the development of IDASA. It was a strange relationship, with Van being part time as it were, and me being full time, but it seemed to work out well. I think I am better at organising, conceiving ideas, inventing, perhaps a little more ready to take risks. Van is more issue-oriented, extraordinarily intelligent and politically astute. He made sure that there was careful thought and consultation before we made any concrete decisions. He was appointed director of policy and planning.

I'm not sure, but I think he was also a little nervous about where IDASA was going at that stage. Nevertheless, we had a successful partnership and Van Zyl remained an active participant who gave critical input on all major events organised by IDASA. The friendship between us, which began when we became MPs, deepened in the much tougher world of extra-parliamentary politics. We never looked back. It wasn't long before our staff complement had grown to a point where we had to move to new premises in Cape Town. The requests that poured in for our assistance made us realise that the only way we could cope would be to open more branches, first in Johannesburg, then in Durban and Bloemfontein, making management of the organisation more challenging than ever.

From the outset, the state security apparatus took an active interest in what we were doing, and we had no doubt that there was someone at all our meetings who would report back on our activities. In the second half of the 1980s, the situation in South Africa was extremely tense. Most of the time, the country was in a state of emergency; the security police were extremely active and I had to keep a pretty tight hand on those who represented us in the various offices. In particular, all official statements from IDASA had to be cleared before they were made public, because they could so easily be misinterpreted. We had to tread a fine line, and it was difficult to follow an open, democratic process and maintain a disciplined approach at the same time. Our main concern was how to move towards negotiation politics. We had seen the crude politics of oppression and witnessed the politics of opposition. It seemed to us that if we were going to have any real future in South Africa, there had to come a time when the apartheid government and the major opposition sat around a table and discussed possibilities, rather than killing or imprisoning and harassing each other. That was our goal.

In the first edition of our journal, *Democracy in Action*, I wrote: 'Essentially, IDASA is trying to promote a culture, or a climate, of democracy in a time when almost every vestige of democracy has disappeared ... [I]f IDASA can make a contribution towards the resolution of our present conflict, our efforts will have been worthwhile. Negotiation is always preferable to violence and confrontation.' The methodology we used was to organise a succession of public meetings in the main centres, along with conferences and workshops to which we invited everyone from the far right to the far left, and the entire political spectrum in between. Obviously, there were some who couldn't participate in these discussions because they were in prison or deep underground, and of course there were those in exile. We did meet a number of the underground operatives from time to time, but always individually and always late at night, because we didn't want to endanger their lives.

The risks we took in order to make and maintain contact were quite amazing, but it was clear that we couldn't operate any other way. Equally surprising was the incredible number of people who attended our workshops. The Conservative Party sent speakers and delegates, who very forcibly put their point of view; we managed to persuade one or two National Party members of parliament to attend; there were people from NUSAS and later from SASO, from the Christian Institute, the South African Council of Churches, many academics from universities throughout the country. We even persuaded trade unionists and members of the business community to come to our conferences and workshops.

In 1988, Beyers Naudé agreed to become chairman of IDASA's board of trustees. This was an enormous honour for the organisation. Both Van Zyl and I were great admirers of his and knew him well. It was wonderful to have the endorsement of a man of such integrity, humility and personal courage, so strongly supported by his equally courageous wife, Ilse. At a later date, Beyers agreed to write a letter of support when we were struggling to raise funds for IDASA's work. His letter was one of our most treasured possessions.

CHAPTER 15

The Dakar encounter

T HE EVENT THAT REALLY PUT IDASA ON THE MAP WAS OUR
decision to meet a group of exiled leaders from the banned ANC. We
had thought about this for a long time, but what really precipitated it was
a meeting between Van Zyl Slabbert and Breyten Breytenbach on Gorée
Island, which is a short boat ride from Dakar, Senegal. They were both there
for a conference and thought this would be an ideal place for a meeting
with the ANC. Gorée is an island full of sinister memories of slaves being
transported to the new world.

Van Zyl and I had visited Lusaka, Zambia, with Colin Eglin and Peter
Gastrow in 1985. Gastrow was the person who really helped us arrange this
trip. He and his wife, Shelagh, had been to Harare and had met a journalist,
Howard Barrell, who had good contacts with the ANC in Lusaka. Peter asked
Howard to act as the go-between to set up a meeting of the Progressive
Federal Party leadership and the ANC.

It took several weeks to arrange, but eventually we received the message
that the ANC would welcome a visit from the PFP leaders. Our first meeting
was strange and subdued after we'd been left waiting at a hotel for a couple
of hours. We met Thabo Mbeki, Aziz Pahad and Mac Maharaj, along with
a number of other ANC members, but these three were the people we saw
and shared views with on a regular basis over a long period. I remember
thinking, over one dinner at the Polo Club, that my idea of the ANC as
a group of revolutionaries didn't fit well with the rather upmarket venue!
It was there that Mac Maharaj asked me about my own background. When
I told him where I had come from, he replied: 'Oh, I see … you are one of
those liberal idealists. I hope you will never lose your idealism.' Looking
back on that fascinating meeting, I've often asked myself whether the
ANC leadership held onto the idealism that was so evident when we first
met them.

We were extremely naive but we listened carefully and exchanged our
different views of a future South Africa. Thabo Mbeki stood out from the
rest from the very beginning. He was warm, open, frank and humorous.
Even at that relatively early stage, we saw him as a future president. We came

to know him much better after we had left parliament, meeting him in London, Paris and New York. Van and I arranged our itineraries to coincide with his and I remember that we always took a bottle of duty-free whisky as a gift. One of our meetings lasted almost an entire night at the hotel where Van and I were staying. It must have been about three or four o'clock in the morning when Van Zyl stood up, somewhat unsteadily, and said he had to go to bed. The problem was, we were in my room, so I couldn't do the same. Thabo had extraordinary energy and seemed to be completely unmoved by the amount of whisky that we had all consumed.

Another of our meetings took place at a well-known seafood restaurant in New York, so our encounters were not always cloak and dagger affairs in some dark alley or hotel room. We met where we could and, although we enjoyed each other's company, we talked about serious issues, not least of which was the possibility of a much larger meeting with senior members of the ANC. We thought it would be helpful to put together a group of mainly Afrikaners who were in many instances quite close to the National Party, either through family ties or allegiance. Some of those we had in mind had influence, others didn't. We thought this would help to start a serious dialogue between those in exile and those in South Africa who were deeply concerned about the conflict in our society and wanted to work for a new order.

The ANC reaction was fairly lukewarm to begin with, not because they were opposed to the idea, but because they thought it would be totally impossible. In the first place, they didn't think a significant group of white Afrikaners would take the risk of travelling outside the country to meet them, and, secondly, even if that did become a possibility, the security forces would prevent it from happening.

As a result of our fairly regular meetings with Thabo – and in many instances he would have Aziz Pahad with him – the word began to spread among the ANC leadership. I think the initial suspicions were allayed and we could start planning for a possible meeting. Each time we met, we reported progress, and finally we got the nod to go ahead and see if we could bring it off.

Van and I made another visit to Lusaka in 1986, to discuss the proposed meeting. There were many questions about where it should take place – the ANC was anxious that it should be as far away from South Africa as possible – and about the timing, who from the ANC should attend, who could we get from South Africa, what the agenda would be, how would we pay for everything. There were a myriad other questions as well.

While we were in Lusaka, I was sitting at the hotel bar having a beer while waiting for some of the ANC members when a man came and sat next to me and ordered a drink. I didn't know who he was so we didn't start a conversation until he nudged me, put out his hand and said, 'Hi, I am Chris Hani.' He was very quiet and I think he wanted to see for himself whether we were genuine, rather than simply taking the word of others who had told him of our visit. He was a hard-line Marxist and we talked mainly about economic justice in South Africa. Certainly, at that juncture, he was deeply committed to a socialist structure for the economy. He didn't attend the gathering in Dakar and I never met him again, but my impression, from that meeting and some of his speeches that I read, was that Hani was a highly intelligent, serious man who would certainly have been a strong rival to Mbeki and others for the presidency of South Africa.

Van and I were together in Swaziland on that dreadful Easter weekend in 1993 when Hani was assassinated. His death very nearly blew negotiations for a democratic South Africa right out of the water and could have had tragic consequences. In the immediate aftermath of the shooting, which was later found to be a right-wing conspiracy, the political atmosphere throughout the country was explosive; only timely and wise intervention by Nelson Mandela on radio and television restored a modicum of calm. I think Chris Hani was sorely missed during the talks and process that led to democracy in South Africa, and he is still missed to this day.

During our various pre-Dakar meetings, we explained to the ANC that our major concern was to put negotiation politics firmly on the agenda. We made it clear that we had no power or authority, no mandate, although the proposed conference could be a precursor to genuine negotiations with those who had both the authority and the mandate to find a peaceful solution to South Africa's ills. After our second meeting in Lusaka, it was clear to us that if we could organise such a conference the ANC would cooperate. As soon as we returned to South Africa, we compiled a list of people we thought would be willing to risk getting together with the ANC. The bulk of the people we approached were white Afrikaners. We couldn't call them and discuss this on the phone, nor could we write to them. We knew that correspondence was monitored by the security police and obviously our telephones were tapped. So it was an arduous task trying to contact people and tell them in person about the idea and determine whether or not they were willing to attend. Even though most of those we approached were white Afrikaners, we felt it was important to include Jakes Gerwel, Franklin Sonn and Randall van der Heever, who were coloured. We also invited close colleagues like Michael Savage and Heribert Adam. We needed some moral support! A full list of those who attended the Dakar meetings appears in an appendix to this book.

Renowned poet, writer and anti-apartheid activist Breyten Breytenbach was of enormous assistance to us, and it is possible that without his involvement this initiative would never have taken place. He was based in Paris and had a close association with Danielle Mitterrand, the French president's wife. She had a small foundation that we could use as a repository for funds, as we received them. It was impossible for us to receive the money in South Africa. Madame Mitterrand was a close confidante of President Abdou Diouf of Senegal and, through Breyten, she approached Diouf and asked if he would host the meeting. This was not an easy decision for an African leader to make. White South Africans were lumped as racists through and through, and he took quite a risk in agreeing that we could come to his country. Madame Mitterrand attended the subsequent meetings in Dakar as well.

We spent a great deal of our time trying to contact foundations, mostly in America, and also potential donors that we had come to know through IDASA in other countries, particularly Switzerland and Scandinavia. We couldn't raise funds in South Africa, because what we were proposing was illegal. In any event, we found that, by and large, the business community and foundations were extremely conservative and wouldn't give IDASA money for anything, let alone an illicit meeting with so-called terrorists and communists. We would need a great deal of money, since we planned to take some sixty people from South Africa and hoped that about eighteen ANC delegates – based in various foreign parts – would attend the meeting. IDASA would have to cover the travel and accommodation costs of the entire group.

Some of the Scandinavian countries gave us money but didn't want to be the only source of funding, so we had to knock on doors as far afield as America. We visited the Ford Foundation and various other major donors, but got nowhere. Towards the end of our American trip, the executive director of the National Endowment for Democracy in Washington made a case for us to his board while we waited nervously outside. He finally came out to say that he was sorry, but the board felt our proposal was too risky and would probably never happen, so they were not prepared to make a contribution. But he did us an enormous favour – he told us of a man called George Soros. We hadn't heard of him, but soon learnt that he was an extremely wealthy man – a billionaire, in fact – who had made his money on the stock exchange. Of Hungarian origin and in many ways a maverick, Soros had set up institutions and foundations all over Eastern and Central Europe in an attempt to bring about democracy.

To my utter surprise, I managed to contact Soros on a Friday afternoon. He agreed to see us at noon the next day, in New York. We took the first available flight and made our way to the city's select Upper East Side to meet Soros and his heavily pregnant wife. She kindly prepared a small lunch for us, which was supposed to include smoked salmon, but she admitted that the cat had got to it first!

We weren't especially interested in the food, but fortunately Soros was very interested in Karl Popper, an Austrian-born advocate of open society, who is generally regarded as one of the greatest philosophers of the twentieth century. Van Zyl knew Popper's work well, so he and Soros immediately found common ground. As their discussion proceeded, I was watching the clock and becoming increasingly agitated as our allotted hour ticked by. Finally, with about ten minutes left, I said to Soros: 'We really would like to tell you what we want to try to do.' He listened attentively as we outlined our plan, then pooh-poohed the whole idea. He said it would never work, and, in any case, it was far too late. 'Your country is down the tubes. I don't think it is worth supporting.' Then he paused and added: 'I must say, it reveals amazing foolhardiness or courage and determination, and I don't mind trying to help people who think big. I'm going to make you a contribution. If you actually bring it off and you need more help, come back to me.' We hadn't a clue what he was going to give us but he got up, asked his wife for the chequebook and wrote out a cheque. He put it in an envelope, sealed it and showed us to the lift. On the way down to the ground floor, we ripped the envelope open and found a cheque for $50 000! He subsequently gave us a further $25 000.

Years later, when Soros asked Van Zyl and me to start the Open Society Foundation in South Africa, he called me aside and said: 'You know, I was so wrong about your country going down the tubes. It was pretty close, but you and others pulled it off, and I'm delighted. Well done.' We always found George Soros straight and direct, sometimes quite abrupt, but he never held grudges and was always ready to acknowledge if he was proven wrong. A controversial figure, he has done so many extraordinarily good things that many countries in the world owe him a huge debt of gratitude.

As our 'war chest' filled up, we managed to persuade the Swiss government to assist us, and they agreed that their ambassador in Dakar would take care of all our hotel bills. What surprised me about this was that, by law, Switzerland had to make public any government donations to any organisation, as well as the purpose of such funding. That they agreed to contribute towards such a controversial undertaking was greatly to their credit, and, once the meeting in Dakar had concluded, the required public disclosures were duly made.

Once we realised that we had sufficient funds to pay the costs of the visit to Senegal, we contacted the delegates we had approached and asked them to book their flights individually so as not to draw the attention of the authorities by having a block booking. We assured them that they would be reimbursed, and they were. We agreed that Van Zyl should go ahead and meet with Thabo and Aziz in London, to make absolutely sure that the ANC was still on board and to finalise the last-minute preparations with Madame Mitterrand. It was nerve-wracking waiting for the evening when we would fly out of South Africa, and I kept waiting for the media to get hold of the story, for it to become public and for the state to clamp down and bar our departure. It was only on the very day we left that the story was leaked. As we gathered in small groups at the airport in Johannesburg, nervously greeting each other, we were suddenly almost overwhelmed by the arrival of a large number of journalists from radio, TV and the print media. We obviously had to give interviews, but we tried to say as little as possible, and we then escaped to board the flight. Once we were airborne, I walked up and down the aisle, and, I must say, we were a very nervous, giggly bunch, acutely aware of the risks that we were taking. On the whole, the only real question the delegates kept asking me was: 'Are you absolutely sure that the ANC will be in Dakar?' I assured them that they would be, although I knew that I would not be convinced myself until I actually saw them there.

We met up with Van Zyl, Thabo and Aziz in London and spent a day at a hotel. We then proceeded to Paris to finalise the necessary diplomatic arrangements that would allow us to enter Senegal as guests of President Diouf. We flew to Dakar in a Central African Airways plane that seemed very old. Several of the seats were broken. It was a long journey and the tension was palpable. However, when we landed in Senegal, we found the ANC delegation, led by Thabo Mbeki, waiting to greet us on the apron at the airport. It was about 1.30 a.m. and yet they were all there, smiling, extending hands of friendship to us. There were also quite a number of people from the Senegalese government, journalists and some curious onlookers, and Van Zyl and I were enormously relieved that we had got this far and could now move towards the meetings that we had been planning for so long.

The next day there was a huge welcome arranged by President Diouf. I recall seeing young men on stilts, countless dancers, musicians, an abundance of food and hundreds of people gathered in the open air to meet, greet and welcome us. We were astonished at the warmth of the reception, which augured very well for the spirit of the meetings. The next day, 9 July 1987, we met in the conference room at the Hotel Sofitel, where we were staying. We began by introducing ourselves, giving our names and briefly explaining why we had decided to make the trip. It was very moving. I remember Thabo standing up and saying: 'My name is Thabo Mbeki, I am an Afrikaner.' Everyone roared with laughter and I think some of the nervousness disappeared and we all began to feel a lot more at ease.

The conference was organised around four main topics: strategies for fundamental change in South Africa; the building of national unity; the structures of government in a free South Africa; and the country's post-liberal economy. We had some robust discussion, much debate, plenty of arguments and many differences, but we tried to focus on what kind of future the ANC saw for South Africa. What were their ideas in terms of a new constitution and constitutional safeguards? What was their economic policy? We also advanced our own ideas. We debated the armed struggle at length, with the ANC explaining why it had been embarked on, why it was necessary and – most of all – that they had seen no alternative, but emphasising that the armed struggle was only part of an overall strategy. Most of us made it quite clear, certainly in the open discussions, that while we could understand their reasons for taking up arms, we could not support the use of violence by either the ANC or the South African government.

I think it would be true to say that, as a direct result of the Dakar discussions and questions, the ANC started doing a lot more homework on their economic policy and ideas about a new constitution. We agreed that if they sent their constitutional proposals to us, we would arrange for interested human rights groups and opponents of apartheid to discuss some of the ideas, and send them our comments. One issue that came up again and again was the future of the Afrikaner and the place of the Afrikaans language. Hermann Giliomee, Laurie Schlemmer and others kept raising the subject, despite several assurances given by the ANC, until finally Pallo Jordan got up and, in impeccable Afrikaans, told them they were being absurd to constantly worry about one language. He was surprised they weren't worried about the language issue as a whole. Since English would obviously be the accepted first language in a future South Africa, what would happen to Zulu and Xhosa, for example? This seemed to placate Giliomee and his small group for a while, but once they returned to South Africa it was clear that they had not been reassured about the position of Afrikaans in a democratic society; indeed, to this day Giliomee remains obsessed with the Afrikaner and his language.

We met from early morning until late into the night on each of the three days that we were in Dakar. While there were many serious discussions, there was also a fair amount of socialising, having drinks at the end of the day and talking more generally. We learnt something of the background of individual ANC delegates who were largely faceless in the South African media. It was moving to hear where they had come from – some from remote rural areas – why they had gone into exile, how they missed their families, the country, the food and the scenery. Their love for South Africa was obvious. Their homesickness was deep and palpable. I believe that getting to know one another at a personal level made a rich contribution to what would be needed in the future.

After everyone else had gone to bed at night, Van Zyl, Thabo and I would meet and work on a statement, which I would read to the assembled media each morning before we started the day's discussions. The media attention was overwhelming. There were print, radio and TV journalists from Europe, the UK, the USA, Australia and South Africa. The official daily statements were agreed to by all participants, and while some journalists were astute enough to obtain personal interviews with different people at different times, our discussions were closed to the media. The official and final Dakar press statement (included as an appendix) had the endorsement of the entire group.

Among those we had invited was Braam Viljoen, whose twin brother, General Constand Viljoen, had been the SADF chief until 1985. Immediately before we boarded our aircraft in Johannesburg, Braam had called me aside and said: 'I have to talk with you and Van Zyl and Thabo Mbeki as soon as we get there, because I have been approached by the security police.' I was staggered by this revelation, but agreed that we would talk on our arrival in Senegal. At the first opportunity, I called Van Zyl, Thabo and Braam together and he told us that the security police had heard about the meeting in

Dakar, were very interested and wanted to get a message to Mbeki. 'A cabinet minister, nameless, would like to meet Mr Mbeki,' said Braam. On his return to South Africa, he was to tell the security police whether or not Mbeki would agree to such a meeting.

Mbeki's face was a picture as he listened to Braam, but his response was immediate and to the point: 'Which cabinet minister? Why does he want a meeting? Where does he want to meet? What are the conditions? What is the agenda? When he tells us all that, I will give him my reply.'

Braam had no idea who the cabinet minister was, nor did we ever find out, but when we got back to South Africa he informed the security police that the ANC was ready to meet under certain conditions. Security was fundamental, and if they wanted to take it any further they would have to answer the questions that Mbeki had raised. I don't know if anything ever came of this approach, but so much was starting to happen that I wouldn't be surprised if a meeting did, in fact, take place.

The conference in Senegal was an unbelievable experience. When we met with the ANC in mid-1987, South Africa was locked in a state of emergency and the ANC were branded as killers, terrorists, communists. The gap between the government and those waging the liberation struggle appeared to be as wide as ever and polarisation ran deep. But, unbeknown to us, discussions had already started between the National Party and Nelson Mandela. Clearly, the ANC were talking not only to us but to other groups as well; in due course, even members of the security and intelligence establishments were asking for and holding meetings with the ANC. Talking to the 'enemy' was clearly an idea whose time had come. In the place of the politics of repression and the politics of resistance, negotiation politics was beginning to get the attention it deserved, and I believe the Dakar conference made a notable contribution to the official negotiations when they opened three or four years later.

From Dakar we went to Ouagadougou and received an incredible welcome from the people of Burkina Faso. We also made an unplanned visit to Ghana, after that country's president not only insisted that we do so, but even sent a private aircraft to take us to Accra. At a public parliamentary meeting, a group of angry Ghanaian intellectuals castigated the ANC for meeting with the 'white boers'. I think we all appreciated Thabo Mbeki's calm and deliberate, yet quite clear defence of the need to meet with people from South Africa, whether white, black, coloured or Indian. His response was widely reported and I think it was of great reassurance to many of the more conservative members of our group.

After these heady days in darkest Africa, it wasn't easy to return home. We had given little thought to the reaction in South Africa, and I had actually arranged to meet my family in Italy and take a break. Van Zyl had also planned to take some time off, in Paris. But when we heard the strident voices coming out of South Africa, where threats were being made by the government and right-wingers, it seemed to me it would be wrong to allow the people we had invited to Senegal to face the breaking storm alone. So, much to the dismay and anger of my wife, daughter Kathy and son Nicky, I decided to forgo our family holiday and go back to South Africa with the group.

It was just as well that I did. While still in the air, we kept getting messages about the situation on the ground, and finally, as we approached Johannesburg, where we were to attend a prearranged press conference, we were informed that our arrival at the airport was under threat, and that the pilot was going to land the aircraft as far away from the terminal as possible. Those of us proceeding to other destinations would have to go straight from one aircraft to the next, without passing through customs and immigration. We heard later that there were about two hundred armed members of the radical Afrikaner Weerstandsbeweging (AWB) waiting for us. Astonishing though it was, the South African authorities had allowed a khaki-clad mob bearing arms to enter the international airport terminal, where they sang and chanted racist, right-wing slogans and threatened that they would 'get' us and 'destroy' us; that we were traitors and disloyal; that the names of Slabbert and Boraine were unfit to be mentioned; that we deserved to be in prison.

Those of us who were bound for Cape Town boarded a domestic flight on the tarmac and flew home to more of the same. The aircraft landed at the furthest point from the terminal and we were taken directly home by bus or, in my case, car. Excellent service, to be sure – but it was not what we wanted and there was nothing we could do about it. We heard later that the government had banned all press conferences for twenty-four hours – an extraordinarily strange order, issued by the department of justice. Apart from the physical danger of the situation at the Johannesburg airport, I was most upset that we had been deprived of what would have been a marvellous opportunity to share our experiences with our fellow South Africans.

We did hold a media conference the next day and tried to answer tough questions from journalists, some of whom were openly antagonistic and accused us of consorting with people who had committed acts of violence.

In doing so, they said, we had not only compromised ourselves but had also condoned the use of violence and aided and abetted armed attacks on South Africans. The journalist from the National Party's mouthpiece, *Die Burger*, was particularly obnoxious. My response was that such allegations were quite absurd. There could be no future negotiations without the ANC being at the table, and while we had no mandate, authority or power, the Dakar conference was the symbolic start of a peaceful settlement in South Africa.

It had been a hazardous, tempestuous and exciting journey, which was followed for quite some time by related headlines every day, various statements and many interviews with those who had made the trip. Unfortunately, a number of the delegates suffered serious consequences. Several of them, including academics, lost their jobs, while a minister of the Dutch Reformed Church was told to leave his congregation. PW Botha attacked us for more than an hour in parliament, the minister of defence stated publicly that we deserved to be jailed, and the minister of justice threatened to revoke our passports, calling us disloyal pariahs. Those of us who had been on the receiving end of threatening phone calls before experienced them more than ever.

But Dakar also brought about a significant shift in the minds of many people. State propaganda had convinced the majority of white South Africans that the ANC was made up of faceless terrorists. I think IDASA gave the ANC a human face. Certainly they were aggressive opponents of apartheid, but they longed to come home and wanted to be part of a new dispensation. Despite the sustained activities of the security forces in the townships – the deaths, attacks, harassment, imprisonment, state of emergency – there was a simultaneous and growing feeling that maybe, just maybe, South Africa could emerge from the apartheid era not by way of bloody conflict and scorched earth, but by way of dialogue between all role players.

Interestingly, the backlash over Dakar was not confined to government or right-wing politicians. I heard from Jakes Gerwel that Allan Boesak felt we were getting far too much attention after Dakar and was certain that we were exaggerating our links with Mbeki and others. He invited Gerwel and Charles Villa-Vicencio to accompany him to London, where he told Mbeki that Van Zyl and I were making extravagant claims about our relationship with both him and the ANC, and suggested that Mbeki should denounce us publicly. According to Jakes, Mbeki listened to Boesak, then said: 'We will discuss and debate and be in touch with anyone we think can assist us in bringing about fundamental change in South Africa, and that includes

Slabbert and Boraine. So I'm afraid I'm not going to follow your advice.' My understanding is that Boesak had paid for the trio's airfares, and they flew straight back to South Africa! What a strange world South Africa was, and is.

When the ANC was unbanned and Thabo Mbeki returned to South Africa, we saw him frequently, Van Zyl more often than I, because they were both in Johannesburg, while I was in Cape Town. What amazed me was the change that seemed to come over Mbeki, during the negotiations and when he became deputy president in 1994 and president five years later. By the second term of his presidency, he was no longer the warm, open person that we met while he was in exile. Both Van Zyl and I were deeply disappointed that the relationship we thought we had with Mbeki was not nurtured after he came home. Perhaps he realised that neither of us would be uncritical supporters of the ANC. Nonetheless, I believe he missed a major opportunity by not making use of Van Zyl's services. He is not the easiest man to have in a group, but he is a brilliant political strategist, and it is truly tragic that his voice has not been heard to better effect.

CHAPTER 16

Embracing the future

E VEN BEFORE OUR HEADLINE-GRABBING JOURNEY TO DAKAR, there was considerable activity at different levels of South African politics. Amid notable signs of flux within the various parties, and against the background of escalating countrywide resistance and a continuous state of emergency, the government had called yet another general election in May 1987.

Having resigned as South Africa's ambassador in London, Denis Worrall teamed up with Wynand Malan, who quit the National Party, and Esther Lategan to form the Independent Movement. Another NP stalwart, Jannie Momberg, later also joined Worrall.

As the battle for opposition turf heated up, the resignation of Horace van Rensburg, the PFP's incumbent MP for Bryanston, was a significant blow for the party. His reasons were that the PFP was weak on security issues, sympathetic to the ANC and even anti-Afrikaner! This played right into the hands of the NP's powerful electoral machine, which lost no time telling voters that the PFP was unable to protect white South Africans because of its liberal stance.

In the election, the PFP lost seven of its twenty-six parliamentary seats, and, to the shock of liberal South Africans, the ultra-right Conservative Party won twenty-three seats, making it the official opposition. The party had been formed in 1982 when a group of NP right-wingers, led by Andries Treurnicht, broke away from the NP in protest against PW Botha's proposed tricameral parliament.

As for the Independents, Worrall lost narrowly to Chris Heunis in Helderberg. Malan retained his seat in Randburg but Lategan lost in Stellenbosch. A general realignment in opposition ranks led to the formation in 1989 of the Democratic Party, bringing Malan, Worrall and Momberg under the same umbrella as the PFP.

As internal 'unrest' and external pressure mounted against apartheid – including foreign trade sanctions – the National Party's response was the deliberate militarisation of every aspect of society. The presence of the security forces was increased in almost every town and city and village or township. Through the Machiavellian structures of his National Security Management System, Botha's 'total strategy' against the 'total onslaught' pervaded even local politics. Simultaneously, rumours were rife about government feelers being put out to the ANC. Certainly, we had found evidence of such overtures during our meetings with Thabo Mbeki in Dakar, but of far greater significance were early reports that talks were taking place between the minister of justice, Kobie Coetsee, and Nelson Mandela. This was of great concern to the ANC in exile, which didn't know the state of Mandela's health and whether or not he was in touch with developments taking place on the political and resistance fronts.

They needn't have worried. Throughout those discussions, which culminated in a secret meeting between Mandela and PW Botha at Tuynhuis on 5 July 1989, the jailed ANC leader remained firmly committed to the organisation's principles and refused to negotiate with the government from behind prison bars. However, the fact that Botha received Mandela at all was a further indication of growing government awareness that the opprobrium of the international community and the resistance from within and beyond the country's borders was becoming too much for them to handle.

But, while South Africa held its breath and waited for the shift in policy that had to come, people continued to die and tragedy befell ordinary people on virtually a daily basis. Soon after we returned from Dakar, Mxolisi Eric Mtonga was murdered in the 'independent' homeland of Ciskei. He was the hard-working and dedicated coordinator of IDASA's East London office, a young man with a family, and it was with shock and distress that we learnt of his death on 24 July 1987. We were horrified by his brutal murder which, as I stated at the time, bore all the hallmarks of an execution, though it was made to look like a car accident. Several months later, I received a tip-off from someone in Umtata that the Ciskeian security police had been involved in his death. I wrote to the then president of the Ciskei, Lennox Sebe, and told him that I had this information. I also named names and said that, unless he took appropriate action, I would make my information available to the press. He must have taken fright, because six senior members of his security forces, including two generals, were arrested and put on trial. Some of them spent a number of years in jail after being found guilty of killing Eric.

The work of IDASA proceeded apace. We set about arranging a series of workshops and conferences for different groups of people. Prominent among these was a women's conference in Harare organised by my wife

Jenny and the IDASA staff. We were lucky enough to have the strong support and presence of Zimbabwe's First Lady, Sally Mugabe. She was extremely helpful in arranging for women from South Africa to meet women from the ANC who were in exile. She was a mediator and handled the conference, together with Jenny, with remarkable skill and empathy. We were very sad to hear of her death a few years later.

Another significant conference was held at Victoria Falls, which we thought would be an appropriate location for a gathering of artists, musicians, poets and writers. The delegates included Breyten Breytenbach, Antjie Krog, Marlene van Niekerk, Njabulo Ndebele, Sandile Dikeni, Don Mattera and Albie Sachs. This meeting was particularly evocative, with various people reading their poems or statements and sharing their music. One glorious evening, we listened to Breyten recite some of his Afrikaans poetry by candlelight. It was very moving and helped us to appreciate anew that music and the arts can transcend politics. Yet, it has to be said that such sessions were interspersed with much discussion on South Africa's political future. After all, it was 1988, and there was no discernible shift in the policies of the apartheid state.

The ANC had brought its own security team to the conference. One morning, in the early hours, Steve Tshwete came to my room and told me they had apprehended two men who had been trying to break into some of the hotel rooms. My immediate thought was that this was a criminal act, but Steve showed me a list of names that had been found on one of the men, who had admitted being sent to Victoria Falls as assassins for the South African security forces. I was still sceptical, until I looked at the list and saw both Tshwete's name and my own on it! I tried to find out what happened to the intruders, but Steve assured me that they had been dealt with by the ANC's security people. To this day I don't know the names of the would-be killers, or what happened to them, but their mere presence was yet another indication of how dangerous it was to try to unite the people of South Africa and bridge the huge divisions that had existed between us for so long.

When the time came for us to leave, we stood together quietly, waiting for the bus to the airport. On one side were the passport holders – who could go home to South Africa – and on the other side were the exiles, who could not. It was all too much for Antjie Krog, who broke down and wept. Barbara Masekela, one of the leading ANC women and a poet in her own right, put her arms around Antjie and comforted her.

Further meetings between the ANC and lawyers, youth groups and members of the business community took place outside the country as, slowly but surely, the ground was being prepared for a negotiated settlement. It was necessary to encourage not only South African residents but also the ANC to accept that this was the way forward. In all our discussions, we tried to focus on a new constitution and a viable economic policy for a democratic South Africa. IDASA hosted debates throughout the country on the constitutional principles sent to us by the ANC, which meant that discussion about a founding document that was acceptable to all was taking place long before the interim constitution was written.

Another significant intervention by IDASA was the holding of a conference on the Freedom Charter. It is safe to say that at this conference, held on 15 and 16 July 1988, there was more talk and exchange of ideas on the Freedom Charter than there had been since the Congress of the People at Kliptown, thirty-three years earlier. The University of Cape Town's Robert Leslie Building was festooned with brown and gold banners proclaiming IDASA's ideals: 'Working Towards Democracy' and 'Working Towards Non-Racialism'. More than four hundred delegates attended the conference and even more were present to listen to Van Zyl Slabbert's closing speech. There was a great deal of enthusiasm, and speakers, both black and white, were drawn from a cross-section of South African society, including politicians, academics, the Natal Indian Congress and Soweto civic leaders.

In my opening address I made three points. First, the Freedom Charter should be seen as a dynamic rather than a static document. As a document of the utmost importance and significance, it should be seen as open-ended, with no limits to new ideas and demands, I suggested. We should be aware in particular of the social, economic and political implications, but we had a responsibility to join a discussion in which many of us had not taken part three decades before.

Secondly, I emphasised that we could not participate in the ongoing search for freedom, truth and justice in South Africa unless we were directly involved in the struggle that this entailed. 'Hopefully, we are not here simply as armchair critics who either applaud every clause of the charter or seek to negate any or all the clauses,' I said. 'To participate in this debate is to participate in the struggle for freedom.'

I asked delegates if they could remember where they were on 26 June 1955 when the Freedom Charter was adopted. I confessed with dismay that I was a university student at the time, and didn't even know that the Congress of the People was taking place. In the last book he wrote before he died, Alan

Paton gave an account of how the Liberal Party decided not to participate in the congress because of reservations concerning the Congress of Democrats, which was regarded as being affiliated to the Communist Party. It was a sad indictment of good people who had denied themselves a great moment in history because of reluctance to get involved, I said.

Finally, I highlighted not only the content of the charter, but also the process by which it had come about. I reminded delegates of the discussions and debates that took place far and wide throughout South Africa, in strong contrast to the approach taken by the government. 'If there is one lesson which this government needs to learn, it is that the only successful way to resolve the present conflict in our country is through the democratic process,' I pointed out.

In January 1989, PW Botha suffered a stroke, which ushered in a new era of possibility for South Africa. FW de Klerk, the minister of education, was elected leader of the NP, but Botha insisted, in his inimitable style, on holding onto the position of state president. He also insisted, to the very last, that he had made a full recovery, but in August, amid growing suspicion that he was no longer in full possession of his faculties, resistance within his own party – and his cabinet – finally forced him to step down, a disgruntled and extremely angry man. De Klerk became the new president of South Africa on 15 August and, just one week later, the ANC issued the Harare Declaration, which expressed its willingness to seek a negotiated settlement.

In May, the NP had called another general election for September, just two years after white South Africans had previously gone to the polls. Under the leadership of Zach de Beer, the newly formed Democratic Party won thirty-six seats, but the Conservative Party remained the official opposition. The CP's increased share of the vote in what would be South Africa's last all-white election reflected a right-wing backlash against an NP led by De Klerk.

De Klerk was very different from his predecessor. Suave, sophisticated, well educated and intelligent, he could read the political situation much more clearly and dispassionately than Botha. Nevertheless, it came as a huge surprise to the overwhelming majority of South Africans, and indeed the international community, when De Klerk made his famous speech at the opening of parliament on 2 February 1990, announcing that the ANC, the PAC and the Communist Party were to be unbanned and that political prisoners, including Nelson Mandela, were to be released.

Nine days later Mandela, his wife Winnie at his side, walked out of Victor

Verster Prison at Paarl, a free man for the first time in twenty-seven years. There was rejoicing throughout the country, although many whites were apprehensive, believing that he would seek revenge for the treatment meted out to those who had opposed apartheid. Far from doing so, however, Mandela set the tone for the immediate future by declaring almost at once that all the people of South Africa had to find a way of living together in peace and justice. This remarkable expression of a desire for reconciliation dominated the years of negotiation until he became the first democratically elected president of South Africa in 1994.

On that Sunday afternoon in the late summer of 1990, Jenny and I sat in front of the television set at our home and watched as Nelson and Winnie Mandela emerged from the prison gates. We wept at the remarkable sight of a man who had endured twenty-seven years of incarceration and hardship because of what he believed in. Then, imbued with the enthusiasm and joy of millions around the world, we jumped into our car and drove into the heart of Cape Town, to join thousands of others waiting on the Grand Parade for the great man to arrive. Traffic congestion and the throngs of well-wishers lining his route meant that the wait was considerably longer than expected, but, for the most part, the spirit was good among the crowd waiting to hear Mandela's first words in public since he had been banished to Robben Island in 1964. When it came, long after the scheduled hour, his speech augured well for the future and was the foundation on which the later negotiations were built.

Through the good offices of Methodist ministers, I had received two verbal messages from Mandela while he was in prison. The first was to thank me for saying on a radio programme that politics ought to be a part of one's religious life. The second message came after I had joined his daughter Zinzi on the platform at a 'Free Mandela' rally at the University of Cape Town. Like so many others, I yearned to meet Mandela after his release, but felt reluctant to make any approach, mindful that a large number of people deserved to be ahead of me in the queue. I was therefore both surprised and deeply moved when I received a message from his office to the effect that 'Madiba wants to know why you haven't come to see him.'

I promptly rectified the situation and spent a wonderful half-hour with him in March 1990. It was an incredible experience to be face to face with him at last. We talked for a while about IDASA, its future role and our meetings with the ANC in Dakar. He agreed to write a letter of support for IDASA, which helped our international fund-raising efforts enormously.

Both this letter and the one written by Beyers Naudé are reproduced at the back of this book, because they meant so much to us at the time, and still do.

Possibly the most remarkable thing about my first meeting with Mandela was that he inquired about my son: 'What about your son Andrew who was detained? Is he all right?' His showing such concern for one of thousands of people who had been in detention, and remembering his name, was a precious moment for me, and indeed for our family. But this was and remained the character of Nelson Mandela – always personal, always intimate, never the formal, cold, distant leader.

During the period after his release, IDASA still had an important task to perform, because the negotiations lasted a tempestuous four years and were intermittent. There was considerable violence, many threats and breakdowns in communication, and part of our job was to act as an intermediary between the various parties and try to keep them returning to the negotiation table.

We were not alone in this, but it certainly took up a great deal of our time. The situation was not helped by FW de Klerk's reiteration, in April 1990, of PW Botha's August 1988 assurance to the National Party congress in Durban that there would be no black majority rule in South Africa. Thabo Mbeki had returned to South Africa from exile on 27 April 1990 and, on 2 May, former sworn enemies representing the apartheid government and the liberation movements finally sat down together to talk about the future of our country and all its people.

IDASA continued to hold public workshops and conferences on a large number of issues such as peace, transformation, a Bill of Rights and a new constitution. Among the areas on which we focused in particular was KwaZulu-Natal, because of Mangosuthu Buthelezi's threat to boycott the proposed democratic elections. In this regard, we worked closely with Jacob Zuma, who had returned from exile as the ANC's head of intelligence. I recall a late-night dinner with Zuma at which I was impressed by his astute leadership and policy of deference to Buthelezi in order to persuade him to participate in the election. Since then, the circumstances surrounding Zuma have changed substantially.

Throughout the period of negotiations, IDASA continued to receive attention from the security police. A number of our staff were detained, including Monde Mtanga, who spent 487 days in detention, and Janet Cherry, from Port Elizabeth. Students on their way home from IDASA meetings were routinely stopped and the literature that had been freely available at the meetings was confiscated. Many of the people who attended our meetings were questioned and harassed, and of course our staff warranted special attention. My office was firebombed on two occasions, wreaths were placed at our homes and threats were a daily occurrence, but somehow we managed to survive and continue the work that we had started, namely the encouragement and support of negotiation politics.

Around 1993, I began to think the time had come for me to leave IDASA. With a new political dispensation on the horizon, I believed that we ought to ensure black leadership wherever possible, and that included IDASA. I also began to feel that, even though compromises were being made and deals struck in the political sphere, memories, particularly among blacks, of the hardships and obscenities of apartheid could not simply be ignored, and had to be dealt with, somehow. Memory was critical, acknowledgement and accountability were essential, and this was where I would turn my attention.

I informed the IDASA board that I was going to tender my resignation and would give them three months to find a successor. Dr Nthato Motlana, who was then the chairman of the board, was categorical in his response: 'We'll give you three years before you even start thinking about leaving.' This was flattering, especially coming from a man I much admired, but I insisted that it was time for me to move on and I left soon afterwards. Professor Wilmot James was appointed executive director in my place. I am not sure that it worked out well for him or for IDASA, and he left after a couple of years.

It is gratifying that IDASA, now the Institute for Democracy in South Africa, has continued to occupy a major place in civil society. Under the capable leadership of Paul Graham, the institute has moved in a different direction, and rightly so. South Africa is no longer a country under siege due to the laws of apartheid; it is a democracy, and IDASA's major thrust has become consolidation of that democracy. I am thrilled, and even a little proud, that something which started off in such a small way in 1986 is still going strong more than two decades later.

Before leaving IDASA, I had begun exploring what other countries in transition had done and was keen to learn what, if anything, from their situations could be applied to ours. I organised an international conference of both experts and people on the ground from Chile, Argentina, El Salvador, Germany, Poland, Hungary, the Czech Republic and several other countries. It was an exciting gathering in February 1994, well attended by the ANC and many other organisations. Afterwards, we published a book titled *Dealing with the Past*, which contained the major lectures as well as an introduction and conclusion written by me. The book was widely distributed and it wasn't long before we had to reprint it; even then, we soon ran out of copies.

The conference was followed by a visit from two prominent ANC members, Albie Sachs and Kader Asmal. They asked if I would write something that could be given to Nelson Mandela, outlining options in terms of a truth commission for South Africa. I thought about this deeply, consulted a number of my close colleagues and then wrote a paper and sent it to Mandela. We subsequently met and talked for about twenty minutes. He was in the closing stages of a hectic election campaign, but I pointed out both the potential benefits and disadvantages such a commission might offer. He asked me to convey my suggestions to Thabo Mbeki and Joe Slovo, which I did, but with the elections upon us I heard nothing more.

On 27 April 1994, the first democratic election ever held in South Africa commenced. Scenes from that day will live forever in the memories of those who participated in the historic event. There was jubilation, weeping, shouting, dancing in the streets and strangers hugging one another, in a country-wide celebration of joy. The ANC won convincingly, with more than 60 per cent of the ballots, and Mandela formed his government of national unity.

A week or two later, I had a telephone call from Dullah Omar, the newly appointed minister of justice, who said he had my letter about a truth commission in front of him, and that we should talk. I had already started a tiny new organisation, Justice in Transition, consisting of Paddy Clark and me. Funded entirely by the Open Society Institute in New York, largely through Aryeh Neier, who was president of that organisation, we worked extremely hard, organising some twenty-seven workshops.

I never saw Justice in Transition as a long-term project, but rather as a facilitator during planning and preparation for a truth commission. No election on its own, however important that was, and no negotiation process, however admirable that was, could offset the long shadow cast by apartheid. When all the joy and tumult of becoming a democracy died down, South Africa was still a sick country, deeply divided and in dire need of healing. The multi-party talks, the deal-making, the compromises, the acceptance by one group of another, all made a rich contribution to a new future, but the legacy of apartheid still had to be dealt with. Nothing had been done to assuage the grief and anger of a pernicious racist system's hundreds and thousands of victims. That was not in dispute, except perhaps among a diehard minority of whites. What was at issue were the nature, extent and methods required to bring about healing and reconciliation.

To this end, a second conference was held in June 1994, with many more South Africans and a few visitors from abroad, including the former president of Chile, Patricio Aylwin, and José Zalaquett – known to many as Pepe – a leading lawyer who became a good friend. Dullah Omar was the keynote speaker and we forged a remarkable relationship that I found extremely positive. Throughout the process that resulted in the Truth and Reconciliation Commission, Dullah was courteous, kind and astute. We met often in one another's homes and it was nothing short of a personal tragedy when he died before our work was done. It was also a great loss for South Africa.

As before, the conference submissions were published in a book, titled *The Healing of a Nation?*, which was made available to as many people as possible. We also organised radio programmes in five languages, which were broadcast nationally. Before the year was out, the concept of a truth commission was being discussed and debated throughout the country. This was precisely what we wanted. If the envisaged truth commission were to have any success at all, it would have to be not only of, but also by and for, all the people of South Africa, especially those who had spent entire lifetimes shielded by the mantra of 'I didn't know'.

PART V

Truth and reconciliation

CHAPTER 17

Lest we forget

THE IDEA OF A TRUTH AND RECONCILIATION COMMISSION WAS controversial from the outset. Obviously, there were those who would have preferred that a veil be drawn over the past, particularly the grave and widespread violations of human rights. There were others who, I think, genuinely felt that the fragile new dispensation would be under threat if there was too much examination of the past and that it would make sense to simply focus on the future challenges of consolidating our young democracy and developing a human rights culture.

Despite many reassurances, a strong stream of criticism came from the National Party, the Freedom Front, the Inkatha Freedom Party and the security forces in particular. FW de Klerk predicted that the TRC 'could undermine the goodwill and sense of national unity that has begun to take root since Mandela's inauguration'. In the same speech, he warned that South Africa would be foolish if it 'precipitately tore out the stitches from wounds that are only now beginning to heal'. The right-wing Freedom Front expressed similar views, with Constand Viljoen, the former SADF chief who had become this party's leader, stating that the commission could become 'a witch-hunt against the Afrikaner'.

In reply to such criticism, Dullah Omar stated in his address to the truth and reconciliation conference: 'I wish to stress that the objective of the exercise is not to conduct a witch-hunt or to haul violators of human rights before the courts to face charges. It is a necessary exercise to enable South Africans to come to terms with their past on a morally acceptable basis and to advance the cause of reconciliation.'

We were fortunate in that we not only had a minister of justice who was fully supportive of the idea of a commission, but also that President Nelson Mandela made it clear on a number of occasions that he was behind the project. Throughout the months of planning and preparation, Mandela was always supportive, urging us to ensure that we would stick to our task, and that once the commission was appointed it would be independent of himself, the government and the ANC. This was what we came to expect of Mandela; he was quick to defend the commission when it finally came into being and enormously helpful to both Archbishop Desmond Tutu and me.

So the stage was set. We had learnt from a number of other countries, we had consulted widely, and the commitment of the government was clear. Now we had to start with the difficult task of drafting the necessary legislation from scratch.

The process was much slower than I ever imagined it would be, but this gave us a chance to spread the word even further. It was also an opportunity for us to respond to the strong challenges from critics and opponents of the concept.

Despite being only a small organisation, Justice in Transition was able to produce material that could be widely circulated. We published 150 000 booklets titled *Truth and Reconciliation Commission* in six languages. We also conducted a two-day history workshop that involved twenty-four leading historians from all over South Africa.

One of the most important initiatives was the documentation of human rights violations. The aim was to compile an accurate and professional record based on information already gathered by various human rights organisations throughout South Africa and even beyond our borders. This was done in cooperation with a number of NGOs, and records were checked, cross-referenced, completed in some cases and stored on a database, so that when the commission began its work it would have access to a large body of material.

The database was set up in preparation for the hearings and to save a great deal of time, but there was also another reason: Dullah Omar told me that it had come to his knowledge that former generals of the SADF were preparing a series of documents concerning human rights violations by the ANC and political parties that were in opposition to the National Party government. He was concerned that this material would be publicly released on the eve of the TRC's launch and felt it was important that we had sound historical material at hand to counter this SADF initiative. In the end, no such documents were ever produced, though the SADF constantly referred to atrocities committed by the ANC and its supporters, both inside and outside South Africa. From the very beginning, most of us underestimated the preparatory work being done by the SADF. The military machine was set in motion at an early stage, as became evident when some serving or former defence force members appeared before the commission. We soon learnt that organisers and supporters of the anti-TRC campaign were meeting regularly to discuss strategy to offset the commission's work.

During the preparation phase, Dullah Omar put together a group of people to assist in the drafting of the bill that would be widely distributed for discussion and debate before being presented to the parliamentary portfolio committee on justice. The small group met regularly and consisted of Medard Rwelamira, a Tanzanian lawyer and academic who was teaching at the University of the Western Cape; Johnny de Lange, an ANC member of parliament and chairman of the portfolio committee; Willie Hofmeyr, also an MP; Enver Daniels from the justice department; Omar himself; and me. As we met over many months and often late into the night, others were drawn into the process, including representatives of the Black Lawyers' Association, Lawyers for Human Rights, the Legal Resources Centre, the National Association of Democratic Lawyers and various other human rights organisations. Prominent individuals who also assisted with early drafts of the bill included such highly respected advocates and judges as George Bizos, Mohammed Navsa and Richard Goldstone, while Albie Sachs wrote an insightful and wise commentary on one of the early drafts.

Important international contributions came from Professor Carl Norgaard, at the time president of the European Human Rights Commission, his wife Helle and Pepe Zalaquett, who was a member of Chile's National Truth and Reconciliation Commission.

The workshops conducted under the auspices of Justice in Transition were enormously helpful to the drafting committee. Many concerns and ideas that emerged from the workshops were referred to the committee. We sought and secured the cooperation of many other NGOs, and, with their assistance, presented some twenty-seven workshops throughout the country, which produced good feedback and critique. We also prepared five radio programmes in several of South Africa's eleven official languages. Many of the workshops were attended by lawyers, psychologists, academics and church leaders, who gave serious consideration to the implications of the proposed commission. A consistent theme was that the basic idea of consciously examining the past was essential. This was the feeling not only of victims of human rights atrocities, but also of professional people who had worked with them and for organisations that opposed apartheid. There was general agreement that, if healing were to take place in a deeply divided society, the truth would have to be faced. This would not automatically result in reconciliation, but it certainly would assist the process.

Medard Rwelamira and I drew up an administrative structure and discussed it at some length with the director-general of the department of justice, who in turn made his views known to the minister. After another workshop on administration of the commission, a more refined structure was submitted to the minister for consideration. Technical workshops were also held and there were many discussions within the department of justice concerning logistics, infrastructure, staffing and other administrative matters.

The TRC would consist of three committees. The Human Rights Violations Committee would be responsible for the victim hearings and for findings concerning those who appeared before the commission. The Amnesty Committee would hear applications from perpetrators and decide if they qualified for amnesty. The Reparation and Rehabilitation Committee would be responsible for drawing up a policy regarding the needs and rights of victims, for submission to government.

The most controversial aspect of the commission was the fact that it could grant amnesty to perpetrators. The amnesty provision was not introduced by the TRC, nor even initially by parliament; it was the consequence of negotiations between the National Party government of the day and the ANC. The clause was inserted in the draft constitution at the very last moment – in fact, at around three o'clock in the morning. It was included largely because generals, both from the army and the police, had approached Mandela to remind him that they had defended the negotiations for four years, ensuring maximum security for all the participants. They expressed their concern that, having done this, a new government led by the ANC might prosecute them for past infractions and send them to jail for many years. In the absence of due consideration for their future, they threatened, they were in a position to make a peaceful election impossible. Mandela was furious at this threat, but appreciated that there was going to have to be some provision to ensure a peaceful election, followed by the ushering in of a new dispensation in a country that had never known democracy, so that a sustainable peace could be realised.

It was for that reason that the amnesty clause was inserted in the draft constitution and later ratified in the final constitution that governs South Africa. In writing the TRC legislation, we hedged the demands for amnesty so as to ensure that it was not a blanket provision, but could be granted only on an individual basis and only in the event of full and public disclosure of human rights violations. Amnesty would only be given to acts that were associated with a political objective, and which were in proportion to the objective pursued.

In the wording of the legislation, the commission was charged with 'facilitating the granting of amnesty to persons who make full disclosure of all the relevant facts relating to acts associated with a political objective and comply with the requirements of this Act', and with 'establishing and making known the fate or whereabouts of victims and ... restoring the human and civil dignity of victims by granting them an opportunity to relate their own accounts of the violations in which they are the victims, and by recommending reparation measures in respect of them'.

One of the most important aspects of the process leading up to the establishment of the commission was the work of the portfolio committee. In keeping with the general spirit of openness, this parliamentary committee publicly debated the issues for many weeks. These meetings were open to the public, and a large number of institutions, organisations and individuals were invited to submit evidence for consideration before the penultimate draft of the bill was prepared. The response was enormously encouraging, with evidence being given by the Catholic Bishops' Conference, the Black Sash, Amnesty International, the chief state legal adviser, the South African Bar Council, Lawyers for Human Rights, the World Conference on Religion and Peace, and a host of others. Inevitably, some of these contributions were harshly critical, but in the main they were supportive.

I submitted a presentation on behalf of twenty-one NGOs. Justice in Transition had organised a two-day workshop for these organisations to go through the draft bill, clause by clause. I made a number of suggestions regarding various aspects of the proposed legislation, but the most important was in relation to Clause 15, which made provision for the Amnesty Committee to meet behind closed doors. In representing civil society, we felt this was a step backwards, and while it is true that every other previous truth commission had met behind closed doors, we felt it was of the utmost importance that the South African process should be open. I concluded my argument by pointing out that the TRC as envisaged was already compromised: 'There are many, many South Africans who would want the state to go much further, who would opt for a Nuremberg court style approach and would want trials and prosecutions.' For that reason, I continued, openness was essential:

> In our wisdom, we have opted for amnesty and reconciliation, but if we attempt to work behind closed doors, we are saying to victims who have suffered enormously, and to the survivors of gross violations of human rights, that not only will justice be limited, but even that limited justice

will not be seen to be done. There is enormous suspicion in South Africa because of the cover-ups of the past, and the very least we can do is [to ensure] that the commission must hold in tension on the one hand a fragile democracy, and on the other a commitment to a human rights culture; and therefore, there is an irreducible minimum, and that is the search for truth. We will never be able to achieve that entirely, but the search remains paramount. There is incentive for people to come and receive pardon. The fact of the matter is that those who have perpetrated gross human rights violations should at least be asked to tell the truth as they have experienced it. That is the very least of the demands that can be made of them. But that ought to be seen to be done. The commission can be a torch for healing and reconciliation, it can restore dignity to survivors, it can be a catharsis for South Africa. It can contribute towards respect for the rule of law and a human rights culture in our country. We should therefore not spoil it by cloaking the Amnesty Committee with secrecy. Let the commission do its work in the light.

Among the most severe critics who made presentations to the portfolio committee were the IFP, the Freedom Front and the South African Police. From the very beginning the IFP expressed strong opposition to the very notion of a truth commission. Firstly, the party argued, it was not the business of government to try to reach the truth: 'The multi-faced soul of our country contains a polarity of truths which no government may express in a unified report.' This criticism overlooked the fact that the commission's findings would not be a government report but a parliamentary one, representing all political parties, and that the commission would not consist of government members but of a nominated group of South Africans from a cross-section of society. They would submit their findings and recommendations to parliament and only parliament itself could accept or reject that report.

The IFP's second major criticism was that the slender resources of the new South Africa should not be 'wasted' on a truth commission, but rather used for other purposes. More seriously, the IFP expressed its deep concern about what it described as an 'ill-conceived idea of having a truth-finding exercise driven by the confessions of those who are in jail and seek amnesty by rendering statements under the spotlight of the press'. They were clearly worried about the publicity that would flow from the hearings. They also opposed the powers of the commission, particularly in respect of subpoenas, search and seizure.

My mother, Isa Blanche Boraine

My father, Michael Charles George Boraine

My grandfather, Frank Evans

My brothers, Aubrey and Ronnie, and me

Our wedding day on Gilnockie farm in Rhodesia, May 1958

With Jenny and her mother, Margaret Clark

Our first child, Andrew Michael,
aged three months, 1959

Outside our house in Oxford,
ready to write my final exams, June 1962

In New York to defend my PhD thesis, 1969

John de Gruchy and me with the first copy of 'Breakthrough',
when I was head of the Youth Department of the Methodist Church

Ursula and Pam join me in looking at the poster for 'Give One Year of Your Life'

Election day, 12 June 1974

Celebrating victory with Jenny

Then there were seven: René de Villiers, Colin Eglin, Gordon Waddell,
Helen Suzman, Alex Boraine, Rupert Lorimer and Van Zyl Slabbert

A teargas canister that was released
at a public meeting in the Rondebosch
Town Hall, before the 1977 election

I won two elections against the
NRP's David Graaff, despite the
defacing of election posters

With Colin Eglin, chairman of the PFP, and Van Zyl Slabbert, leader of the party.
I was chairman of the federal executive

A cartoon by Bob Connolly after defence minister PW Botha said in parliament:
'I am after some people's blood, including the Honourable Member for Pinelands'

According to this cartoon by Tony Grogan, the NRP's David Graaff could count
on support from National Party voters against me in the 1977 election

With Jenny and Andrew, after his release from
four months' detention without trial, 1980

With Steve Tshwete on Goree Island
in Dakar, Senegal, 1987

Part of the team who went to Dakar to meet the ANC

At Leverkusen in Germany, 1988. One of several follow-up meetings with ANC leaders after Dakar, this workshop focused on economic policy for a democratic South Africa

Jenny and me with our children, Nicky, Kathy, Andrew and Jeremy, 1994

With Desmond Tutu and Dullah Omar, minister of justice, in 1995

The commissioners who served on the Truth and Reconciliation Commission

The TRC in crisis. Behind Tutu and me are John Allen and Yasmin Sooka

In my TRC office with Paddy Clark

With our six grandchildren: Maya, Tara, Angie, Grace, Dan and Mano, 2003

With Madiba at his home in Cape Town, 2006

Mangosuthu Buthelezi and other IFP members eventually appeared before the commission, but their general attitude was both negative and destructive. Tutu and I appealed to Buthelezi on a number of occasions to cooperate with the commission. He was adamant that his party had resolved not to do so and he was unable to change that. My own view was and remains that he was one of the key architects of opposition to the commission, and that, if he had made a statement of support, the IFP leadership as well as the rank and file would have followed suit. Despite their sustained opposition, it is interesting to note that Dr Harriet Ngubane, an IFP MP, served on the selection committee for the commissioners and did a fine job.

General Constand Viljoen, representing the Freedom Front, appeared before the portfolio committee on 6 February 1995. In his opening statement, he urged the committee to move away from the wording in the draft bill as it pertained to amnesty, and to retain the provisions of the interim constitution which, he argued, called for general amnesty.

Secondly, he indicated his uneasiness about a lack of 'even-handedness' and urged that the legislation be tightened to ensure that the commissioners were not given too much leeway, which might result in biased assessments.

General Viljoen expressed considerable concern about the cut-off date for the period to which amnesty would apply. The original date was 5 December 1993, when agreement was reached on the post-amble to the constitution. This was perhaps an arbitrary decision, but in order to encourage peaceful opposition in the run-up to the election scheduled for April 1994, and to avoid impunity, it was the date that had been chosen. The one valid point made by the general was that, at the time the post-amble was drawn up, the Freedom Front, the IFP and the PAC were not party to the agreement: 'For them, the conflict of the past did not come to an end on Friday, 5 December 1993, because the aspirations and demands of those parties were not met. In fact, the final accord between my party and the ANC was only completed on 23 April 1994.'

Viljoen linked his concerns to an argument that the legislation should apply not only to perpetrators, but also to victims of gross human rights violations. 'If the cut-off date remains 5 December 1993, it will mean all victims of gross violations of human rights after that date will be excluded from the provisions of reparation and rehabilitation,' he pointed out. This would certainly be no fault of the victims, and Viljoen thus urged that the date be changed to either 27 April (the first day of the democratic elections) or 11 May 1994, the day after Nelson Mandela's inauguration as president.

A major concern for Viljoen was the emphasis on the pursuit of truth and the revelation of perpetrators' names. He stressed that he had no objections to seeking truth and reconciliation, but he severely criticised the NGO contribution to the debate. His view was that many of the NGO people who had played a role in the formulation of the commission were 'invariably moralists and some even sentimentalists, and whilst they are good people, their judgement in the field of public life is based on prejudice and they ought not to be trusted because of their high ideals and their frustration'. He even suggested that propagation of these ideals could result in 'some form of fanaticism'. The implication was that such people couldn't be pragmatic and that this was why they had emphasised the need to name perpetrators as a precondition for national reconciliation.

Quite clearly, General Viljoen had no idea that the emphasis on exposure came not from the NGOs, but from the ANC leadership as well as some members of civil society. What may have confused him was the strong emphasis by NGOs in particular on transparency and the need for amnesty hearings to be held in public.

At its highest level, the South African Police opposed establishment of a truth commission from the first. Like those of the IFP and the Freedom Front, the SAP objections were based on principle, but they also included a number of suggested amendments and improvements to the draft legislation relating to matters of pivotal and substantive importance.

As with General Viljoen, a major thrust of the SAP's argument supported collective rather than individual responsibility for acts of violence committed during the political conflict of the past. They argued that the leadership of the National Party and the ANC were primarily and collectively responsible for creating a climate conducive to furthering their political objectives. Both parties were on record (in ANC publications such as *Sechaba* and *Mayibuye* and in the records of the NP government's State Security Council) as making statements to the effect that the power struggle had resulted in a state of war; the NP had even created and actively implemented the 'total onslaught' doctrine, the SAP pointed out.

Orders issued by the political leadership of both parties had been ambivalent. This position was taken over and over again by members of the security forces when they appeared before the TRC. According to the SAP's submission to the portfolio committee on justice, 'Although direct instructions were sometimes given, the normal practice was that subordinates would act upon the implied authority which stemmed from such ambivalent commands. This included the actions of the Civil Cooperation Bureau and the implementation of strategic communications projects under the State Security Council as well as the activities of Umkhonto we Sizwe Special Operations.'

Their point was that, in their judgement and experience, 'individuals entrusted with carrying out the orders of the National Party government were left to their own initiative and devices and were personally commended on an individual and group basis by members of the cabinet'.

In short, the SAP argued that, before any legislation could be promulgated and any truth commission could start its work, it was imperative for the government of national unity to 'come clean' on the following:

> Firstly, acknowledgment of principal and collective responsibility and liability for actions aimed at the achievement and furtherance of political aims and objectives of the past; secondly, acceptance of principal and collective liability for crimes and acts committed by individuals which must fall within the ambit of 'acts associated with a political objective' in furtherance of the above, for which amnesty shall be granted; thirdly, full public disclosure by political leaders of all means employed towards the furtherance of political aims and objectives including structures, strategies, elements of propaganda, deeds of terror and destruction, the use of state machinery and its apparatus, covert projects, etc. Finally, public acknowledgment of the fact that ambivalent orders and commands over a long period of time created a situation in which the execution of such orders was left to the discretion of individuals who were forced to operate under a system of implied authority.

The Promotion of National Unity and Reconciliation Bill was published by the newly appointed government in November 1994. It was the subject of examination, scrutiny, additions, deletions and amendments by the portfolio committee on justice. After hearing the evidence and finalising the bill for debate, the minister of justice, Dullah Omar, introduced it in parliament on 17 May 1995. In his introductory speech, the minister focused on many of the important issues that had been in dispute during the short life of the draft bill. He stressed, however, that the proposed legislation 'provides a pathway, a stepping stone, towards that "historic bridge" of which the constitution speaks, whereby our society can leave behind the past of a deeply divided society, characterised by strife, conflict, untold suffering and injustice, and commence the journey towards a future founded on the recognition of human rights, democracy and peaceful coexistence and development opportunities for all South Africans, irrespective of colour, race, class, belief or sex'.

All the political party leaders and members participated vigorously in the debate that followed. It was, in fact, the longest debate of the newly elected democratic parliament. Objections to certain clauses were raised and thoroughly debated, but no significant changes were made to the bill, particularly because party representatives had been given the opportunity to put their case while the draft bill was still before the portfolio committee. At the end of the day, all the parties voted in favour of the bill, with the exception of the Freedom Front, which voted against it, mainly because the cut-off date had not been altered, and the IFP, which abstained because it was not convinced that 'even-handedness' would prevail. (In the end, the cut-off date was changed to 27 April 1994, after renewed representation by Viljoen.)

The bill was signed into law on 19 July 1995 and came into effect on 15 December, when the commissioners were appointed. President Mandela had decided that he would not nominate members and appoint the commission. Instead, he asked a specially appointed committee to draw up a shortlist before he made the final decision in consultation with his cabinet. The committee consisted of the following members of parliament: Harriet Ngubane (IFP), Ray Radue (NP), Rosier de Ville (FF) and Baleka Kgositsile (ANC). It also included four members of the NGO community: Bishop Peter Storey, Jayendra Naidoo, Jody Kollapen and Brigalia Bam, and was chaired by Professor Nicholas Haysom, legal adviser to the president.

This decision was widely advertised, and all organisations, political parties, churches, agents of civil society and individuals were invited to nominate people they thought would make suitable commissioners. In the end, 299 nominations were received, and the list was whittled down by the committee to a more manageable size. Public hearings followed, allowing all the people of South Africa to participate in the TRC process, either by attending hearings in person or following proceedings on television or radio. This stage of the process took considerable time.

I was surprised to be appointed deputy chairman of the commission and delighted that Archbishop Emeritus Desmond Tutu was chosen to be the chairman. This was an inspired choice by President Mandela, and throughout the life of the TRC, and beyond, Tutu was indispensable and offered remarkable leadership and direction.

The other commissioners included five lawyers, Dumisa Ntsebeza, Yasmin Sooka, Richard Lyster, Sisi Khampepe and Denzil Potgieter; Mary Burton, leader of the Black Sash; Bongani Finca and Khoza Mgojo, ministers of religion; Hlengiwe Mkhize, an academic; Wendy Orr and Fazel Randera, medical doctors; Mapule Ramashala, a medical researcher; Glenda Wildschut, a psychiatric nurse; Wynand Malan, a former National Party MP; and Chris de Jager, who had been an MP for the Conservative Party.

The final list of commissioners didn't please everyone. FW de Klerk was not happy in general, and was particularly displeased with the appointment of Tutu as chairman and me as his deputy. Mangosuthu Buthelezi said that he agreed with the list, but that the TRC chairman and deputy chairman would not have been his choice. His antipathy towards Tutu was well known, and the friendship that Buthelezi and I had once enjoyed had unfortunately fallen by the wayside in the heat of political debate. I think the appointment of human rights activists and lawyers, as well as church leaders, confirmed his view that even-handedness would be impossible.

Among the seventeen commissioners there were seven women and ten men; seven blacks, two coloureds, two Indians and six whites. It was, therefore, a fairly representative group, but when the commission started its work and began to make a number of decisions and statements, criticism from many quarters in relation to balance and impartiality became more and more pronounced. The fact, however, is that by the time parliament actually passed the bill into law, this was an idea that had been well publicised and discussed. I think we can justifiably claim that the TRC was owned not by the president or parliament or the commission itself, but by the people of the country.

South Africa has many virtues and our passage to democracy has been quite remarkable. But there is also a dark side to the country that is punctuated by lawlessness and violence. This was brought home to me in the worst possible way shortly after I was appointed to the TRC. Our family had experienced hardships before, but what befell our daughter, Kathy, was shocking and almost impossible to bear.

On that fateful Sunday, Jenny and I had just returned from a walk in the Constantia green belt. We were having tea, doing the crossword puzzle and reading the Sunday papers. The telephone rang, and when I answered I heard the hysterical voice of Hardy Botha, my daughter's partner. 'Kathy has been attacked. Please come immediately to the Paarl Hospital.' I couldn't believe it and I tried to get some sense out of Hardy as to the extent of her injuries, but he just kept on saying, 'Please come, please come.' We dropped everything and raced to Paarl. I switched on the car's hazard lights and drove as fast as I could. I subsequently received a traffic fine that indicated I was travelling at 170 kilometres an hour.

When we arrived at the hospital, Kathy was in a small room, and as we looked at her, our hearts sank. We were extremely frightened. Her face looked as though it had been split in half. She was stunned and barely conscious. She told us later that she was still afraid that the man who had attacked her would follow her to the hospital and finish her off. She was terrified until one of the doctors, an older man, came and held her hand. 'It was amazing what that did for me. It connected me back with humanity and I felt reassured.' The doctor put her on a drip and told me they were waiting for an ambulance to take Kathy to the N1 Hospital, which was far better equipped to deal with the gravity of her injuries.

Jenny accompanied Kathy in the ambulance. As they sped off, she asked us to please make sure that her daughter Tara (only seven months old at the time) was safe, so Hardy and I went back to their home and I checked that Tara was all right in the care of a group of concerned neighbours. As soon as possible, I left for the hospital. The traffic was heavy but I arrived shortly after the ambulance. We were met by an orthopaedic surgeon and a neurosurgeon. They took her into theatre immediately and we waited, desperately anxious. Eventually, the neurosurgeon came out and told us that there was no brain damage as far as he could ascertain, but that Kathy's injuries were grave; her skull was fractured in two places, her jawbone, cheekbone and nose were broken and she had a bad injury to her knee. They would operate on her leg immediately and then place her in intensive care for observation, before deciding what further measures to take.

It was a week before they could operate on Kathy's head and face, because the swelling was so severe. Jenny and I gathered the family together at our Scarborough cottage and we held a vigil with candles and music, just talking quietly, waiting for news from the hospital. But she was in surgery for a very long time – ten hours – and, finally, I couldn't handle the interminable wait any longer. I raced off to the hospital and sat there until the doctors emerged from the theatre. They were most reassuring. Her brain membrane had been torn, but they believed they had managed to repair all the damage and that she would make a full recovery. This was a huge relief, not only to Hardy, Jenny and me, but also to our sons, family and friends who had rallied around and been incredibly generous with their love and kindness.

A few days after the attack, and before the major surgery, the police had gone to see Kathy in the hospital. They showed her some photographs and she immediately recognised her assailant. Earlier, I'd had a visit from Dullah Omar. He was shocked and sympathetic and assured me that the person who had done this would be arrested speedily, not because it was my daughter, but because her attacker was clearly a menace, and other potential victims needed to be protected from him.

A couple of weeks later, Kathy was released from hospital, on crutches. She and Tara came to stay with us. Jenny took her to the identity parade and once again, through the glass window, she immediately recognised the man who had attacked her. Because of the severity of her injuries, the prosecutor decided, after discussion with the surgeons, that the charge should be attempted murder rather than common assault.

Two months later, I took Kathy to the court in Paarl for the trial. It was a terrible ordeal for her, and for me, but it had to be done. I had been full of rage against this person who had so viciously attacked my only daughter, but when I arrived at the court and sat immediately behind him standing in the dock, I saw a young, slightly built, short figure and listened to his story of poverty, living in a shack, his young life devoted almost entirely to house-breaking, and I felt pity rather than anger. Kathy told me later that she felt the same, although she did make this point: 'I was at first desperately afraid of him, that he would come back. When I saw him, I had more pity than anything else. He had clearly had a miserable life, ended up becoming a brute of some kind. But to claim my own power back, my own self, you do feel angry as well. In a sense it's part of trying to work it all out. I remember how confusing it was for me. My brothers had said to me, "Why didn't you respond? Why didn't you hit him at least once?" I remember thinking, I am so pathetic. It just renders one so helpless. I needed the strength of that anger to recover.'

The court case didn't take long. The accused was found guilty of attempted murder and, despite all the questions put to him by the magistrate, he never really explained why he had attacked Kathy. He simply admitted that he was trying to kill her. He had never set eyes on her before, but in a paroxysm of rage he wanted to kill her. He was sentenced to fifteen years without the option of parole.

I learnt a great deal from the violence that visited my own family. While

I would never wish that experience upon my worst enemy, there was a lesson to be learnt from it all. I was about to go into a truth and reconciliation commission, and for months on end my fellow commissioners and I would listen to stories of excruciating violence, not only random and impulsive, but also the violence of the state. In a way, having violence touch our family so closely helped me to have a deeper understanding of the feelings, the anger, the hopes of thousands of victims who came to the commission.

CHAPTER 18

Lifting the veil

IN TERMS OF THE GENERAL PUBLIC AND THE TRUTH AND RECON-
ciliation Commission's objectives, the real beginning was in East London
on Tuesday 16 April 1996. The months leading up to this, our first public
hearing, had been intense. Our first weeks were concerned in the main with
setting up offices, appointing staff, coping with administration and dealing
with the press. But our energy and thinking were directed towards the first
victim hearings. We were under constant pressure from the media and others
to get these under way, and the question asked most often was: 'When are
you going to hear from the perpetrators?' Our response never varied: clearly,
our first responsibility and priority was to give a voice to the voiceless, the
victims of the apartheid system.

This involved interviewing hundreds and hundreds of victims throughout the country. We had to get it all down in writing and then find out
whether they were prepared to tell their story in public, or whether they
simply wanted their story to be documented as a record of their experience.
We couldn't do this ourselves, so we appointed statement-takers, some
volunteers, some paid. They did an outstanding job in taking down the first
statements of the victims. Other preparations included the appointment
and training of briefers, who would be alongside victims when they testified;
booking halls; publicity and interviews. We were moving into the unknown
and went out of our way to be as ready as possible, without knowing exactly
what we were in for, doing everything possible to prepare thoroughly for
something that none of us had experienced before.

But East London, where we held the first public human rights hearing,
was where the TRC really came to life. We met in the very large cavernous
city hall and spent time preparing it so the first victims would feel comfortable and not overwhelmed by the occasion.

We also had to deal with the question of security. In addition to tele-
phonic threats to both Desmond Tutu and me, the police informed us that
their intelligence was cause for deep concern about our safety. We were
both assigned bodyguards and our homes were protected day and night.
Wynand Rademan, one of the new breed of policemen, stayed with me

for the duration of the TRC and was fiercely loyal to both me and the commission. I did wonder, sometimes, if the security measures really served much purpose, however, because when I returned home late at night I often found the security guard outside the house fast asleep! At other times, I was grateful for the precautions. On one occasion we were awakened at about 3 a.m. by bright lights shining into our property and the sound of many vehicles outside. Someone had apparently been trying to gain entry to our house, the guard had sounded the alarm, and a host of police officers went crashing over fences and down alleys and streets in search of the intruder, who managed to elude them.

As I walked into the East London City Hall with Tutu on that first morning, the curtain was raised on a drama that would unfold over the next two and a half years. I think what helped enormously from the very beginning was that the commission didn't consist of stern-faced officials cloistered in a private chamber, but rather a stage with a handful of black and white men and women who listened intently to stories of horror, sorrow, amazing fortitude, supreme heroism and anger. The audience was there too, and, thanks to the wonder of television and radio, a wider audience of millions was able to follow proceedings. It was theatre, perhaps; it was certainly a ritual, deeply needed in the healing of a nation. In the main, the actors were ordinary people with powerful stories to tell. The stars were never the commissioners, but rather the victims, who were treated as VIPs. Adding to the drama was the fact that we had barely started the proceedings that day when we were told by the police that there had been a bomb threat and that we had to evacuate the hall. It was at least ninety minutes before the sniffer dogs indicated that there was no bomb and we could resume.

Tutu had asked me to welcome each of the witnesses before they began testifying. The very first was Nohle Mohape, whose husband, Mapetla, had been killed in police detention in 1976. As I watched her approach the table where victims would be seated, I felt my heart pumping and a frisson of excitement, underscored by concern. So many things could go wrong; so many people could be hurt if those who despised the TRC found some way of getting into the absolutely packed hall. There was complete silence as she took the oath, and then I said to her: 'We are mindful of the suffering that you have endured in the past. Many of us remember as though it was yesterday when Mapetla died in police custody. We remember the anguish and horror of those days and we know also, apart from the personal grief that you have experienced, that you yourself have been a victim of human rights violations. We know that you too have been detained and were in solitary confinement, and we salute you as someone of great courage. We thank you for coming here today. This is testimony to your commitment, to truth, to justice, to reconciliation and to peace between you and all people and all South Africa.'

Mrs Mohape was quietly determined to tell her story. Throughout that first day I sat on the edge of my seat, my body stiff with anxiety and my heart filled with great sadness as I listened to ordinary people telling their extraordinary stories of sorrow and loss. I bit the inside of my cheek in order to try to be more composed, and surreptitiously wiped my glasses of the tears that could not be held back. It was the beginning of a very long journey.

When Mrs Mohape told the packed hall that she was happy to finally be able to recount her husband's suffering and death, I knew that whatever else was going to happen, this commission was right and necessary for the healing of South Africa.

We were astonished at the size of the international and national media contingents from radio, television, newspapers and magazines, but even more surprising was the quiet dignity of those who were grateful for the opportunity to finally break the silence that they had lived with for so long, the chance – at last – to give expression to their sorrow and anger. The second day was even more moving than the first, probably because of the story told by Nomonde Calata. She was the widow of Fort Calata, one of the so-called Cradock Four who had been brutally murdered in 1984. I had met and known Fort and remembered travelling from parliament to the Eastern Cape when the bodies of the Cradock Four were found. Who could ever forget Nomonde's cry of anguish in the middle of her testimony? She broke down, threw her head and entire upper body back and let out a cry that seemed to come from her very soul. It was like a howl in the darkness, an expression of all the horror of the apartheid years, that transformed the hearings from a litany of suffering and pain to an even deeper level. It was broadcast on radio and television many times during the life of the commission. It seemed to be, as writer and poet Antjie Krog put it, 'the beginning of the Truth Commission – the signature tune, the definitive moment, the ultimate sound of what the process is about'.

The Eastern Cape had been the strongest centre of opposition to apartheid in South Africa, and its people had suffered most at the hands of the security police. We listened in awe and horror to the widows of the Pebco

Three, as they were known, and many others who gave first-hand accounts of abduction, disappearance, detention and imprisonment, torture, and loss of loved ones to the police and the military.

Another victim in that first week was Ernest Malgas, a struggle veteran who had been harassed and arrested many times and had spent fifteen years in jail. I had met him some years earlier through IDASA, but the man I saw before me in East London was no longer upright and powerful; he had grown old, had suffered a stroke and was in a wheelchair. He had been severely tortured while in prison and I asked him to describe his ordeal, because we needed to verify and corroborate accounts of torture and other human rights violations. He struggled to describe a particular technique known as the 'helicopter', which involved suspending the victim upside down from a stave of wood and beating and kicking him, often until he was unconscious. Unfortunately, revisiting this experience was just too much for Malgas, who broke down and wept. This, in turn, was too much for Tutu, who put his head on the table and sobbed. I brought the hearing to an end, because there was clearly no way we could continue.

The emotional reaction was so much part of Tutu. Generally full of fun and humour, he felt the victims' pain intensely. Often he would just sit with his face screwed up, struggling to cope with the horrific stories we heard. I had known him for some twenty-five years, but during the TRC's lifetime I came to know him at an entirely different level. He was undoubtedly the cement that held the commission together.

We had served together on committees when we were both linked with the South African Council of Churches and I had watched his progress from ordinary priest to the first black archbishop in South Africa. His journey had taken him to many of apartheid's trouble spots and he had seen at first hand what was happening in the townships. He protested and proclaimed, he argued and became angry, but he was always compassionate. In a documentary film comparing several truth commissions in different parts of the world, Tutu was asked what it was like when the South African TRC started its work. 'It was hell! It was hell!' he replied. He was referring not only to the trauma of the hearings, but also the challenge of trying to keep a commission together under trying circumstances. We both believed that the TRC was a microcosm of South Africa, so inevitably there were real differences, often conflict, and even racism. But through it all, Tutu was magnificent, and I cannot praise him too highly for the leadership he exercised. When he was diagnosed with prostate cancer in 1996 and told by his doctors that he should go to New York for two months of treatment, I was worried about him, and about leading the commission in his stead. I wasn't concerned about the work or the administration or the organisation, but holding together a group of independent-minded people under difficult circumstances was not the easiest of tasks. I kept in close contact with Desmond while he was in New York, but he was sorely missed.

After the East London hearings, we went to Cape Town for a week of similar hearings, and then it was on to Johannesburg and Durban. Tutu and I were the only two who sat through every day of those first four weeks. From then on, we simply seemed to be travelling every week of our lives. It was like being on an express train. One hearing followed another, with little opportunity to catch our breath. We were moving through uncharted territory; we didn't know what to expect and had to learn on the job. It was as challenging as it was traumatic, and we had very little time for reflection or second-guessing. We simply had to plunge in and get on with the process, which held us captive for the duration.

We were away from home and far from our families, and I sorely missed Jenny as well as Kathy and our granddaughter, Tara. But when I did go home, it was a sanctuary. There was a sense of acceptance and peace and I remember so vividly how Jenny would try to keep Tara quiet so that I could rest. But for me to hold Tara, to roll on the floor and play with her was like a healing balm. I have to say that the occasional whisky and soda didn't hurt either! Those brief moments at home gave me the strength to continue.

It wasn't long – though too long for the media – before the first perpetrator hearings took place. They were very different to those of the victims. These were tough, hard men who had either a police or military background. They came and told stories of their activities in assassination squads, harassment and torture. This was the other side of the coin: in many cases, perpetrators who had already been identified by victims, in earlier hearings, now corroborated what we had been told about their actions. This was of tremendous value to the commission, because until the perpetrators began owning up, most white South Africans believed that the victims were lying, exaggerating, venting their hatred of whites. There was a spirit of absolute denial – but having to listen to perpetrators admitting what they had done, how they had killed, abducted and tortured people, burnt or thrown bodies into rivers, forced people to accept that the victims had not lied. No one would publicly lay claim to such horrific deeds unless they had happened. This brought about a shift in perception. No longer was there denial. Now the plaintive cry of whites became, 'I didn't know. I didn't know this was happening in my country. I wasn't involved. I didn't do it. I'm sorry about it but it wasn't me, it was the government.'

These were the same people who had voted for the National Party in every general election since 1948, increasing their majority each time. It was not a question of not knowing; it was that they didn't want to know. In a sense, this reaction was also an example of just how successful apartheid had been. We had been segregated since we were children, with coloureds, whites, Indians and blacks kept deliberately apart. Our schools were separate, our buses, trains, beaches, cinemas, theatres, schools and all public amenities were separate. In addition, it was true that most of the horror occurred in the townships, and very few whites would ever have had cause to enter those areas. How they avoided reading or hearing news reports about what was going on and were oblivious to the admonitions and statements made by Tutu and so many others, how they missed accounts of what some of us had been saying in parliament for so many years, I will never know, however.

As important as the perpetrator hearings were, for the next eighteen months victim hearings throughout the country were, in many ways, the heart of the commission. We heard of the deaths of Steve Biko and Neil Aggett; David Webster, Suliman Saloojee and Bheki Mlangeni; the attempted assassination of Albie Sachs and the details of many, many others who were assaulted and tortured in detention. One of the most bizarre and distressing hearings dealt with the death of Siphiwe Mtimkulu. His mother, Joyce, was scheduled to give her evidence before the commission at one of our early hearings in Port Elizabeth, but her testimony was opposed in court by a notorious Eastern Cape security policeman, Gideon Nieuwoudt.

I will never forget that hearing. The audience was by far the biggest we had ever had. There must have been close to 3000 people packed into the venue. The mood of anger, excitement and expectation was palpable. I was extremely nervous, perhaps for the first time. One of my fellow commissioners on this occasion was Bongani Finca. When I realised that a court order granted to the security police had muzzled Joyce Mtimkulu and that she would not be allowed to give her evidence, I knew there was going to be a strong and angry response from the crowded hall.

I said to Bongani: 'I will be speaking in English, but I want you to translate word for word into Xhosa – don't even wait until I have completed a sentence. I want you to follow me very closely so that everyone knows exactly what I am saying.' In his own, wonderfully reliable way, he did what

I asked, and together we told the audience that, although Joyce Mtimkulu was not allowed to speak on that day, we offered our absolute assurance that she would do so freely at some future time. The audience was restive; there were oohs and aahs and shouts of dismay, anger and resistance, but thankfully they settled down. Ironically, many of those who appeared before us that day spoke of the security policeman they believed had abducted and killed Siphiwe Mtimkulu, but had to refer to him as 'Mr X'. He featured prominently in their testimony.

Several months later, clutching a lock of hair from Siphiwe's head in her hand, Joyce Mtimkulu did testify before the commission in Port Elizabeth. Having previously succeeded in gagging her by means of the court order, Gideon Nieuwoudt duly sought amnesty for the assassination of her son. His application was refused and he was eventually indicted by the National Prosecuting Authority for Siphiwe's murder. However, Nieuwoudt died of cancer before he could stand trial.

The names of those mentioned at the hearings as testimony to the truth, and as a way of memorialising those who suffered the illegal actions of the state, read like a role of honour: Anton Lubowski, Ashley Kriel, Stanza Bopape, the Guguletu Seven, Rick Turner, Sizwe Kondile – whom security police officers seeking amnesty admitted to killing, then burning his body while they drank and barbecued just a short distance away – Brian Nqalunga, Florence and Fabian Ribeiro, Joe Cele, Zwele Nyanda, Keith McFaddon, Bram Fischer and so many, many others on a seemingly endless list. But we didn't hear only from those who had endured violence at the hands of state agents. We also heard from families who had suffered as a result of the St James Church massacre, the ANC landmine campaign, the bombing of Magoo's Bar by Robert McBride, torture and summary trials in ANC camps, the bombing of the Heidelberg Tavern, and the widespread necklacing which took place in townships throughout South Africa. The stories were most often grim and gruesome, but what impressed all of us was the remarkable courage of the victims who appeared before us and the generosity of spirit shown by many towards those who had abused them and killed their loved ones. The cumulative story told to the TRC was one of darkness, but it was often illuminated by the lightness of being of people who were willing to move on, even to forgive.

At the request of many concerned parties, but also on our own initiative, we also held a series of special hearings. There was one for children, which was held in camera so that they couldn't be besieged by the media. A special hearing for women was also closed to the public and the media and took place before an all-woman panel of commissioners. While there were many women who wanted to testify in public about sexual abuse by the police and the military, and who did so, there were also some who felt able to tell their stories only in private.

We invited business leaders to attend a special session because, obviously, business is involved with government and we wanted to hear their account of their activities in relation to the violence and illegality of state action. We also asked members of trade unions to give their point of view, which they did very bluntly. They were harshly critical of the business community, who they said 'were in bed with government'. A special hearing on the health sector dealt particularly with doctors who had worked in prisons and colluded with officials to deny the torture that was taking place. Special hearings on prisons and military conscription were also held. We listened with considerable interest to members of various church groups who gave evidence at a two-day hearing, and it was particularly gratifying to hear top officials of the Dutch Reformed Church offer their apology for complicity with the National Party and its apartheid policies.

The armed forces hearings were highly unsatisfactory. It was difficult to pin down any of them. Unlike the foot soldiers, the generals and senior officers were both devious and unhelpful in responding to our questions. We probed deeply, but with little success. We listened to the police, the SADF, MK and APLA. None of those who appeared before us was convincing. Everything that emerged during the special and institutional hearings made it overwhelmingly clear that torture was not an isolated occurrence in some prisons or villages, towns and cities, but was endemic in South Africa throughout the apartheid era. To suggest, as some of the National Party leaders did, that 'there were a few bad apples' was demonstrably untrue.

The special hearings also extended to lengthy sessions with representatives of all the major political parties. They made their submissions and presented us with voluminous memoranda containing their views on the apartheid years. Once we had spent some time reading these documents, party representatives were recalled to answer our questions. Some were more frank than others, but there were many disappointments. Desmond Tutu and I got into hot water following our press conference after listening to FW de Klerk for a full day. It was our view that, while he did acknowledge some responsibility and offered some apology, his insistence that he didn't know what was happening at the hands of his security forces was difficult to swallow – so much so that Tutu literally broke down. The National Party decided to take us to court and demanded that Tutu retract his statements and tender a public apology. What we found impossible to accept was De Klerk's denial that he was ever party to any of the state's illegal actions against opponents of apartheid. He had, after all, been both head of state and chairman of the State Security Council.

Similar retractions and apologies were demanded of me, in addition to which I was to be compelled to resign as deputy chairman and a member of the commission. I certainly had no intention of doing so and had the full backing of both the TRC and President Mandela, who told me that I should expect opposition, but that I should fight back. Though I was not happy about it, we did issue an apology. I felt that if anyone needed to make a frank and open apology, it was De Klerk and the National Party, but in order to allow the commission to continue its work, I reluctantly acceded to this part of the demand.

Some of the most difficult hearings were those dealing with the Soweto uprising of 1976 and the Boipatong massacre that took place on the night of 17 June 1992. Forty-eight people, many of them women and children, were killed that night in an extremely poverty-stricken area. We went to that hearing with a sense of dread and foreboding. It was a miserable day, cold and wet, and the people were huddled together in a hall that offered very little comfort. All the memories of that fateful night, when so many people were killed in their homes, came crowding back. The hall seemed to be filled not only with victims and family members of the dead, but also with ghosts, demanding to be acknowledged. I stood outside for a long while, trying to summon the courage to enter the hall, but, as we entered the bleak room, we heard the sound of singing. Quite spontaneously and in no way thanks to us, these poor people who had experienced so much sorrow and loss had started singing a well-known hymn. It filled the hall, bringing with it at least some measure of light and hope, reminding me, not for the first time, how often religion – in the best sense of the word – had given succour and comfort to so many black people in particular, who had no place in the white man's scheme of things.

While all these hearings were taking place throughout South Africa, a special committee was hard at work noting the requests and ideas of victims regarding reparations, doing research into what other governments and countries had attempted to do throughout history in this regard and preparing a report that was debated many times by the full commission, so that we would have a comprehensive set of recommendations regarding monetary and symbolic reparations that we could present to the state on conclusion of our work.

Perhaps the most difficult challenge facing the commission centred on two very powerful people: Winnie Madikizela-Mandela and PW Botha. They were very different – worlds apart in culture, position and race, yet two of the key actors in what can be described as the South African tragedy. Botha, who died in October 2006, was requested by the commission to attend a special hearing so that he could give an account of his successive stewardship as South Africa's defence minister, prime minister and state president. We went out of our way to make it easy for him to appear, but he was resolutely intractable in rejecting any advances we made. He saw the commission as a circus, with Tutu as the ringmaster and the rest of us dancing around! Not even personal intervention by Nelson Mandela could persuade him to attend a hearing. Mandela met with some members of PW's immediate family, urging them to encourage the old man to cooperate with us, and even telephoned Botha and offered to attend the hearing with him, if this would assist compliance with our request, but to no avail. Finally, we had no alternative but to subpoena Botha, only to be informed by his lawyers that he would refuse to accept the summons. In terms of the TRC Act, anyone who refused a subpoena was guilty of contempt. Our only recourse, therefore, was to hand the matter over to the Cape attorney-general, Frank Kahn, to decide what action should be taken.

Botha appeared in the magistrate's court at George on 23 February 1998. He was his usual arrogant and defiant self. The scene was almost war-like, with the entrance to the court lined on both sides with barbed wire to prevent clashes between supporters of Botha and the ANC. There were placards supporting Botha and others supporting the TRC. The court case was not our preferred route, but at least it meant that the man who had been in charge of the military and the State Security Council, who devised and sanctioned many of the policies of the National Party government, was being held to account. He was no longer the president; he was now the accused.

Botha was found guilty of contempt and his lawyers successfully appealed against the verdict, which was set aside on purely technical grounds in March 1999. We were deeply disappointed by this finding and, although we could have taken further legal action, we decided not to do so. The TRC was coming to the end of its tenure, and we had shown that Botha was both accountable and not above the law. During the course of the case in the magistrate's court, we had placed on the record many of the questions and allegations that we would have put to him at a public hearing, so there was really no point to pursuing the issue. In an editorial in the *Argus* on Monday 7 June 1999, the editor wrote, inter alia: 'History will be the final judge of Mr Botha and there is no doubt that it will give a very harsh verdict.'

Winnie Madikizela-Mandela was an entirely different experience. She enjoyed widespread and enthusiastic support from the majority of people in South Africa and had many friends abroad. She was known in ANC circles as the Mother of the Nation. She was intimately connected with the Mandela United Football Club, which she had started. They certainly never played football, but several of them died while they were members of that club and under Madikizela-Mandela's care. Several youngsters were abducted by Winnie Mandela while under the protection of the Methodist Church and many had been badly injured.

It was a long and difficult hearing. Over a nine-day period, scores of Winnie's supporters congregated outside the hall where we met, along with the mothers and family members of some Mandela United Football Club members. Their silence – indeed, their very presence – was a powerful rebuke of President Mandela's ex-wife.

At the heart of the Madikizela-Mandela hearing was the murder of Stompie Moeketse Seipei and the disappearance of Lolo Sono. Lolo's father, Nicodemus, told the commission that Madikizela-Mandela was the last person seen with Lolo, whom she had accused of being a police informer. The grieving father testified that when he last saw his son in Madikizela-Mandela's minivan, 'He was beaten up. His face was bruised. It was actually pulped.' He had urged Madikizela-Mandela to leave his son with him, but she finally said: 'I am taking this dog away. The movement will see what to do.' Despite searching for Lolo and calling at Winnie's home many times after this, Nicodemus said, she refused to give him a clear answer about his son's whereabouts and eventually refused to see him at all.

Another witness, Nomsa Shabalala, testified that her son, also a member of the Mandela United Football Club, disappeared after being in Madikizela-Mandela's house. At the end of her evidence she said: 'I would request Winnie to give Siboniso back to me. I want him or his bones and remains. If Winnie doesn't know anything, that is what she says, I also say that she knows, deep down inside of her she knows.' Tragically, the remains of Lolo Sono and Siboniso Shabalala were never found and Madikizela-Mandela categorically denied the accounts given by their parents. To the very end, she also denied any part in Stompie Seipei's death.

In fact, the hearing ended with very little acknowledgement by Madikizela-Mandela of many of the accusations made against her by so many witnesses. I am sad that she never applied for amnesty. I think it could have helped not only Winnie herself, but also the commission and the parents of the children who were murdered or went missing. It could also have been of great help to South Africa.

The commission's findings regarding Madikizela-Mandela included the following:

> Ms Madikizela-Mandela was central to the establishment and formation of the Mandela United Football Club which later developed into a private vigilante unit operating around Ms Madikizela-Mandela and from her houses in both Orlando West and Diepkloof. The Commission finds that the community anger against Ms Madikizela-Mandela and the Football Club manifested itself in the burning of the Mandela home in Orlando West in July 1988, which led to political, community and church leaders requesting that she disband the Football Club.
>
> The Commission further finds that the Mandela United Football Club was involved in a number of criminal activities including killing, torture, assaults and arson in the community. It is the Commission's view that Ms Madikizela-Mandela was aware of the criminal activity and the disquiet it caused in the community, but chose deliberately not to address the problems emanating from the Football Club. The Commission finds that those who opposed Ms Madikizela-Mandela and the Mandela United Football Club, or dissented from them, were branded as informers, and killed. The labelling by Ms Madikizela-Mandela of opponents as informers created the perception that they were legitimate targets. It is the finding of this Commission that Ms Madikizela-Mandela had knowledge of and/or participated in the activities of Club members, and/or that they were authorised and/or sanctioned by her.[1]

The TRC interviewed and took statements from more than 22 000 victims. There were close on 8 000 applicants for amnesty. We held hearings in every major city and many rural towns and villages throughout South Africa, and because we decentralised our operations and had offices in various provinces, we were able to complete the hearings for victims as well as the special and institutional hearings in the time designated by the Act.

Unfortunately, and mainly because of the legal requirements, we were not able to complete the amnesty hearings, which continued for a further two years. Of all the witnesses who appeared before us, I think the most telling remark was made by Peter Storey, the former bishop of the Methodist Church, during the Madikizela-Mandela hearing. His evidence was succinct, clear and to the point. He concluded by saying: 'The primary cancer may be and was and always will be the apartheid oppression, but the secondary infection has touched many of apartheid's opponents and eroded their knowledge of good and evil. One of the tragedies of life is that it is possible to become like that which we hate most, and I have a feeling that this drama is an example of that.'

His observation was not well received by Madikizela-Mandela's lawyers or her many supporters, but, as far as I was concerned, it hit the nail on the head.

Two events marred the closing days of the commission. The five-volume report, due largely to outstanding work by Charles Villa-Vicencio and his team, was in the hands of the printers when FW de Klerk, incensed by the findings made against him, brought an urgent action against the commission. This action requested the Cape High Court to prevent the commission's findings being included in the report. The hearing, with Judge Edwin King presiding, took place on 28 October 1998, the day before the report was due to be published. In order not to delay the publication, an agreement was reached not to include the findings. The page was removed, but was replaced with one printed with a black square to indicate that something had been removed. Villa-Vicencio had the unenviable task of retrieving Volume 5 of the report and replacing the page, and still managed to get all the copies to Johannesburg in time for the public launch.

The second blow was the announcement that the ANC had applied for an interdict to prevent the publication of the findings against it.[2] We were due to hand over the report to President Mandela at noon on 29 October, and the court was still sitting in Cape Town long after 10 a.m. Fortunately, we received the news before noon that the court had dismissed the ANC's application with costs. We were therefore able to hand over the report, but it was a very subdued occasion, not the joyful one we had anticipated. But in one way we were greatly encouraged that we had incurred the wrath of De Klerk and Mbeki, because it underscored the impartiality of the commission.

CHAPTER 19

Truth and consequence

MORE THAN A DECADE AFTER THE TRC, THERE IS STILL ENOR-mous interest in its work. A number of feature films have been made using the TRC as the central theme, as well as many documentaries, one of which, *Long Night's Journey Into Day*, was nominated for an Oscar. It has become increasingly difficult to keep up with the number of books written about the commission, to say nothing of the poems and plays, conferences, workshops, graduate and doctoral theses, and the subject continues to draw interest. By the end of 2007, the South African cast of Michael Lessac's play, *Truth in Translation*, had performed at several venues in South Africa as well as in Rwanda, at the Edinburgh Festival, in London and Paris, and it was scheduled to be staged in a number of major centres in the USA during 2008. The second half of 2007 also saw the SABC mark the tenth anniversary of the TRC with a series of interviews with many of us who were directly involved.

It is not difficult to understand why the South African commission grabbed the imagination of so many people throughout the world. Obviously, the magical name of Nelson Mandela is one of the reasons. Though at no time a member of the commission, he was a central character; his sheer humanity and commitment to reconciliation from the day he walked out of prison and throughout his tenure as president of South Africa set the tone for our work. Desmond Tutu is an icon in our country and well known and respected in many parts of the world. I think that his involvement led many people to think about the possibility of introducing a similar instrument in their own lands.

In addition, there were certain characteristics of the TRC that were unique and novel, and which, I think, contributed to the sustained global interest. It is probably true to say that, when considering the establishment of a truth commission, there is no country that does not immediately think of contacting some of us from the TRC. Without exaggeration, the South African exercise has become the yardstick by which all other commissions are judged.

However, that is not to say that one can simply take the South African model and export it, holus bolus, to be imposed on countries that are very different from our own. Each country has its own history, culture, politics and possibilities. Each country has to look at many models and take what is best from them, while also learning from mistakes made by the South African commission.

I have dealt thoroughly with the TRC in my earlier book, *A Country Unmasked*. However, it could be helpful to briefly reiterate some of the favourable conditions that helped to facilitate the commission's work, as well as some of its unique features. I will also consider some of the shortcomings of the TRC, as well as its positive outcomes.

The first favourable condition was the fact that the newly elected ANC government was a strong supporter of the TRC, and that President Mandela offered such powerful leadership. This meant that the commission was almost part and parcel of the new dispensation, even though it was not the subject of pre-democracy negotiations. It is impossible to understand the life and work of the TRC unless one sees it in the context of a difficult, but also highly successful, process that ultimately led to a new constitution, a new parliament and a new beginning for South Africa. The TRC was built on fruitful political negotiations.

Secondly, the existence of a strong civil society gave enormous depth and foundation to the work of the commission. Long before it came into being, there were numerous discussions, debates, consultations and meetings that influenced the TRC's structures and modus operandi.

Furthermore, the international community's interest in what was happening in South Africa greatly assisted the commission. Many countries sent delegations of human rights activists, academics, politicians and others to attend sessions of the TRC, and, of course, they took their experiences home and to missions that they travelled to throughout the world. In addition, we received considerable financial assistance, and, in particular, a large number of well-trained foreign investigators joined our team for the duration of the commission's work. This gave us access to their expertise and gave credibility to the TRC's investigative process.

Finally, the rich contribution of Archbishop Desmond Tutu to the TRC cannot be overestimated. All the commissioners and a highly trained and skilled staff played a role, but he was the centre point, and because of his stature and influence the commission was able to fulfil its mandate. It is difficult to imagine the TRC without his inspiring leadership.

There were also certain unique features that characterised the TRC. One of these was the fact that, long before it started its work, there was considerable emphasis on consultation and involvement of as many people as possible. Unfortunately, in many countries commissions are appointed with almost no reference to the people, and, as a result, it often takes a long time for a commission to gain support from the community.

In addition, the TRC was a parliamentary rather than a presidential commission. In both Argentina and Chile, the commissions were appointed by the respective presidents. We felt strongly that, with a new democratic parliament, the mandate given to the TRC should come not only from the president, but also from a representative assembly.

A further unique element of the South African model is that our TRC was the first to hold its hearings in public. I cannot stress sufficiently how important this was and is. Not only was the TRC afforded a great deal of integrity by being transparent, but people throughout South Africa could participate in proceedings. We didn't hold hearings in only the major centres, but travelled the length and breadth of the country to peri-urban areas and small rural towns. In all of this, we were wonderfully supported by the SABC's TV and radio broadcasts, as well as by the print media. Antjie Krog on radio and Max du Preez on television were empathetic and brilliant in their coverage of the commission's work. We were fortunate that the editors of all the major newspapers seconded senior staff to cover the commission from beginning to end. Radio coverage was especially critical. Hearings were well attended in all parts of the country, but access to radio ensured that the trauma and testimony of victims and perpetrators became a national experience rather than being limited to those who were physically present.

The South African TRC was unique in terms of the powers granted to it. As a parliamentary commission, we could request certain powers that previous commissions had not enjoyed. The powers of subpoena and search and seizure were used sparingly, but were invaluable.

The TRC embraced an extensive mandate. We didn't confine our hearings to individual victims and perpetrators of human rights violations. We also decided to hold special and institutional hearings, because the impact of apartheid was felt in every area of life. There were special hearings for children and for women, as well as for key representatives of political parties, the legal fraternity, faith communities, business leaders, labour unions, the health sector and prison authorities. It was the hope of the commission that, by giving institutions an opportunity to spell out their role during the apartheid years, they would think more creatively about the role they would play in the new South Africa. This would assist in the institutional transformation that is essential if a country is to change for the better. It is not enough merely to hold an election and change the top people, or even the government; institutions are structures that can either limit positive and creative change or assist it.

The holding in tension of the commission's authority to grant amnesty to those who qualified by meeting all the legal requirements, while at the same time determining the fate of missing victims, restoring the dignity of those who related the violations they had suffered and recommending reparations, gave South Africa's commission its truly unique character. We were charged with hearing both the stories of victims and confessions of perpetrators.

The amnesty clause was possibly the most controversial aspect of the TRC, and was strongly criticised both inside and outside South Africa. The international legal community opposed it on the grounds that amnesty could encourage impunity, whereas it was important that perpetrators of gross human rights violations be charged in a court of law. What has often been overlooked is that South Africa never offered a general amnesty; it was always conditional, possible only in exchange for the whole truth, and limited by several specific factors.

Firstly, amnesty had to be applied for on an individual basis; there was no such thing as collective indemnity. Secondly, applicants had to complete a prescribed form, published in the *Government Gazette*, which called for extremely detailed information relating to the specific human rights violations. Thirdly, applicants had to make full disclosure about their deeds. Fourthly, in most instances applicants would appear before the Amnesty Committee, and the hearings were open to the public and the media. Fifthly, there were time limits. Only gross human rights violations committed between 1960 and 1994 would be considered for amnesty, and applications had to be submitted between December 1995, when the TRC legislation was promulgated, and May 1997. Finally, actions were eligible for amnesty only if they had a political objective, and if they were in proportion to the objective pursued.

Nevertheless, despite the conditionality of the South African amnesty, not a single truth commission anywhere else in the world has followed our example. Many commissions have borrowed from the South African model in other respects, but not regarding amnesty. I think this is unfortunate. While I appreciate the apprehension among human rights practitioners and legal scholars that amnesty could lead to impunity, I think it is a grave error to lump all amnesties together. Amnesty has been a useful tool and has served over hundreds of years to resolve pressing problems in many countries where conflict and deep divisions were present. I think a major advantage of conditional amnesty was that we were able to obtain information that we could never have secured from the victims, because they themselves were seeking answers about what had happened to their loved ones. The fact that perpetrators were able to give detailed information regarding gross human rights violations not only ensured a degree of accountability, but also gave great comfort to victims, because it seems that victims, not only in South Africa but all over the world, have a deep desire for the truth, even though it may be dreadfully hurtful.

When we wrote our final report, we made it absolutely clear that our intention was to avoid impunity, and we emphasised the need for accountability in the following terms:

> Where amnesty has not been sought or has been denied, prosecution should be considered where evidence exists that an individual has committed a gross human rights violation. In this regard, the Commission will make available to the appropriate authorities information in its possession concerning serious allegations against individuals (excluding privileged information such as that contained in amnesty applications). Consideration must be given to imposing a time limit on such prosecutions.
>
> Attorneys-General must pay rigorous attention to the prosecution of members of the South African Police Service (SAPS) who are found to have assaulted, tortured and/or killed persons in their care.
>
> In order to avoid a culture of impunity and to entrench the rule of law, the granting of general amnesty in whatever guise should be resisted.[1]

Aryeh Neier, president of the Open Society Institute in New York and a very strong opponent of blanket amnesty, reinforces the point well: 'Indeed, in the specific circumstances of South Africa it is not easy to quarrel with Archbishop Tutu when he contends that the Truth and Reconciliation Commission process of providing amnesty in exchange for acknowledgment and full disclosure, with prosecution as an alternative for those who do not acknowledge and disclose, served the country better than a process that would have relied solely on prosecutions.'[2]

In an address to the Library of Congress/NYU Law School symposium in 2000, Sandra Day O'Connor, formerly a judge of the Supreme Court of the United States, made the following observation:

Amnesty does not necessarily undermine accountability ... South Africa, drawing on the experience of countries such as Argentina, established a Truth and Reconciliation Commission that provided only conditional grants of amnesty. The preamble of the Reconciliation Act which established the Truth and Reconciliation Commission identifies its goals as 'reconciliation, amnesty, reparation and the search for truth'. The Commission considered 'gross violations of human rights' which include 'the killing, abduction, torture or severe ill treatment of any person'. These 'gross violations of human rights' are limited to acts that were crimes under the apartheid legal system and liability extends not only to acts committed by the apartheid regime but also acts committed by members of the liberation movements such as the African National Congress. Although the negotiated end of apartheid included the agreement that some form of amnesty would be available for outgoing leaders in return for a peaceful transfer to a fully democratic society, blanket amnesties were not given. Instead, conditional grants of amnesty are given to those who acknowledge their crimes by providing complete and truthful testimony regarding their actions. The Commission investigates the testimony and decides whether to grant the application for amnesty. If amnesty is denied, then prosecution can proceed. Perpetrators whose crimes are deemed 'disproportionately' heinous or not motivated by politics can also be denied amnesty.

There are, she continues, several advantages to this process:

First, because the amnesties granted under this process are not designed to exculpate the state's own agents but instead to expose and acknowledge the crimes of the previous regime, the process promotes truth and accountability. Second, the focus on reconciliation and healing ensures that the process looks forward to strengthening the new democratic regime rather than looking backwards toward retribution. Finally, the process signals a break with the past regime and can be used to build political legitimacy for the new regime. The South African approach appears to effectively balance these two goals, encouraging public accountability without the destabilizing effects of a fully fledged trial.[3]

It is unfortunate that many international lawyers seem not to have taken into account the balance exhibited by Sandra Day O'Connor in her examination of different options in confronting a violent past. There appears to be a dogmatic demand for prosecutions in societies scarred with divisions that still run deep, and this can pose serious risks to attempts to work towards a sustainable peace. It also creates difficulties in the establishment of a human rights culture and the consolidation of democracy.

It is critically important to understand power relations and the continuing power of former generals. As a delegate at a human rights conference in Aspen, Colorado, aptly put it in 1988, 'beware the sleeping lion on the porch'. In countries emerging from large-scale and lengthy conflict, the demand for rebuilding the economy will be acute. Resources are scarce and the cost of long-term trials is prohibitive. There is a kind of legal fundamentalism that excludes all other options and approaches, and, if this prevails, it can actually discourage reconciliation in the country concerned. The focus is squarely on the perpetrator and punishment, while the victim is pushed to the sidelines. It is unfortunate in the extreme that the recently established International Criminal Court makes no provision for amnesty of any kind, or even the option of a truth commission. It has already become apparent that this leaves the ICC very little room to manoeuvre in cases such as that of northern Uganda, for example.

It should be quite clear that I am not arguing for blanket or general amnesty, nor an amnesty imposed by the previous regime. In this respect, Ron Slye assists us by focusing on the possibility of legitimate amnesties. In an excellent article titled 'The legitimacy of amnesties under international law and general principles of Anglo-American law' he poses the question, 'Is a legitimate amnesty possible?' In discussing various types of amnesty, including the amnesic, compromise and corrective kind, he argues for accountable amnesties. 'Accountable amnesties are amnesties that provide some accountability and more than minimal relief to victims.'[4] He suggests that to qualify as accountable, an amnesty must be democratic in its creation and must not apply to those responsible for war crimes, crimes against humanity and other serious violations of international criminal law, but must impose some form of public procedure or accountability on its recipients. It must also provide an opportunity for victims to question and challenge an individual's claim to amnesty, offer some concrete benefit, usually in the form of reparations to victims, and be designed to facilitate a transition to a more human rights–friendly regime, or form part of a comprehensive programme of reconciliation, aimed at addressing long-standing and serious societal tensions and injustices. He concludes: 'The South African amnesty is the only one to date that comes close to qualifying as an accountable amnesty.'

It is to be hoped that the international community takes note of this argument and seeks to distinguish between different kinds of amnesty, rather than dismissing all attempts to introduce some form of amnesty, in countries that are in transition to democracy from dictatorship or authoritarian government. Conditional amnesty, such as that granted by the TRC, could be a useful tool in bridging the conflict of the past and a new society, as has been shown in South Africa.

On a visit to South Africa, Kofi Annan, the former secretary-general of the United Nations, made the following comment when discussing the International Criminal Court *vis-à-vis* the TRC:

> The purpose of the clause in the Statute (which allows the Court to intervene where the State is 'unwilling or unable' to exercise jurisdiction) is to ensure that mass murderers and other arch-criminals cannot shelter behind a State run by themselves or their cronies, or take advantage of a general breakdown of law and order. No one should imagine that it would apply to a case like South Africa's, where the regime and the conflict which caused the crimes have come to an end, and the victims have inherited power. It is inconceivable that, in such a case, the Court would seek to substitute its judgment for that of a whole nation which is seeking the best way to put a traumatic past behind it and build a better future.[5]

It is true that the argument has moved on, and some maintain that if the South African model were to be introduced today it would be unacceptable, because, in terms of international law, people who have committed war crimes and crimes against humanity cannot be considered for amnesty. This is the ideal for which we should strive, but justice, like politics, is the art of the possible. A single example will make the point. As I write, Sri Lanka is locked in conflict, with serious human rights violations being perpetrated by the Tamil Tigers and government forces. One day, peace talks will start again. When that happens, is it conceivable that the government and the rebels will be tried in a court of law as part of the resolution of conflict? This is hardly likely.

A final unique feature of the TRC, which was also highly controversial and often disputed, was its impartiality. It was not a witch-hunt; it was not a focus on the Afrikaner, although many people accused us of this; it was not a focus on the National Party alone, as the architect of apartheid policies. The focus was on all of us – on those who imposed a vicious system as well as those who opposed it. Our reasoning was that wherever human rights violations occurred, they should be addressed and accountability sought. This brought us into head-on conflict with the ANC, which believed – wrongly

– that we were assigning moral equivalence to the state and the liberation movement. At many of our hearings, in our written work and in particular in the commission's final report, we made it very clear that this was not the case. We laid critical and key blame for what happened in South Africa on the state, and we illustrated that unambiguously. However, we also had to say that, in opposing the state, certain violations took place outside the country in the ANC camps, as well as inside South Africa. Many of us recoiled in horror at the necklacing of people suspected of being informers. In addition, the clash between different groups within the opposition movement often led to violence. In this we were guided by the Geneva Convention, which allows for a just war, but makes it clear that the party which opts for a just war has to accept moral and political responsibility if, in the course of that war, it commits human rights violations. This did indeed happen, and we felt it should be included in our report. The result was that we were attacked from all sides when the report was published.

The NP and its leadership, particularly FW de Klerk, did not like our heavy emphasis on state responsibility. The ANC didn't like being charged with certain human rights violations. No one seemed to like the report, which suggests that perhaps we did a good job in the end. This emphasis on inclusivity, in terms of overall responsibility, was a key feature of the commission and it was adopted after very heated and spirited debate.

In his book, *Overcoming Apartheid*,[6] social scientist James L Gibson came to the conclusion after more than 3 000 individual interviews that the general truth, as described by the commission in terms of what happened in South Africa during the period under review (1960 to 1994), was accepted by the majority of the country's citizens. The sample included black, white, coloured and Indian respondents. This is not to suggest for a moment that the commission discovered the whole truth. Far from it. However, the general truth that apartheid was not a noble experiment but a vicious system that affected the lives of millions, and that there were many parties to the conflict, was and is accepted by South Africans. This points to at least a measure of reconciliation. The emphasis was on a common memory that would allow all South Africans to agree that this did happen, and that it must never happen again; that despite our divisions and differences, we can and must work together. It is this memory which is accepted by those who applied the apartheid policies, those who opposed them and the large group in the middle, who denied any knowledge of what was really happening around them.

To reach that point in such a short space of time, after so many years of oppression and degradation, was a giant step forward, even though South Africa still has many steps to take. In an article published in *Business Day* in September 1994, journalist Simon Barber argued: 'The goal of the inquiry [i.e., the TRC] cannot be perfect justice but should rather be national reconciliation and the development of a "shared memory" which makes possible both forgiveness and its essential precursor, sincere penitence, and which, just as importantly, vaccinates the democracy against further abuses of power ... [I]deally, truth must precede forgiveness.'

Countries around the world can learn not only from the successes but also the shortcomings of the TRC. The South African model failed in some important respects. Firstly, the commission did not gain the support of the white minority, South Africa's former ruling class, which was complicit in the injustices of the apartheid era. Initially, this group's reaction to the TRC was mainly hostile or somewhat indifferent, as if this process had nothing to do with them. It took a while for the message to get through that all whites, irrespective of their political views, were beneficiaries of the apartheid system, and the commission tried hard to encourage them to participate in our work. Tragically, very few even attended the public hearings. This was partly because whites in general felt uncomfortable about the disclosures that were being made by victims. They were suspicious of the proceedings, uncertain and fearful. There was a sense of guilt, but also a feeling that they wouldn't be welcome among a predominantly black audience attending the hearings. They were so wrong.

One of the things that stood out for all of us in the TRC was the remarkable, almost unbelievable, generosity of black South Africans, even towards self-confessed perpetrators. Many blacks came to me, and I am sure to other commissioners, time and time again and urged us to publicly invite whites to attend the hearings. We did so, but it was almost always only the usual suspects – those who had been involved in fighting against apartheid, members of the human rights community – who accepted the invitations and gave support. They came in good numbers over the years that the TRC existed, but we really failed to involve the white community as a whole. Fortunately, the commission reached out across the country through radio, television and the print media and made a considerable impact on white opinion – but it never pierced the hard shell of white complicity.

Secondly, the TRC did not uncover the whole truth. This is particularly true of the involvement of the military in the governing of South Africa during the 1980s. The generals were evasive and smart, and the 'not guilty' verdict in the 1995 trial of the former minister of defence, Magnus Malan, and a host of top-ranking military officers and IFP officials on charges of having been responsible for the massacre of thirteen people, including women and children, at KwaMakhutha in 1987, made it so much easier for the top brass to treat the commission with disdain and even contempt.

Thirdly, the TRC did not succeed in securing even a minimal amount of justice in relation to those who actually drew up the policies of apartheid that resulted in death squads, torture, detention without trial and assassinations. Many of the documents had been destroyed in the run-up to the negotiations and during the period when the National Party was still in power. There was no paper trail linking senior politicians, generals and the many other security force leaders. As always, it was the foot soldiers who took the blame, even though they were acting under the orders of their superiors.

Fourthly, the commission failed to persuade the ANC-led government to grant swift and adequate reparations to victims. This had a major impact on those who had put their trust in the commission, who believed that they would, indeed, receive some form of compensation, as recommended in the TRC report. The government failed dismally to fulfil its responsibilities by not acting timeously on the recommendations made by the commission, and when they finally did offer some form of reparation, it was considerably less than we had proposed.

The commission strongly recommended that those who had applied for but been denied amnesty, as well as those who refused to seek amnesty but against whom there was a *prima facie* case, should be prosecuted. The window of opportunity was never intended to remain open forever – but here, too, despite the government appointing leading lawyers to investigate cases that we referred to them, there was a serious dearth of follow-up.

In August 2007, former minister of law and order Adriaan Vlok and retired police commissioner General Johan van der Merwe were charged with attempted murder by means of administering poison to the clothes of the Reverend Frank Chikane in April 1989. At the time, Chikane was an outspoken anti-apartheid activist, secretary-general of the South African Council of Churches and vice-president of the United Democratic Front. While visiting Namibia and the United States, he fell extremely ill every time he dressed in clothes from the suitcase he had packed prior to his departure. Eventually, after he had been hospitalised several times in a critical condition, doctors in America discovered that he was suffering from organophosphate poisoning. More than a decade later, investigations showed that the deadly toxin had been produced as part of South Africa's top-secret chemical and biological warfare programme, Project Coast, and applied to some of Chikane's clothing by security policemen who intercepted his luggage at the Johannesburg airport.

The accused pleaded guilty and were each sentenced to ten years in prison, wholly suspended for five years on condition that they were not convicted again during that period 'of a crime in which assault or the administration of poison or any other hazardous substance form an element, or of conspiracy to commit such a crime'.

They had entered into a plea bargain with the state and the court hearing was a farce. There was no cross-examination, and the victim – by then a senior minister in President Thabo Mbeki's office – was not called to testify. The court record makes it clear that an order to act against high-profile members of the liberation struggle was issued during the latter half of the 1980s and that a list containing the names of persons to be targeted was handed to senior members of the security establishment. However, due to the nature of the Vlok/Van der Merwe case, we still don't know who issued the order or whose names were on the list.

Not long after the Vlok/Van der Merwe plea bargain, Mbeki told parliament that the government was considering a pardon for people who committed political offences, even if they had not applied for amnesty. A special inter-party committee had been appointed to consider each application on merit.

In my view, a great opportunity was missed for Vlok, Van der Merwe and many of their colleagues to come clean. I had told Vlok during a live television debate that he owed it to the people of South Africa not only to talk about the attempt to kill Chikane, but also to divulge all incidents relating to the order to act against anti-apartheid activists. In view of the way the Chikane case was dealt with, however, it seems highly unlikely that any serious attempt will be made by the state in future to bring to book those who lied to or withheld evidence from the TRC, or refused to apply for amnesty.

I believe that our demands on the perpetrators should have been stronger. I think of East Timor, where its commission decided that those who were to receive a form of amnesty should take part in some specific community service. This would be difficult to impose and not easy to implement, but nevertheless I think we should have done more to ensure that perpetrators made some kind of atonement in the form of community service, particularly in black areas.

Lastly, I want to sketch briefly what I consider to be some of the main positive contributions made by the TRC. In an introduction to *The Healing of a Nation?*, which incorporated the major lectures given at a conference held in June 1994, I made the point that there was no quick fix for the healing of a nation. There were no magic formulae that would offer an instant remedy for the sickness that had reached epidemic proportions. I tried to emphasize that the healing we sought could not be achieved merely by holding conferences, nor writing books, nor even through appointing a truth and reconciliation commission. Discussion, debate, analysis and the recording of the truth can be a significant part of the healing process, but no more than that. It was clear that South Africa would need to build a new society and that this could only be achieved over several generations. The wounds incurred in the bitter period of repression and resistance were too deep to be trivialised by imagining that a single initiative could bring about a peaceful and stable restored society.

Obviously, therefore, the impact and contribution that the commission could make to both truth and reconciliation was limited, not only by the time factor and its mandate, but also because this is a task that has to be performed by all the institutions and people of South Africa. We were simply a precursor to what needs to happen.

Our responsibility was not to reconcile the nation. Indeed, the process of reconciliation had begun at the negotiation table, long before the TRC was set up. Our job was to encourage continuation and development of the process and support the promotion of reconciliation within every area of society. The commission acknowledged in its final report that the process of reconciliation had a long, long way to go. Many ordinary South Africans have experienced a measure of reconciliation, but much work still lies ahead. This is particularly true in the area of economic justice. This was a prominent and constant theme in the debates and discussions of the commission. Many of us made the point, over and over, that we can speak words of reconciliation and uncover a fair amount of the truth, but, unless we address the yawning gap between rich and poor, the disparities between the haves and the have-nots, unless we assist the poorest of the poor to have

basic living conditions – decent housing, clean water, clinics and schools –
we will remain forever unreconciled. Indeed, unless considerable resources
are committed to tackling these fundamental issues, we could be sitting on
a time bomb.

On the subject of the eradication of poverty and the responsibility of
both the private and public sector in this regard, the TRC accepted that
business in general benefited from operating in a racially structured context.
However, the commission was anxious to point the way ahead rather than
dwell on the past, and made specific recommendations relating to the future
role of the private sector, namely:

> It will be impossible to create a meaningful human rights culture with-
> out high priority being given to economic justice by the public and
> private sectors. Recognising that it is impossible for the public sector
> alone to find the resources required to expedite the goal of economic
> justice, the Commission urges the private sector in particular to consider
> a special initiative in terms of a fund for training, empowerment and
> opportunities for the disadvantaged and dispossessed in South Africa.

The commission went further and recommended that

> a scheme be put into place to enable those who benefited from apartheid
> policies to contribute towards the alleviation of poverty. In submissions
> made to the Commission, a wealth tax was proposed. The Commission
> does not, however, seek to prescribe one or other strategy, but recom-
> mends that urgent consideration be given by government to harnessing
> all available resources in the war against poverty.[7]

Recognising the political and economic significance of the land question,
the commission also recommended that the business community, together
with other interested parties and in cooperation with the Land Commission,
'undertake an audit of all unused and underutilised land with a view to
making this available to landless people'.[8] Further recommendations related
to affirmative action, compensation for black, Indian and coloured business
people who lost their businesses or other means of income during periods
of unrest, and the elimination of child labour wherever it still exists.

I have referred to many individuals who were assisted by the commission, and it would be helpful to mention a few of these. One was Lucas
Sikwepere, who appeared at a hearing in Cape Town in 1996. He had to be
led up to the platform, because he was blind. He had been shot in the face
by the police, and later, having become more politically active as a direct

result of losing his sight, he had also been very badly tortured. He told his story in some detail, and when asked if there was anything else he wanted to add, he said: 'I feel what has been making me sick all the time is the fact that I couldn't tell my story. But now it feels like I got my sight back by coming here and telling you the story.'[9]

Tim Ledgerwood, a former conscript in the SADF, alleged that he had been severely tortured by the security police. The process of telling his story to the commission, he said, had deeply affected his life, because he now felt an enormous freedom to talk to others about his experiences as well. He said he felt '[a]s if I've been freed from a prison in which I have been for eighteen years. It is also as if my family has been freed ... The silence is ending and we are waking up from a long bad nightmare.'[10]

Duma Khumalo, speaking on behalf of the Khulumani Support Group, reported a similar healing process after meeting with many of the victims who had appeared before the commission: 'It is the intervention of the Commission that restored the dignity of so many people that was lost during the political era in our country. People had no one to listen to their griefs or pay attention to some of these griefs until the establishment of the Commission. Then many of the victims came forward and started, for the first time, to talk about their past griefs.'[11]

Cynthia Ngewu, whose son was killed by the police in the infamous 'Guguletu Seven' incident, explained to the commission that in her view reconciliation involved the healing of perpetrators as well as victims: 'What we are hoping for when we embrace the notion of reconciliation is that we restore the humanity to those who were perpetrators. We do not want to return evil by another evil. We simply want to ensure that the perpetrators are returned to humanity.'[12] Ngewu was bereaved and deeply angry, but, remarkably, she thought not only of her own particular needs, which were great, but of the needs of the very people who killed her son. If this is not the beginning of reconciliation in a particular person as well as in a particular community, then I don't know what is.

Remarkable testimony also came from Beth Savage, who was seriously injured in an attack on a function at the golf club in King William's Town. She not only spoke about the circumstances and the serious injuries that she sustained, but expressed a wish to meet those who were responsible. Her wish was fulfilled in April 1998, when Thembelani Xundu sought amnesty. As a result of her meeting with Xundu, Beth Savage told a newspaper, her nightmares related to the attack had ceased.

The willingness to forgive and start again cut across men and women, black and white. Johan Smit, whose son was killed by a bomb planted at the Amanzimtoti Shopping Centre in 1985, told the commission that he had forgiven those who killed his son and had met the parents of the young ANC supporter who planted the bomb. 'It was a great relief seeing them and expressing my feelings towards them,' Smit said. 'I felt glad that I could tell them that I felt no hatred for them. I bore them no grudge.' Asked by one of the commissioners whether he had found some relief in knowing what had happened and being able to talk to the family of the man who had killed his son, he replied: 'Yes, it gave me peace because I knew what was happening. I thought if I placed myself in the other person's shoes, how would I have felt about it? How would I have liked not to be able to vote, not to have any rights, and that kind of thing? So I realised that I would not have liked it, how it must have felt for them.'[13]

J Msweli told the commission in 1996 that her son Simon had been tortured, violated and mutilated, and had died as a result. She felt very strongly that it was important for those responsible to acknowledge their responsibility: 'I want the people who killed my son to come forward because this is a time for reconciliation. I want to forgive them, and I also have a bit of my mind to tell them.'[14]

A further example of the countless incidents involving forgiveness and reconciliation is the story of Neville Clarence and Aboobaker Ismail. Clarence was a former South African Air Force captain who had been blinded in the bombing of the SAAF headquarters in Church Street, Pretoria. Ismail had planted the bomb outside the building. He told the Amnesty Committee that he regretted the deaths of people in the course of the armed struggle.

When the two men met before the hearing, Ismail told Clarence: 'This is very difficult. I am sorry about what happened to you.' The blind Clarence said that he understood, adding, 'I don't hold any grudges.' They agreed to meet again. A little later, Clarence spoke to the media. 'I came here today partly out of curiosity and hoping to meet Mr Ismail. I wanted to say that I have never felt any bitterness towards him. It was a wonderful experience ... Reconciliation does not just come from one side. We were on opposite sides and, in this instance, I came off second best.'[15]

But others who appeared before the commission told us that it was impossible for them to forgive, that they needed more time, that they didn't know if they would ever be able to do so. Many of them expressed a hope that those responsible for their loss and injury would come before the commission; perhaps they would be able to forgive once acknowledgement had been made.

It also has to be said, however, that even when full acknowledgement was made at the amnesty hearings, many victims and families of victims still found it difficult to forgive. I can only reiterate that it was not the intention of the commission to demand forgiveness, to pressurise people to forgive; our task was to create an opportunity for those who were able and ready to forgive to do so.

In my view, the great strength of the storytelling by some 22 000 people who came to the commission was not only that the silence was broken, but that a process had begun. Many organisations, including churches, schools and universities, set up their own storytelling exercises, so the experience of the commission was duplicated all over the country. These instances of individual reconciliation are important, and while they do not mean that South Africa has been reconciled, we cannot overlook the generosity of spirit that characterised so many of those who appeared before the commission. Numerous people were helped by the experience and many of them sought to stretch out a hand to those who had caused their suffering.

A final example of how some good can come from tragedy concerns the killing of Amy Biehl and the consequences that flowed from her death. Amy was a young American Fulbright scholar, working in South Africa. She was well known to many of us, and in fact some of us met with her and others the day before she was brutally murdered. She often went into the townships around Cape Town and, on this particular occasion, was taking three friends home to Guguletu.

While she was driving along one of the main streets of the township, a group of young black men on their way back from a PAC rally stopped Amy's car and dragged her out. When she tried to run away, they chased her and stoned and stabbed her to death. Her attackers were apprehended, charged and sentenced to long terms of imprisonment, even though they were very young. When the three perpetrators applied for amnesty, to the astonishment of many, Amy's parents, Peter and Linda Biehl, appeared before the committee to support their application. They applauded the work that their daughter had been involved in, pledged to continue that work and said they believed that the only way forward was for these young men to be given a second chance. I am sure that this influenced the Amnesty Committee considerably, and amnesty was granted.

The follow-up was that the Biehls established the Amy Biehl Foundation and, together with her killers, set up a youth club in Guguletu in 1998. The club was still going strong in 2007 under the leadership of one of the young men who had been convicted of killing Amy. Peter Biehl had died in the interim, but Linda continued to spend a considerable amount of time in South Africa, running the foundation and working in the club. Astonishing as the Biehl story is, it reflects the spirit of many who participated in the commission.

There can be little doubt that, during public hearings for both victims and perpetrators, some truth was revealed, some healing took place and some reconciliation was achieved. Reconciliation in South Africa is a process that started not only when enemies sat on opposite sides of the table, but also when victims told their stories and perpetrators confessed their atrocities. It is a process that would have to continue long after the commission had completed its task. There is a real danger of cheap reconciliation, particularly when it comes from those directly responsible for apartheid's hell, who cry 'Peace! Peace!' where there is none. Reconciliation must go beyond words if it is to be taken seriously.

The South African TRC was deeply influenced by the African philosophy of *ubuntu*. Constitutional Court judge Yvonne Mokgoro helps us to appreciate the rich meaning of this Nguni word. It describes an African world view, a guide for social conduct as well as a philosophy of life. *Ubuntu* represents personhood, humanity, group solidarity and morality. It is literally translated as 'a human being is a human being because of other human beings'. South Africa needs to rediscover the core meaning of *ubuntu* if it wishes to continue the process of reconciliation. With crime statistics soaring and a high incidence of violent crime, particularly against women and children, it seems as if *ubuntu* is a romantic notion that is practised in the breach. To recognise and to affirm our common humanity in South Africa is essential if our social fabric is not to be torn asunder.

PART VI

*Transitional
justice*

CHAPTER 20

Teaching justice
in a time of terror

T OWARDS THE END OF THE TRUTH AND RECONCILIATION
Commission's proceedings, I began to think about what I was going to
do next. I had kept a diary and knew that I wanted to write a book giving the
inside story of the TRC, but it would be problematic to do this and earn a
living at the same time. I was a white male, nearly seventy years old, and our
work as a commission had provoked very strong feelings, particularly from
government, so there didn't seem to be any obvious place for me to put my
energies to work. The ANC wanted to demonstrate that as a government it
could 'go it alone', as it were. This was perhaps understandable, if misguided,
but it limited my options. I began to ponder various possibilities, but my
duties with the TRC were so demanding that I soon put such thoughts to
one side.

Early in 1996 I had been invited to speak at a conference that was being
held at a venue just outside Dublin, Ireland. While I was there, the organiser
told me there was someone who wanted my advice about a project that he
and others were hoping to start in South Africa. The day was bleak, cold and
miserable, so I suggested we should seek shelter from the rain and meet in a
small pub, with a fire burning in the grate and good Irish whiskey available!

John Healy, the executive director of Tara Investments, about which I
knew very little, duly picked me up and took me to a snug pub where we
had a long chat. He asked me about reliable NGOs in South Africa that
would make responsible use of financial assistance, particularly in the field
of human rights. I gave him the names of several that I knew, and after a
pleasant discussion we went our separate ways.

It wasn't long afterwards that I received an e-mail from John, saying that
he was visiting South Africa and would like to visit the TRC and continue
our talks over lunch. We met at the Vineyard Hotel in the Cape Town suburb
of Newlands. With John was Harvey Dale, who was introduced to me as a
tax law professor from New York University. They were warm and friendly
and asked numerous good questions about the work of the TRC, and then
– somewhat pointedly – asked me: 'What are you going to do when the

commission has fulfilled its mandate?' I told them I was keen to write a book, but that I was still thinking about it. They said if they could be of any assistance to me in the future, I shouldn't hesitate to contact them.

I didn't think much more about their offer but, about six months later, they were back in South Africa. This time, I was told that Harvey Dale was not only a tax law professor and director of New York University's philanthropy programme, but also the president of Atlantic Philanthropies, a major foundation based in New York that identifies worthy causes and people to support in various ways. Harvey suggested that I might want to apply for funding so that I could write my book. I was obviously delighted and said I would certainly do so, but pointed out that foundations often take a long time to process applications. He assured me that I would have a reply within a week. I was sceptical, but took him at his word and drew up a proposal for the book, including a modest budget. Within a week, as promised, I received a reply, telling me that the project had been accepted, but that the budget was hopelessly inadequate and should be revised. I was also told that I could go wherever I wanted in order to write the book. I could return to Oxford University, go to London or anywhere else that I chose, and they would support the endeavour.

I was astonished at the broad vision shown by Atlantic and the concern and care of Harvey and John. With some assistance from John, I drew up a new budget and decided that I wanted to go to New York. Many years before, Jenny and I had spent time in Greenwich Village, home of the New York University campus, and because of my new friendship with Harvey I felt that New York was where I wanted to be. I had earlier been invited to Columbia University as a visiting professor and also had the option of spending a year at the United States Institute for Peace (USIP) in Washington, so I was still unclear which institution I would be linked with. Soon, however, I received a letter from John Sexton, dean of the NYU Law School, inviting me to be a visiting fellow for three to four months.

Jenny and I deliberated long and hard and decided that it made sense to put some distance between the TRC and me, so that I could write what I wanted, with greater objectivity. We were exhausted from two and a half years of work with the TRC and it wasn't easy to extricate oneself from that life. I worried about this a great deal, but the time had come to move on. In January 1999, we set off for New York with high hopes.

An apartment was made available for us at 240 Mercer Street, close to the law school, and we received a warm welcome. John Sexton in particular is a remarkable man, gifted and unusual in that he not only had a law degree from Fordham University but also a PhD in religion. He was an excellent lawyer, a good teacher and an outstanding dean. By the time we arrived at NYU, he had elevated the law school to being one of the top three or four in the US. I settled into my office – a little cubicle, really – in the basement, and started to think and write.

Jenny and I fell in love with New York all over again. It is a remarkable city that gives one energy rather than taking it away, and living in the Village, home to so many poets, writers and artists, was an enormous privilege. Just walking in the streets, meeting people, going to fabulous restaurants, occasional theatre, movies and wonderful museums was a wonderful break from the harrowing period at the TRC. So many people imagine New York to be cold and unfriendly, but this was not our experience; we made many good friends who were kind and generous.

On 20 April, the New York University *Annual Survey of American Law* dedicated its fifty-sixth volume to the chairman and deputy chairman of South Africa's Truth and Reconciliation Commission. Among the speakers at the dedication were Hillary Rodham Clinton; South Africa's ambassador to the United States, Sheila Sisulu, who introduced me; and the Reverend Canon Williams, who introduced Desmond Tutu. We made history, in that this was the first time the award had been made to non-lawyers, the first time it had gone to non-citizens of the United States and the first time that it was awarded to two people.

We were astonished that we were being honoured in this way. Normally the *Annual Survey* dedicates a volume to 'a preeminent jurist, scholar, or legal practitioner'. The year before, in fact, Clinton herself had been the recipient. The ceremony was very special and was attended by journal members, John Sexton, members of the faculty and invited guests.

Sheila Sisulu was extremely generous in her introduction:

> Looking at Alex Boraine, you could assume that he was representing white men on the TRC. No, he wasn't. Alex Boraine represented for us that rare breed of people in South Africa who, in the dark days of apartheid, stood up to be counted … [H]e not only strongly criticized apartheid when he was in parliament but, more importantly, he spoke to those of us who did not have a voice in parliament in order to be able to speak meaningfully and truthfully of what it was that apartheid was doing to the majority of the people of South Africa … [F]urther, when it was not fashionable to speak to the African National Congress, he was

one of the initiators of those meetings with the ANC, which was banned, so he was risking imprisonment by insisting that these talks had to take place. In those dark days of apartheid he had Jenny by his side, supporting him in taking the risk of speaking out, and sharing his values and visions. I want to quote what he said when the TRC was winding down: 'The process will not be completed until all South Africans who benefited from apartheid confront the reality of the past, accept the uncomfortable truth of complicity, give practical expression to remorse, and a commitment to a way of life which accepts and offers the gift of humanness.'

While deeply appreciative of such recognition from a distinguished black woman, I still had a job to do, and I started to block out the material for the book. At one of our regular meetings, John asked me if I had any thoughts about the law school, any observations as someone coming from outside. I got as far as 'John, I have an idea ...' before he interrupted me and said, 'I want that idea. Hang onto it, develop it and let's talk again.' That was the way John worked. He had a remarkable energy; he sought ideas and was never closed to suggestions. The very next day, I heard from one of the most senior professors, a close confidant of John's and his fellow director, Norman Dorsen. He called me and said, 'I understand from John that you have an idea. Let's have lunch.'

We went to a little French restaurant in MacDougal Street and I told him I thought there were many developments taking place in countries that were in transition. Already there was a growing body of literature, discussion and debate about how one deals with the past and the nature of justice in transitional societies, particularly in post-conflict environments requiring widespread recovery, rebuilding and starting all over again. This was something that ought to be taught at a prestigious law school such as NYU's, I said. Norman liked the idea and asked me to draw up a proposal. I felt a real debt to the law school; they had taken me in and made it possible for me to write my book in return for only a few public lectures, and I really wanted to be of help. So I began to sketch out a proposal, with a lot of help from Norman, who used his red pencil quite brutally! After several drafts, he handed it to John and they asked me to draft a possible two-semester course outline on transitional justice.

With fourteen weeks in each semester, the plan would have to cover twenty-eight weeks of teaching as well as a bibliography – a great deal of work. I got stuck in, though, not only because I felt this was something that could make a difference to NYU, but also because I was getting many requests from other countries to produce short courses on transitional justice. I had conducted seminars on the subject over one or two days on visits to Northern Ireland and Eastern Europe which had been useful, but I realised that we needed a more substantial and deeper course of study. Starting just such a course at NYU could serve as a model that could be introduced elsewhere and, indeed, similar courses were subsequently introduced at many law schools in the USA and Northern Ireland. Transitional justice as a specialised subject is here to stay.

I submitted the completed course outline about a month after being asked to do so, and, without my knowledge, Norman presented it at a faculty meeting, got approval for it to be introduced and then sought the necessary funding. Atlantic Philanthropies made a three-year grant available and the course became the first of its kind at any law school, anywhere. When John asked if I would teach the course, I was shocked. While I was glad to be a part of developing a course in transitional justice, I was not a trained lawyer. Certainly, I had learnt a great deal about the law as an opposition member of parliament for twelve years, which encompassed the drafting, redrafting and criticism of proposed legislation. I had also written new proposed legislation and assisted in the drafting of the TRC bill, but that was hardly the same as being an adjunct professor at a first-rate law school. However, I was attracted to the idea and flattered by the offer.

Jenny and I discussed it. We were in two minds. We were anxious to go back to South Africa – our children and grandchildren were there; it was our country. But, on the other hand, this was a remarkable opportunity that seldom comes the way of someone my age and with my lack of qualifications for the job. Finally, we accepted. We returned to South Africa for a couple of months and I continued to work on my book. By August 2000 we were back in our apartment at 240 Mercer Street, and I began to teach.

In some ways, it was a baptism of fire. I had taught before, but never had young lawyers in their sixth or seventh academic year as students. What amazed me was that there was so much interest in the course that we finally had to draw lots to decide who would be accepted and who would be left out. That first day, I walked into the classroom and looked at the eager faces and shining eyes behind which were brilliant legal minds, and almost fled from the room. I had to work like a dog to keep ahead of my students, spending days preparing my lectures, and slowly but surely I gained confidence and accepted that I had a contribution to make, that there were areas that were unfamiliar to my students and that this was a worthy undertaking. It was a very special class. The students were all superb people, extraordinarily bright, and I think they appreciated that they were pioneers, in a sense. We were engaged in a joint enterprise, and the students worked hard, but we also had a lot of fun. What also made it special was the fact that I was visiting some of the countries we were studying so it wasn't merely an academic exercise. I was able to use case studies from these visits in a very personal and up-to-date way.

We spent the next four years in New York. Thanks to NYU's generosity, we were able to return to South Africa for a month or so twice a year, but we also began to build a group of good friends in America, not only at the university and law school but in a wider circle. Everyone was remarkably kind and these were people who meant a great deal to us.

I made several trips to Northern Ireland, which was still in the throes of trying to resolve a long history of violence and conflict, as well as Bosnia and Serbia. I also visited countries such as Indonesia, which wanted me to talk about the South African model for conflict resolution and justice in transition. All this time, I was still working on my book as well, and eventually I simply didn't have enough time or energy to teach and travel and write.

Matters came to a head when Priscilla Hayner, whom I had met in South Africa when she visited the TRC, told me that she was working as a consultant for the Ford Foundation, which was thinking seriously about whether or not to become involved as a donor agency for other truth commissions. My response to her was twofold: firstly, I felt that one should think in much broader terms than truth commissions only, since transitional justice covers a far wider field. Secondly, I suggested that she should persuade the Ford Foundation to bring together a group of people – from NGOs to legal academics and human rights workers – to discuss the possibility of a new institution or organisation.

Both Priscilla and the Ford Foundation agreed, and Paul van Zyl, a fellow South African and a close friend, joined our small team. He had been the executive secretary of the South African TRC, and, having recently completed another degree at NYU Law School, was working for a law firm in New York. The three of us began to talk about the possibility of a new institution.

The seminal workshop duly took place at the Ford Foundation headquarters in New York. Among those who attended were Aryeh Neier, president of the Open Society Institute, Juan Mendez, professor of law at Notre Dame University, Susan Berresford, president of the Ford Foundation, and several senior officials from Ford. There were also representatives from

Human Rights Watch, Lawyers for Human Rights (now known as Human Rights First) and Amnesty International. Many of those who attended were nervous. Some of them felt there was no need for yet another organisation, as there were already many doing the work that we envisaged. Others felt that there might be room for a small organisation; that any new body should be based in the southern rather than northern hemisphere and certainly not in New York; that any available funding should rather be channelled to existing small NGOs in different parts of the world, particularly in Africa. The latter view was strongly supported by Graeme Simpson, who was then executive director of the Centre for the Study of Violence and Reconciliation in South Africa (ironically, he now holds a senior position at the ICTJ and is based in New York) and by Yasmin Sooka. She had served with me on the TRC and went on to become executive director of the Foundation for Human Rights in South Africa.

I was in despair, because I really believed that there was a niche, a gap to be filled, and that a new organisation could well take on work that was urgently needed. Priscilla knew a number of those attending the workshop well and had listened carefully to their reservations. Just before I gave the concluding address, she gave a fairly cautious response. She talked about the possibility of six to eight people working with existing human rights organisations to develop the concept of transitional justice. Several people had made it clear that they were strongly opposed to 'an 800-pound gorilla' – in other words, a cumbersome organisation – and pointed out that the South African TRC had been exceptionally large. I think they were worried that I would do the same with the proposed new organisation. With a full day of discussion heading for what looked like an impasse, I summed up by saying: 'I'm not afraid of an 800-pound gorilla. What I am afraid of is that the mountain will bring forth a mouse.'

We left it there, but the next morning I got a call from Susan Berresford, who suggested that we meet for breakfast to continue the discussion. I found her open and intelligent, a warm and charming person. She asked me a number of questions and recommended that I should draw up a structural proposal for the organisation I had in mind and spell out its mandate and objectives. Priscilla, Paul and I put together a rough draft and rewrote it again and again before I finally submitted it to Susan.

She liked our proposed name, the International Center for Transitional Justice (ICTJ). We talked about the possibility of setting up a full-time organisation that would focus on societies in transition and assume a holistic approach to justice. From the beginning, I felt that if we were going to do this, we had to do it properly, with access to adequate resources, both human and financial. Susan asked me to put a figure on the project but I felt totally inadequate to do so, and asked her to give me the help of one of Ford's top financial people. She did, and together with Paul and Priscilla, we drew up a somewhat ambitious budget. Paul and Priscilla undoubtedly played a seminal and significant role in the founding of the ICTJ, and would continue to occupy key leadership positions in the organisation.

My next meeting with Susan, at her home, was relaxed. After a while, she asked: 'Well if Ford came into this, what would you expect us to bring to the table?' I hesitated for a long time and then said, 'I would expect Ford to contribute $15 million over the first five years.' There was silence, and then Susan uttered the words that I will never forget. 'That doesn't frighten me.' She told me that I could count on Ford, but there was one non-negotiable condition: the foundation would only back the project if I agreed to remain in New York to lead this new organisation as president or chief executive officer. This was something I hadn't considered. I thought my job was to get the project going and then leave it in capable hands, perhaps playing some part in between my teaching and writing and my return to South Africa.

Susan, however, didn't see things that way at all. She contacted a number of key people at various foundations and asked them to put pressure on me, which they did. Jenny and I had a long discussion about our options. She wasn't keen to stay in New York longer than we had originally intended. She was anxious to get home, to be back in our own country with our children and grandchildren. Finally, we agreed that we would stay and that we would do this for three to five years and that Jenny would spend more time in South Africa. That was the beginning of a new chapter in our lives, one that we could never have anticipated. I counted myself extraordinarily lucky, at my time of life, to be starting up a completely new organisation in a country other than my own. The law school wanted me to establish the centre at NYU, but after careful consideration I decided that we needed to be in-dependent. In this way we would be able to work with several universities and have a separate board of trustees. The dean asked me nevertheless to continue teaching my course on transitional justice, which I did.

We were fortunate in that we received other significant grants from the Rockefeller Brothers Fund, the Carnegie Corporation and the McCarthy and Mott foundations, and a generous donation of $5 million over five years from Atlantic Philanthropies. This enabled us to kick off in a serious way, our first task being to recruit well-qualified staff. We also had to find suitable accommodation. It reminded me so much of the initial days of the TRC, when we were rushing around trying to find a building that met our requirements.

While I was on holiday in Cape Town, it fell to Priscilla and Paul to find premises for the ICTJ in New York. They were anxious that we should be as far downtown as possible, because it was cheaper, and eventually they came up with a suite of offices at 20 Exchange Place. I wasn't keen on the location, which I felt was not easily accessible, and tried to persuade them – from a distance – to look for something more midtown. However, they outflanked and outsmarted me. Because I wasn't there, it was difficult for me to argue my case, so we set up shop just around the corner from Wall Street.

Establishing a new international organisation involves an enormous amount of preparation and logistics, ranging from drafting the aims and objectives, a fund-raising strategy, office space and personnel – including recruitment, contracts, benefits and work permits – to the legal status of the organisation, a logo, technological resources, outreach and, most importantly, appointment of a board. I thought long and hard about whom we should approach to be chairman, as this was a critical appointment. Some time earlier, I had met Vincent Mai, who was chairman and executive director of AE&A Investors in New York. He was born in South Africa and, after completing his degree at the University of Cape Town, he and his parents left their Cradock farm because of their strong opposition to apartheid. Vincent went on to become very successful and was involved in human rights work, specifically as it related to South Africa. He is a man of intelligence and warmth, and we took to each other immediately at our first meeting. I told him about our plans and asked if he would serve as the founding chairman of the ICTJ. After some discussion he agreed and he proved to be a tower of strength, serving first as chairman and later as vice-chairman.

It was Vincent who suggested that we approach David Hamburg, former president of the Carnegie Corporation, to join the board. We added the name of Minna Schrag, who had recently retired as a partner in a New York law firm and had also served on the International Criminal Tribunal for the Former Yugoslavia. Additional appointments made later included ambassador Don McHenry (distinguished professor in the practice of diplomacy at Georgetown University's School of Foreign Service) and Jim Ottaway (then senior vice-president of Dow Jones & Co). Vincent also put forward the name of Kati Marton, author and director of the Committee to Protect

Journalists. One of my suggestions was José Zalaquett, professor of human rights at the University of Chile's School of Law, and a good friend.

Another old friend, Richard Goldstone, former judge of the South African Constitutional Court, was appointed in due course, as was Professor Gyimah Boadi from the Ghana Centre for Democratic Development. Other board members included Kofi Appenteng, a partner at the American law firm of Thacher Proffitt & Wood; Norway's chief public prosecutor, Siri Frigaard; Yash Ghai from Hong Kong; Alexis Keller, professor of law at the University of Geneva; Ken Miller, a senior adviser at Lehman Brothers, the global financial services group that has its headquarters in New York; and Professor Samantha Power, from Harvard University's John F Kennedy School of Government. It was a real coup early on to secure the services of Theo Sorenson, a close confidant and major speechwriter for slain US president Jack Kennedy. From the outset, the board was a source of encouragement for me and its collective wisdom and direction have served the ICTJ with great distinction.

We had borrowed furniture and one or two computers, and, to begin with, the staff comprised Priscilla, Paul and me. Then we recruited a bright young Canadian, Mark Freeman, who was an absolute gem and assisted us enormously. Lorraine Belgrave came in as my personal assistant and continued to serve my successor in the same capacity. A wise and wonderful woman, she was a great asset from day one. We received so many invitations to visit diverse places around the world that we soon had to recruit more staff, and slowly but surely we built up our carefully selected personnel. We paid more than some NGOs and offered better benefits, which I think attracted people who were bright and who also wanted a decent career.

One thing that surprised and even shocked some of us was the reaction from certain leading human rights organisations in New York. There were various reasons for this. Firstly, NGOs always have to work hard to raise funds for their projects and I think that several of the organisations that had been in existence for a long time were resentful of the fact that Ford and other foundations had given large grants to a totally new entity. Secondly, I think the fact that I, the founding president of the ICTJ, was a South African and had not lived in New York or the US for very long was resented by a number of people. Thirdly, I was one of the chief architects of the TRC, and many human rights practitioners were suspicious of the South African model, believing that we had sold out justice for the sake of truth. In particular, they did not like the idea of amnesty being granted to people who disclosed in full their human rights violations during apartheid. However, as we continued to grow and expand and make our position clear, many of the early suspicions dissipated. Today, the ICTJ works closely and comfortably with most, if not all, of the major human rights organisations in the world. (The objectives of the organisation are summarised in an appendix).

We had barely moved into our premises when there was a bolt from the blue. On 11 September 2001, I was in my office just after 8 a.m., having a meeting with Mark Freeman. A few other staff members were also already at their desks when one of our staff, Lisa Magarell, came into my office at about 8.40 a.m. and said that an awful tragedy had taken place: a small aircraft had flown into one of the Twin Towers that housed the World Trade Center. I couldn't believe it. Just seconds earlier, I had glanced out of the window and noticed what seemed to be screeds of scorched paper flying past. We were on the fifty-fourth floor and I thought that there had been an accident and that garbage had drifted upwards from street level. I rushed to Lisa's office and, from her window, had a clear view of the aircraft that had, indeed, crashed into one of the towers, which was now engulfed in fire. I was still thinking, what a tragic accident, when I noticed the second aircraft. It was huge and it was moving fast, heading straight for the second tower. I remember that I felt like putting up a hand in warning and yelling: 'Look out, look out! You are going to crash into that building!'

Then there was a massive flash of red and black flames and ash, and the aircraft seemed to slice right through the building. It was at that moment that I realised this was no accident, but an attack on New York. I telephoned Jenny and told her to switch on the television, but we were cut off within seconds. We were in one of the tallest buildings in the area, close to the WTC, and had no idea if other aircraft were about to plunge into other buildings or whether more attacks of any kind were coming. I called the staff together and told them the only thing to do was to evacuate. I still hadn't comprehended the enormity of what was happening outside, but then I went back to the window and saw people jumping out of the stricken towers to escape the flames. That sight is indelibly printed on my mind.

We decided to vacate our offices immediately. Our computers were down, the phones weren't working and we were anxious that the lifts might stop operating at any moment. When we reached street level and went outside, the air was filled with dust and everyone was nervous, not knowing what to do. We just stood there, gaping and talking in hushed tones. I told my staff it was unsafe to stay where we were and that they should all go home. There was no transport; all taxis, trains and buses had stopped. Some of our people lived a long way from the office, but we all set off on foot, heading in different directions. The wisest and most sensible of our group made their way down to the river, boarded ferries and got off Manhattan Island.

I was stupid. I walked towards Broadway, which actually brought me closer to the towers. Our apartment was a little further uptown, a couple of miles away, and as I walked I was soon engulfed in the panic-stricken crowds. I saw some people staggering out onto the street, having survived the attack. They were dishevelled, their dresses torn, suit trousers shredded to ribbons, some without shoes. Everyone looked totally bewildered. Some started to run, and of course then everyone else did too. People were jostling and pushing one another aside. One little girl tripped and fell in front of me, and, as I bent down to help her up, a huge guy came up behind me and shoved me into a pole. I clung on, heard a terrifying noise and looked back to see one of the towers collapsing. I really felt that this was the end. There was a huge plume of black smoke and I was sure that we would be buried under the debris. All around me people were yelling, 'We're all going to die! We're all going to die!' We ran for our lives. I didn't know I could run as fast as I did that day. I finally reached our apartment, covered in black soot, and there was Jenny, in tears. She had been watching television and had heard that the buildings had collapsed. She knew that I would be on my way home and thought I must surely have been killed. It was a deeply emotional reunion, made more intense by the sheer relief of being alive. Only later did we hear that close on 3 000 people died that day.

It was a week before we could return to our offices. Paul and I went to Exchange Place together, wearing masks over our mouths and noses because the air was so foul. We made our way through so many security checkpoints that it seemed New York was occupied by an army – which it was, of course. Heavily armed police stopped us, wanting to see photo identification, asking where we were going, and why. We finally reached our building and deter-mined that we would be able to go back to work within a few days.

We contacted as many of our staff as we could reach and, on our first day back in the office, held a staff meeting. People were sobbing, some with relief, others with lingering shock and fear. We talked about how we had escaped and where we had gone, some spoke about how friends of theirs had died. Only a few weeks earlier, this very sombre group of people had come together with so much promise and enthusiasm, never dreaming we would have to deal with so much trauma on our very doorstep. But, like so many others, we had to come to terms with what had happened, and start doing our job.

On a broader front, I was struck by the reaction of most people in New York and the USA as a whole. They couldn't believe that this catastrophe had befallen the most powerful nation in the world. For months, perhaps even longer, all criticism of the government was suspended. The *New York Times*, the *Washington Post* and the major television channels were mute. President George W Bush could say anything, do anything, and he was beyond reproach. He used this time to instil fear into the American people, and their docility was frightening. When I tried to comment on this phenomenon, I was criticised as being an outsider. I was shocked that intelligent, caring people had become like sheep. It came as no surprise that Bush had overwhelming support when he decided to invade Iraq in 2003.

CHAPTER 21

Helping to heal
history's hurts

T HE DAILY PRESSURE OF THE TRUTH AND RECONCILIATION
Commission prevented me from accepting a number of invitations
from various countries that wanted to hear how South Africa had managed
to turn the corner, as it were, and about the workings of the TRC in particular. However, I did manage to visit a few of these countries and this was one
of the major reasons why I felt, quite strongly, that the enormous task of
trying to assist other countries was not something that could be done by an
individual, but would need strong institutional backing.

One of the places that I visited during the TRC's lifespan was Northern
Ireland. A number of South Africans have spent time there at the request of
political parties and officials, NGOs and churches. In February 1999, I visited
under the auspices of the Northern Ireland Association for the Care and
Resettlement of Offenders (NIACRO) and Victim Support Northern Ireland.
I met with a large number of organisations that were trying to bring healing
to their country and find some stability and peace in a region that had been
wracked by violence. Some of the questions they raised included: What
can Northern Ireland learn from South Africa and its experiences? How do
we begin to deal with the damage we have inflicted on each other and on
ourselves in thirty years of conflict? How do we do this and achieve personal and community healing? How do we remember our history, yet find
creative ways of moving on? How do we preserve our newfound peace while
building unity and reconciliation?

These were deep, substantive questions, and I met with the organisations
on a number of occasions, trying to wrestle with these issues. I stressed that
South Africa was not necessarily the answer to their situation. Northern
Ireland's history was different; its culture was different; its problems in many
ways were different. However, I did say that perhaps there were some lessons
they could learn, as we had done from other countries.

Despite the differences, however, there were a number of similarities
between Northern Ireland and South Africa, the first being the level of
suffering. In both instances, the killing, the abductions and the loss of loved

ones took place over an extended period involving at least three generations. Secondly, the conflict in both countries was such that neither side
could win. There had to be a resolution based on negotiations between the
parties. Thirdly, because the conflict extended over such long periods, both
societies were deeply damaged, with thousands of people becoming victims.
Northern Ireland had thousands of young people and adults with little or
no experience of contact with people from other cultures with whom they
shared a common destiny. This was exactly our experience in South Africa.
In both societies, healing was and remains of primary importance, with
many barriers to be broken down.

A fourth similarity is a lack of awareness by many of their society's
abnormal nature. Northern Ireland had known conflict for so long that it
had almost come to accept this as 'normal', and many had little vision of a
society not at war with itself. This was certainly true of South Africa as well.
Abnormal societies require abnormal or unusual solutions.

In the fifth place, both societies have often been dishonest and are
haunted by truth. While in Northern Ireland, I observed: 'Dishonesty has
permeated the history of this lovely and tragic land. Truth haunts us all.'
I said this against the background of my own society, which has sought
to deny its culpability and complicity.

A final similarity is the apathy and denial experienced in both countries.
In Northern Ireland, as in South Africa, most who have suffered come from
the disadvantaged sections of their community. In the development of truth
that is accepted by all sides, those who have benefited from the conflict
must face up to their responsibility. Truth and progress require at least the
acceptance, but hopefully also the commitment, of all sections of society.

In March 2000, I returned to Northern Ireland and spent a few packed
days meeting with a wide range of people and groups. This time I focused on
the major political parties as well as organisations working with victims, the
most notable ex-prisoner organisations being the Human Rights Commission and the Protestant and Catholic churches. I was struck again by the deep
cleavages that existed in this very beautiful but tragically divided country.
One of my recommendations was to put together a group of people from
both sides of the conflict who could work together and, in doing so, demonstrate that it was possible to have unity in Northern Ireland on a much
larger scale. This was a difficult task. A number of meetings were aborted
when one or more on either side, Protestant or Catholic, didn't like the
direction in which the discussions were going and walked out. But we

finally managed to draw together about fifteen people and decided to call this new organisation Healing Through Remembering. It made a slow start but it survived and continues to do excellent work. I salute these good people who, despite enormous difficulties, have been able to sustain the organisation and assist in the ongoing need for sustainable peace.

Towards the end of 1999, I was invited by Neil Kritz and the United States Institute for Peace to attend a conference in Sarajevo to consider whether or not there was sufficient local support, and, if so, to work out a programme to establish a truth commission in that deeply divided territory. The tragic violence that has characterised the Balkans for more than a thousand years erupted in an epidemic of killing, assault and destruction between 1992 and 1995. The response of the international community to this bloodletting was the appointment of an International Criminal Tribunal for the Former Yugoslavia (ICTY), based in The Hague. There is no doubt that this was an important and necessary step, but I have always believed that it was only one of the needed responses. If the last word is punishment, there is very little likelihood or hope of any measure of restoration and reconciliation for the societies concerned. We needed the tribunal, but we also needed other initiatives to assist in bringing about healing. This is particularly true of Bosnia. Serb, Croat and Muslim live side by side there, but peace has been maintained only by the presence of a large peacekeeping force.

The conference to which I was invited was held in Sarajevo on 3 and 4 February 2000. If ever I needed a reminder that Bosnia was not South Africa, my arrival in that formerly besieged city certainly jogged my memory. I had left Cape Town in the middle of a glorious summer; the temperature in Bosnia was below freezing. The entire area was blanketed in snow and it was impossible to land. After flying in a holding pattern for more than an hour, we landed in almost zero visibility.

I was deeply impressed by reports from a large number of organisations representing women, youth, politicians, lawyers, human rights practitioners and others who pleaded for a commission in their own country, using their own language. All those who spoke referred to The Hague as being a long way away and far removed from where they were.

The conference was held in the Herzegovina Hall at the Holiday Inn, the only hotel in Sarajevo that had remained open throughout the siege. It was badly damaged by mortar shells and there was no access to one floor, which had a gaping hole in the outside wall. I suppose it was an apt setting to discuss truth and reconciliation. There were about 150 delegates and observers. The chairman for the morning was Jakob Finci, who was very active in Sarajevo's small Jewish community, as well as in human rights work. He was trusted because he did not belong to any of the major ethnic groups. The first international speaker was Richard Goldstone, well known in South Africa for his work on the Goldstone Commission and as a judge of the Constitutional Court. He was perhaps better known internationally as the first prosecutor at the International Criminal Tribunal and could speak with authority and integrity on the need for a truth commission alongside the tribunal.

I followed Richard, and in my address I emphasised that 'South Africa is not Bosnia and never will be', but then referred to similarities between the two societies. 'Violence, a litany of human suffering, crimes against humanity, the loss of human and social dignity, the lies, half lies, denial and the deep longing for peace and stability are common to both Bosnia and South Africa. The South African Commission was an opportunity for ordinary people to get on with their lives and this may well help victims in Bosnia also. The approach, the strategy and the structure will be very different, but the elusive search for accountability and peace is universal and human rights are indivisible.'

While there seemed to be unanimity among the people of Bosnia with regard to the establishment of a truth commission, a sentiment endorsed by international speakers who had experience of truth commissions in other parts of the world, there was one very strong dissenting voice. Two representatives from the Hague Tribunal spoke out strongly against the establishment of a commission. They felt that this would interfere with the work of the tribunal and would divert attention away from this forum and its resources. I was astonished at the arrogance shown by these representatives and I think the very long delay in reaching any kind of conclusion was largely the result of opposition from the tribunal.

There are still committed people, led by Finci, who continue to attempt to launch a truth commission. There are some in the former Yugoslavia who believe that the commission should not be limited to Bosnia but should be regional, because the violence crossed the borders of Serbia, Kosovo, Croatia and Bosnia. I think they are correct, but it is an extraordinarily difficult task due to the lack of trust between the various countries that have emerged from the former Yugoslavia.

Although there is no truth commission in Bosnia or in the former Yugoslavia, I think many countries, including South Africa, could learn from one clause in the draft statute that we discussed and debated at the conference. It concerns the need to uncover 'the existence and actions of individuals who refused to participate in the prosecution of their neighbours and who at grave personal risk maintained their sense of humanity and attempted to protect their neighbours of other ethnic or religious groups from abuse'. In my view, this emphasis on telling the 'good news' or 'good stories' is something that other commissions could learn from. I am sorry that we didn't do something similar in South Africa.

Later in 1999, I was invited to join a group of people from the former Yugoslavia, including Kosovo, Serbia, Macedonia and adjoining states, to discuss the implications of the conflict in Kosovo and the NATO bombing. This meeting was held in Budapest under the auspices of the Open Society Institute. It was a remarkable event, with many disagreements about future policy and strategy. One of those who attended was Sonya Licht, president of the Soros Foundation in Belgrade. She expressed interest in the South African experience and asked me for further information. I immediately pointed out the differences between South Africa and Serbia, but outlined what we had attempted to do. Not long afterwards, Sonya invited me to Belgrade. I was due to speak at a meeting in Cape Town on the work of the TRC, and suggested that she should attend that conference to assess what, if anything, South Africa could contribute to the Serbian situation, before I travelled to Belgrade. She did so and told me afterwards that she was more convinced than ever that the South African model was the one that could help people like her, who were in opposition to Slobodan Milošević and sought to move towards a democratic alternative in Serbia.

I went to Belgrade in October 1999. The journey in itself was interesting. Serbia was under very strict embargo at the time and there were no flights in or out of Belgrade. I flew to Budapest and was driven for three hours to the Hungarian–Serbian border. I got out of my car with my suitcase and waited in the rain for someone from the other side to meet me and assist me across the border. Being a great fan of thriller writer John le Carré, I had visions of a dramatic arrest or being refused entry to Serbia. In fact, the border crossing went very smoothly. There was a delay, but it was because the computers were down. I was questioned closely by the Serbian authorities but finally allowed to proceed. We then drove for another three hours to Belgrade.

Serbia showed all the signs of a country enduring a stringent economic boycott and political turmoil; there were black-marketeers in the streets and people marching every night in opposition to Milošević and his policies; a tense, brooding atmosphere overshadowed everything and everyone. I had decided that I would make no public speeches but would keep the visit private. I met with a wide range of people representing alternative academic organisations, students, NGOs, independent media and the Orthodox Church, and attempted to outline the procedures followed by the South African TRC. There was unanimous agreement that the South African model did have a contribution to make, particularly in the area of truth-telling and the need to come to terms with the truth of Serbia's involvement in Kosovo and in 'ethnic cleansing'. A truth and reconciliation commission would give people an opportunity to express their own views and ideas, not only about the past but also about the future.

We agreed that a public conference would be held at the end of April 2000, at which I would give the keynote address, and that invitations would be extended to representatives from Serbia and international organisations.

Unfortunately, my application for a visa was refused. I was devastated, not only because we had spent several months planning the conference, but also because I felt deeply for those who were struggling to keep alive the hope of democracy in Serbia. Fortunately, two of the invited speakers, Pepe Zalaquett from Chile and Patricia Valdez from Argentina, did not require visas and were allowed in.

Once the ICTJ was up and running, Serbia was one of the first countries to invite us in. I am sure that this was because of my earlier connections with that country before the fall of Milošević. The new president, Vojislav Koštunica, was a law professor, a strong nationalist and conservative, but certainly very different from Milošević. I had been asked to meet with the president when he visited New York with his foreign minister, who was later assassinated. He asked if I would assist his country in its quest to become a human rights community and a democratic state. I agreed and said the ICTJ would do whatever it could, but I felt that we should lay down at least six points of agreement so that we could work harmoniously together. The president accepted this with alacrity, as did his foreign minister.

The six points were: (1) there ought to be widespread consultation, particularly with the human rights community, before the president made any move towards a truth commission; (2) it should be a parliamentary rather than a presidential commission; (3) hearings should be public; (4) reparations for victims should be a central feature; (5) a report should be published that would include recommendations to government; and (6) adequate time and resources should be made available so that the commission could do its work thoroughly.

Unfortunately, even though he subscribed readily to these six points, and did so again when I visited Belgrade and met with him and his cabinet, one Saturday morning in 2002, out of the blue, the president announced the appointment of a truth commission. He listed the names of the commissioners and then announced that Alex Boraine would be his human rights adviser! This was without any prior consultation, and, of course, the inevitable happened. Several of those named declined to serve, because they had not been consulted. Human rights organisations were upset that some shady characters had been included, while other very good people were overlooked. I was travelling to Belgrade regularly, and during my next meeting with the president I told him that this had been a totally ill-conceived decision and that I couldn't see the commission succeeding. He acknowledged that perhaps it was a mistake, but said he had been under severe pressure from the West, which was withholding funding that was badly needed by his country, until he made some move towards the building of a human rights culture.

What he didn't add was that the West, as he put it, was demanding much stronger cooperation with the Hague Tribunal. As a result of his precipitate action, I felt I had no recourse but to withdraw from the commission. It simply faded into oblivion. They had hardly any resources, did almost no work as a result, and there has been no truth commission to take its place. Perhaps one day there will be such a commission, which will involve not only Serbia but also Croatia, Bosnia and Kosovo, because violence knows no borders and neither does a truth commission. I can only hope that the time will come when the former Yugoslavia can take stock of and deal with the past and thereby enrich its future and consolidate democracy. We continue to work in the region, but progress towards a human rights culture is slow, though steady.

In October 2002, I received an invitation from Alan Tieger, senior trial attorney at the Hague Tribunal. It was an extraordinary letter, asking me to participate in a most unusual and unique event, which read as follows:

> I am writing on behalf of the Office of the Prosecutor to request your appearance at an unprecedented and historical hearing.
>
> On 2 October 2002, Biljana Plavšić, the former President of Republika Srpska, entered a plea of guilty to a Crime against Humanity for her

participation in persecutions against Bosnian Muslims and Bosnian Croats. The crime charged was the widespread campaign against Muslims and Croats in 1992, including killings, the establishment of inhumane camps and deportation. By entering her plea, Mrs Plavšić became the first person in a leadership position to acknowledge and accept responsibility for crimes against other national groups in the Balkans in the last decade.

Mrs Plavšić issued a statement expressing her remorse 'fully and un-conditionally' and stated her hope that her acceptance of responsibility would offer some consolation to the innocent victims, of all nations, of the war. She also invited leaders on all sides of the conflict to examine themselves and their own conduct. The Office of the Prosecutor publicly acknowledged Mrs Plavšić's plea as 'an unprecedented and courageous decision'.

A sentencing hearing is presently scheduled to be heard on 16–17 December, although the possibility of an additional day remains open. Both the prosecution and the defence anticipate that the hearing will focus on two primary issues: the suffering of the victims and the extra-ordinary nature of Mrs Plavšić's acknowledgment and remorse. In short, the hearing will consider the consequences of her actions in 1992 and the potential consequences of her actions in 2002.

This process, it is hoped, will bring a measure of peace to the victims, deter revisionism and disrupt the circle of retributive oppression. We expect that a number of leading international figures will testify before the court and before the international audience that will be viewing the event live on television. We are hopeful that your voice and the insights drawn from your unique background will form part of this extraordinary hearing.

I hope that you will be willing and able to participate in the hearing. I would be available to meet with you at a date and time of your con-venience to discuss the nature of the hearing and your participation in greater detail. Meanwhile, please feel free to contact me at your con-venience … Because we are attempting to finalise the witness list as far in advance of the hearing as possible, I would appreciate your earliest possible response. I am very grateful for your time and look forward to hearing from you.

Others approached to testify at this special hearing included Madeleine Albright, former US secretary of state, Carl Bildt, a former Swedish prime minister who served on international missions in the Balkan region before becoming Sweden's foreign minister, and ambassador Robert Holmes Frowick, the first head of mission at the Organisation for Security and Cooperation in Europe (OSCE) from 1995 to 1997. He worked with Mrs Plavšić in organising the first free and democratic elections in post-war Bosnia and Herzegovina. Nazi holocaust survivor Professor Elie Wiesel, one of the major figures who appealed to the international community in 1992 and 1993 to intervene against the campaign of ethnic cleansing in Bosnia and Herzegovina, would attempt to explain the importance of leaders acknowledging crimes and expressing remorse.

I went to The Hague on 16 December and testified the following day. It was quite an experience. The fact that Mrs Plavšić was the first prominent leader of the former Yugoslavia to plead guilty to very serious charges of war crimes meant that there was no place for a normal trial, as had been the case, for example, with the former president of Serbia, Slobodan Milošević. The tribunal decided to hold a hearing because of its concern for reconciliation in the former Yugoslavia.

I agreed to appear before the tribunal because the situation was unique, and the role of apologies by significant leaders in certain countries, such as Germany, had an impact on developments within the country itself, as well as on its relationships with neighbours. In a general statement to the hearing, I said the following:

> Systems of criminal justice exist not simply to determine guilt or innocence, but ultimately to contribute to a safe and peaceful society. Thus, they are critical to the process of reconciliation. In my experience, accepting responsibility for terrible crimes can have a transformative effect, not only on the perpetrator, but also on victims and the wider community. Such acceptance, whether by a guilty plea in a criminal case or in some other forum, can be a significant factor in promoting reconciliation.
>
> The ICTY was established not only to determine the guilt or innocence of individual accused, but also to 'contribute to the restoration and maintenance of peace' and to 'contribute to the settlement of wider issues of accountability, reconciliation and establishing the truth behind the evils perpetrated in the former Yugoslavia'. In the case of the accused, Biljana Plavšić, these objectives take on a special meaning.
>
> Biljana Plavšić, former President of Republika Srpska, has pleaded guilty to the crime of 'persecution on political, racial and religious grounds', for acts committed in more than thirty Bosnian municipalities

between July 1991 and December 1992. In doing so, she assumes responsibility for the horrors that many Serb leaders continue to deny. However, we should never forget or seek to minimise the crimes for which she has assumed responsibility: the killing of defenceless civilians; torture, physical and psychological abuse, and sexual violence; the forced displacement of entire communities; establishing detention camps, where thousands of prisoners were kept in inhumane conditions and many killed; and the razing of entire villages. Any effort to achieve justice that fails to recognise the enormity of these crimes will jeopardise the transformative potential of Mrs Plavšić's actions.

The potential importance of Mrs Plavšić's confession must not be understated. As a Serb nationalist and a former political leader, her confession sends a crucial message both about the true criminal character of the enterprise with which she was engaged, and about the legitimacy of the tribunal and its functions. It is important to remember that Mrs Plavšić surrendered herself to the tribunal and voluntarily travelled to The Hague. Too often, the tribunal itself has constituted the focus of anger and grievance among leaders and large segments of the population in Serbia and the Republika Srpska, rather than the war criminals in their midst. Mrs Plavšić has publicly apologised and called on other leaders to examine their own conduct. This acceptance of responsibility may demonstrate to victims that their suffering has been acknowledged. Genuine reconciliation in the former Yugoslavia will remain elusive until responsibility is accepted by those who through bold declaration or silent indifference explicitly or implicitly endorsed the atrocities. Biljana Plavšić has taken this crucial first step.

Mrs Plavšić's confession is the first of many acts of contrition that I hope she will undertake. Her expression of remorse, like any apology, must be understood in the context of not just her words, but also her actions. Appropriate weight should be given to her role in ending a war and seeking to implement the Dayton Peace Accords. Her role in seeking to steer her people away from the violent nationalism that she herself helped to foster should also be recognised.

But there are other important steps toward ultimate reconciliation that Mrs Plavšić is now in a position to take. For example, she has the opportunity to play a key role in elucidating what led others to commit similar crimes, by providing detailed information about her own role and that of others in the criminal enterprise in which she participated. Moreover, she can provide symbolic reparation by continuing to express remorse to the tens of thousands whose lives she helped to destroy.

In my view, it is vital to listen carefully to the voices of victims. All too often their suffering, needs and aspirations are given insufficient weight in the complex calculus of justice. In seeking to blend accountability with reconciliation, in attempting to strike the right balance between punishment and forgiveness, and in an effort to deal with a sordid past but then place emphasis on a more hopeful future, we should be guided first and foremost by those who have borne the brunt of past injustice. Reconciliation can all too easily be undermined if victims feel that their pain and suffering have not been given sufficient recognition in both judicial and non-judicial processes established to respond to gross violations of human rights. However, respecting the experiences and views of victims means not putting words in their mouths or caricaturing them as either insisting on retribution or being amenable to lenience. The fact that the views of victims are as complex and varied as human beings themselves demands proper consideration of their pain and their different perspectives.

I would like to echo the calls made by Mrs Plavšić to leaders on *all* sides of the past conflict to examine their own conduct. Although some apologies have been made in the past two years in the former Yugoslavia, in my view these have been partial at best, and have not been backed up with reparative programmes or actions in favour of victims. Instead, these apologies have generally been accompanied by a lack of cooperation with the ICTY, one-sided trials at the national level and ongoing intimidation of local minorities. If the region's citizens and leaders are *not* prepared to seriously confront the demons of the past, the next generation will bear the consequences.

However, I hope that with time and courage, the cause of narrow nationalism will wane and pluralistic societies grounded in human rights and the rule of law will emerge. The reality is that there is no other choice that can guarantee sustainable peace in the region.

I was asked a number of questions by the judges, particularly Judge Robinson, who wanted to know whether truth-telling in South Africa had brought about any reconciliation. My response was that the witness of victims and perpetrators had played a significant role in easing the very real tensions and even hatred in my own country. I added that whites, who were largely responsible for the apartheid crimes, denied over and over again that the horrific reports published all over the world were true. But, once the perpetrators began to acknowledge their actions, the denial was broken, and this contributed to reconciliation. Summing up my evidence, I said:

I hope very much that Mrs Plavšić's actions will prompt other leaders responsible for similar crimes to acknowledge their culpability, recognise the jurisdiction of this court and accept the appropriate punishment. I think this is a factor that is lacking in the former Yugoslavia. There does seem to be a stubborn resistance and a climate of denial. Therefore, I think that when someone in a significant leadership position actually makes the break, as has been done in this case, there is the potential at least of prompting other leaders to come forward and I hope this happens. I think it is also true that her statements could help catalyse or initiate a process of honest truth-telling and acknowledgement throughout the former Yugoslavia.

In closing, I referred to a conference in which I participated in Sarajevo in 2001. President Jorda, who at that time was president of the Hague Tribunal, made the point that a tribunal can't try everyone or listen to every witness, even though they need and deserve to be heard. A tribunal can't always calculate the patterns and causes of the horrendous crimes that have taken place, and it is difficult for a tribunal on its own to piece together a collective memory, without people at least starting to agree on some basic facts. 'Looking at Mrs Plavšić's record in terms of the seriousness of her crime, her change of behaviour, her acknowledgement and confession, it seems to me that she has sought to grasp a second chance,' I said. 'I think the people of the former Yugoslavia deserve a second chance, to move away from prejudice and hatred of the past to a more tolerant and a more decent future with human rights as its centrepiece.'

When the court was adjourned pending sentencing in the first few months of 2003, I went to Belgrade to see Mrs Plavšić. We met in a tiny, cluttered flat and I asked her, 'Why did you plead guilty and apologise?' She replied: 'First and foremost, I apologised to myself. What I did was not worthy of who I am. I apologised and pleaded guilty for the sake of young people who will come after me, and I had to do this in public and therefore I had to do it before the tribunal. Also, my religion – I am Orthodox – tells me that confession is necessary for absolution of sin. I also pleaded guilty and apologised in the hope that other leaders who have denied their complicity will follow my lead. It's not been easy for me. I have been ostracised. I have had death threats, but I believe it was necessary for me to do what I did.'

In March 2003, Mrs Plavšić was sentenced to eleven years in prison, to be served in a Swedish jail.

Although the ICTJ is a young organisation, people began to hear about us, and this was illustrated by the calls we received for assistance. One Monday morning in 2001 I received a phone call from the then minister of justice in Ghana, Nana Akufo-Addo, asking me to comment on a draft bill for the establishment of a national reconciliation commission. I had never met him and it was a strange situation to discuss a country that I didn't know a great deal about. After listening to what they wanted to do, I suggested that instead of rushing to publication of the bill, the minister should rather share his government's idea with human rights leaders in the country, as this would ground the commission and enable many more to own it. He told me that the president was very anxious to get going, but ultimately agreed that he would follow my advice on certain conditions. The deal was that I would organise a national conference in Accra and attend as a visiting speaker. I would also suggest several international people who should attend the conference. Obviously, local organisations would attend as well.

The conference proved to be a great success, and there was robust debate. We had the leader of the opposition speaking against the idea of a commission. His party had been in power previously and I think they thought they might be victimised or charged with human rights offences. We had the chief justice of Ghana as one of the keynote speakers, along with a number of people from different parts of the world.

There is no doubt in my mind that the original draft bill was greatly enriched by the debate and discussion and the ideas that flowed from the conference. A few weeks later, we were asked to return to Ghana to train the commissioners and to offer advice and assistance. This we did, and I must say the learning process was always mutual. We learnt a great deal as we moved from one country to another, and hopefully we were able to be of some help to them. The National Reconciliation Commission held its hearings in public, which we had advised, and I was invited to speak at the first hearing. The hall was packed and it was rewarding to see in action the fruits of debate and the training and ideas that we had worked out together.

Sierra Leone was particularly challenging, a very difficult country to work in. We had been approached by members of civil society as well as the United Nations to assist with the truth and reconciliation commission they intended to establish, and also with establishment of a special court that would attempt to try those most responsible for atrocities in that war-torn country. Sierra Leone was decimated by rebels who abducted young people aged ten, eleven or twelve and forced them to be child soldiers, fed them cocaine and ordered them to engage in many of the amputations that took place throughout the country.

One hot Sunday afternoon I sat in a hall full of amputees, some of them with both hands cut off, at the elbow or at the wrist, others whose feet had been lopped off. It was an unbelievable experience to listen to the helplessness and hopelessness of people without limbs. It was certainly one of the most moving experiences of my life. We were asked to try to persuade this village of amputees to give evidence before the truth commission. They were reluctant to do so, because people had promised them help before that had never materialised. Understandably, they were extremely cynical and wondered if it was worth their while. By the end of the afternoon they had changed their minds and decided that they would testify, and in due course they did. A middle-aged man rose to his feet and held out his arms – both hands had been severed – and said, 'Look at me. I am helpless. I can't feed myself, I can't even go the bathroom on my own. I have no job. This is not a life. I am a dead man.' They had so few resources; they were an embittered, sad people.

Some help has subsequently been forthcoming, but the government has been slow and international organisations haven't been much help, with the exception of Norway. Sierra Leone went through a terrifying war; there is abject poverty and dysfunctionalism at a number of levels, but I think the truth commission made a difference, as did the special court that operates under the aegis of the United Nations. We returned to train the commissioners, and, because we had experience of doing this elsewhere, I think it worked. There is, of course, enormous need for such training, not only in Sierra Leone, and we are constantly asked to assist different countries.

By 2002, the ICTJ was in full swing. We had recruited some superb and bright people, which enabled us to respond to the many requests that came our way. Apart from visiting other countries, we received many people in our offices who wanted to know more about transitional justice; we wrote articles and visited universities and organisations throughout the United States. Slowly but surely, there was recognition that the ICTJ was no longer the new kid on the block, but an organisation which was here to stay.

That year, I received an invitation to deliver an address at the memorial service for Neelan Tiruchelvam, an active human rights lawyer cruelly killed by a teenage suicide bomber in Sri Lanka. I had never realised before that there were more suicide bombers in Sri Lanka than any other part of the world, including Israel and Iraq. What amazed me even more was that most of the Sri Lankan bombers were young women.

Along with an ICTJ colleague, I visited Colombo first and met with politicians, academics and human rights activists and talked about the possibility of the ICTJ being of some assistance to those who were working for peace and justice in Sri Lanka. A ceasefire had just been announced and peace talks were beginning, but the atmosphere was tense and many of the people we talked to were cynical about the ceasefire. Those who supported the government blamed the Tamil Tigers, and they, in turn, blamed the government. It was a delicately poised situation.

I was anxious to visit the south, where the Tamil Tigers had their stronghold. We flew in an ancient aircraft of Russian origin, finally boarding after sitting on the grass for about four hours. The security was unbelievable and there was a large soldier with an AK47 who patrolled the aisle of the plane during the flight. It was quite hair-raising, because the aircraft was extremely old and seemed to lurch from side to side, not only on take-off and landing but throughout the trip. When we arrived in the south we were told that we were not allowed to travel on our own but had to join an army convoy. So we travelled in military trucks to Jaffna, where I was to speak at the university. We were hoping very much that I would be able to meet with some of the leaders of the Tamil Tigers.

The discussion at the university went well, with lots of questions about the South African model and the future of Sri Lanka. Clearly, most of those in the audience were in sympathy with the demands of the Tamil Tigers for decentralisation, if not federalisation. That night, I was due to meet with some of the Tamil Tiger leaders. We went to a tiny house in a remote area and sat in the living room and waited and waited. There was a bowl of fruit on the table, but no tea or coffee or anything stronger was served. Finally, two or three men appeared and said they were from the Tamil Tigers. We talked through interpreters for about an hour. They questioned me closely about who I was, where I had come from, why I was there, and so on. When the hour was up, they abruptly left the room. I didn't know what had precipitated this, but a few minutes later another group of men arrived. They turned out to be the real Tamil Tiger leaders! They simply hadn't trusted me, which was understandable, but at last we could start talking about issues. It was late at night, but I did challenge them on the question of child soldiers and the killing of civilians. They assured me that, in accordance with the conditions of the peace talks, they were no longer abducting children and were totally opposed to the killing of civilians. Such actions, they claimed, were largely the work of the government.

We returned to Colombo the next day and continued our discussions with several cabinet ministers and those involved in the peace talks. Tragically, a year later the peace talks were called off, violence was renewed, and at the time of writing Sri Lanka is once again locked in fierce conflict, with many lives lost and widespread destruction of property. While there is hope that the peace talks negotiated by Norway will resume at some point, this will not be easy. Feelings run high in a country riven by intense hatred and division, but hopefully the ICTJ can continue to assist human rights groups to hold together and maintain the principles of justice and peace until the day comes when talks resume and the violence ends.

Towards the end of 2002, the ICTJ was approached by Peru for advice on starting a truth commission. Accompanied by Priscilla Hayner and Lisa Magarell, I met with the then foreign minister and several of his senior officials in Lima. Lisa was designated our point person in Peru, and she spent many months assisting and guiding the process. I was enormously impressed by the quality of the human rights workers in Peru. They were smart, intelligent, concerned and well trained in human rights law. Their truth commission is probably one of the best examples of its kind, although there were major initial difficulties and problems to overcome.

The more we worked on different continents, the more experience we gained and the more requests for assistance we received. I am very proud that the ICTJ has gained recognition as the leading transitional justice organisation in the world. It was a new and unusual idea to talk about a holistic approach to justice and there was suspicion that this meant being soft on justice, particularly on retributive justice. What many critics could not seem to grasp is that countries emerging from violence, conflict, breakdown and deep divisions do not only need to have the perpetrators identified and punished, but also require a much wider, deeper and richer approach to justice as they move, hopefully, from dictatorship to a more democratic style of government and a fresh commitment to a human rights culture. The record shows that many of our early critics have since accepted these basic principles, and the fact that we continue to receive scores of invitations for assistance speaks volumes.

One of our weaknesses was an inability to say no, and sometimes we took on far too much. I think this is still a common problem in organisations like the ICTJ, which today is active in at least twenty-four different countries in Africa, Latin America, Eastern Europe and South-East Asia. The expansion within the organisation has been quite phenomenal.

CHAPTER 22

Spreading the
need to know

IN 2004, THREE YEARS AFTER BECOMING PRESIDENT OF THE ICTJ, Jenny and I decided to return to Cape Town. I wasn't ready to leave New York; I thought it might be better for me to stay on for another two years, but Jenny was anxious to go home. She generously suggested that I should stay and complete my five-year term as president, but I thought that would be a mistake. Of course we would have had opportunities to visit each other, but I don't believe long absences are healthy for any good relationship, let alone a marriage.

Although not happy with our decision, Vincent Mai, chairman of the ICTJ board, understood and appreciated our need to go home. In the interest of continuity in a young and rapidly expanding organisation, he immediately suggested that I should assume the chairmanship, while he would become vice-chairman. He also asked if I would consider giving 50 per cent of my time to the ICTJ and opening an office in Cape Town. This was a remarkable offer that I had not anticipated. After I'd thought about it for a while and talked to Jenny and some of my colleagues, Vincent's proposal was put to the board. They had hoped that I would serve my full term, but accepted the alternative, and so did I. I would become director of the Cape Town office, and chairman of the board.

It wasn't easy to leave New York; we had a growing staff complement, lots of exciting work on the horizon and many countries seeking our assistance. Inevitably, the part-time nature of my future involvement would see the gap between head office and the Cape Town branch widen, and sooner or later it would be impossible to stay in daily touch with developments. But there were huge advantages to going home and much to be thankful for. We would be with our children, grandchildren and old friends, Jenny would be able to resume her place in South Africa, and, no matter where one is in the world, there is something about the call of Africa, with all its challenges and problems and excitement, that tugs at the heart strings.

Nevertheless, settling back into our life in Cape Town wasn't easy. Our friends and family had become accustomed to our long absences abroad and there was a need for adjustment on both sides. I would bump into friends in Cape Town who thought I was still based in New York, and, when I went back to New York, people there would be equally surprised to see me. For quite some time, invitations on both sides of the Atlantic failed to reach us due to some confusion about our geographical location. Three years after returning to Cape Town, I was still running into people who would ask: 'Are you still in New York? Are you visiting?' I would tell them that I'd been back in South Africa for a couple of years and some would find that hard to believe.

By the time I arrived home, Paddy Clark, my faithful assistant over more than thirty years, had already set up an office for the ICTJ, which marked our first step towards decentralisation. This made it much easier to settle in. I could walk in and immediately start planning what we would be doing on the ICTJ's behalf in Cape Town and southern Africa.

Under the leadership of Juan Mendez, my successor as president of the New York head office, the organisation has gone from strength to strength. By the beginning of 2008, it had a staff complement of close on one hundred, with branches in Brussels, Geneva, Kinshasa, Monrovia, Bogota, Nepal and Indonesia. Plans were also under way to open an office in Beirut.

As a young lawyer, Mendez had been imprisoned and tortured during the period of the junta in Argentina. When he was finally released, he left his country and went to live in the US. He has an enviable record as a champion of human rights law. As president of the ICTJ, he has been ably assisted by a strong management team and in particular by Paul van Zyl, executive vice-president.

One of my new responsibilities was greater participation in what we called the Fellows Programme, started in 2002. Part and parcel of our objectives was capacity-building. We wanted to run training courses for people who, against impossible odds, were battling to work in the field of human rights. From the beginning, I thought that the training courses ought not to be offered in New York, but rather somewhere in the southern hemisphere, and, knowing the situation in South Africa so well, I suggested that the programme should be based in Cape Town. We needed a partner, so we approached the Institute for Justice and Reconciliation through its executive director, Charles Villa-Vicencio, whom I had known for many years. The ICTJ raised all the necessary funding and recruited the candidates, but, as soon as they arrived in Cape Town, the IJR assumed major responsibility for the programme. It was a good partnership, although not without its problems and difficulties. Everyone sees things differently, and there was sometimes a clash over where the true emphasis should lie, but we were able to resolve these issues.

Since 2002 the programme, run for three months each year, has drawn people from most of the countries in Africa, as well as South-East Asia, Afghanistan, East Timor, Israel, Palestine and the Balkans. Initially, the course was strongly academic, focusing on international law, transitional justice and human rights. However, it soon became clear that the programme needed to include subjects of a more practical nature, and we introduced courses on computer skills, management, budgeting, public speaking, leadership, fundraising and related issues. The main aim was to help trainees understand the central values of transitional justice as it applied to their own countries, as well as neighbouring states. In the first five years, more than one hundred fellows completed the programme and, thanks to the success of the South African model, the ICTJ decided to establish a similar programme in Latin America. Our partner there is Professor Pepe Zalaquett, director of the University of Chile's Human Rights Centre. The language medium there is Spanish, and when the fellows return to their homes they continue the programme through distance learning, an interesting experiment that seems to have worked well. We have also introduced a similar programme in Morocco for French-speakers, mainly from West Africa. The various programmes have produced hundreds of people whom we regard as alumni and with whom we keep in touch. We have also drawn a number of our staff from their ranks.

I was joined in our Cape Town office by Olivier Kambala wa Kambala from the Democratic Republic of Congo. As one of the participants in the Fellows Programme, he had excelled both in contributing during debates and in his writing. A trained lawyer and fluent French-speaker, he was an excellent addition to our staff. He and I travelled to Kinshasa and linked up with Alpha Fall, a Senegalese lawyer, also fluent in French, who had been appointed senior associate in our Kinshasa office. We spent a week in a very dysfunctional city and saw abundant evidence of the grandeur of the Belgian colonists who, under pressure of rising black nationalism in the 1950s and 1960s and international moves to decolonise and grant independence to many African states, had abandoned that country and left it in desperate poverty and disunity. Tragically, the Congolese fared no better under latter-day dictator Mobutu Sese Seko's reign of terror and corruption.

We worked at a tremendous pace, visiting the vice-president of the

DRC, the minister of reconciliation, several other government officials and many NGOs. We had several meetings with United Nations officials stationed there to maintain an uncertain, insecure peace. The UN had 17 000 peacekeepers spread throughout that vast country, where transport was an enormous problem. They had to use a fleet of helicopters and aircraft to get from one place to another. In my view, under the energetic leadership of Bill Swing, the secretary-general's special representative and a former US ambassador, the UN did a superb job in ensuring that the 2006 referendum for a new constitution was well conducted and relatively peaceful, and that the elections duly took place in 2007. Although the peace in the DRC remains uneasy, conditions are certainly much better in every possible way at the time of writing than when opposing factions seemed to be at each other's throat constantly, resulting in huge loss of life and damage to property. There is no guarantee, however, that peace will prevail. This is particularly true of the country's eastern region.

The ICTJ continues to work in the DRC, under difficult circumstances, but that is what our job is all about: assisting countries to deal with their transition from authoritarian rule to a form of democracy. The DRC is a true test of the holistic justice that characterises our work: striving towards accountability; seeking truth; attempting to reconcile deeply divided societies; working towards transformation and rebuilding of key institutions; and demonstrating care for the many thousands of victims through some form of reparation. It is simply not enough to focus only on the perpetrators; a just society requires a holistic approach. There had been some attempts to set up a truth and reconciliation commission in the DRC, but, in our view, its terms of reference were inadequate. The choice of commissioners also left a great deal to be desired. Following Joseph Kabila's election victory in 2007, the proposed TRC fell by the wayside, and it will not be easy to resuscitate the idea in the short term.

In due course, we were joined in the Cape Town office by Abdul Tejan-Cole as deputy director. From Sierra Leone, he has a great deal of experience and is a fine lawyer. His energy and contribution in Cape Town and further afield has been of enormous assistance. I had hoped that he would take over from me as director, but he will return to his own country in 2008 to head up an anti-corruption commission.

Towards the end of August 2005, Jenny and I returned to New York. I had been invited by the NYU Law School to give a series of lectures as a global visiting professor. They wanted me to teach for two semesters, but, due to my work in Cape Town and an enormous amount of travel as chairman of the ICTJ, I could teach a course on emerging democracies for only half a semester (seven weeks). My lectures focused on democracy, with specific reference to South Africa's new constitution, which is probably one of the finest in the world. South Africa came late to democracy and we were able to learn from many other countries in writing our constitution. The course I taught also dealt with developments since negotiations for a peaceful settlement in South Africa began in 1990. It was a satisfying subject to teach; so much of it was familiar, but it was an eye-opener for me to study the constitution in some detail. I realised afresh that it is a magnificent document that safeguards our fundamental rights. As usual, the students were a joy to teach and showed genuine interest in South Africa's journey towards a democratic state. In fact, it was difficult to accommodate the number of students who wanted to take the course.

It was an enjoyable and challenging interlude, and in between my lectures Jenny and I saw many of the friends we had made over the years. I also spent a fair amount of time at the ICTJ offices. At the end of eight weeks, we returned to Cape Town, but this wasn't the last of my travels, even though making any foreign trip these days is not easy, thanks to heightened airline security. I keep in regular touch with Juan Mendez and key senior staff on policy matters that need board support and approval, and, as chairman of the ICTJ, make two or three trips a year to New York. In addition, since my last stint of teaching at NYU, I have been to Japan three times and to Taiwan twice; to Liberia, Turkey, Brussels, Zimbabwe, Turin and San Remo in Italy, as well as the International Criminal Court in The Hague.

At the United Nations University in Tokyo, I spoke at a conference on human rights. I enjoyed meeting people from many parts of the world and discussing tough issues relating to justice and peace. On my second visit, I met Mrs Sadako Ogata, the former UN High Commissioner for Refugees. She had done superlative work in that capacity and, although retired, had been asked by the Japanese government to head up the Japan International Cooperation Agency. We talked about the possibility of her organisation, which has offices around the world, and the ICTJ working together. I am a great admirer of this tiny, dynamic, powerful and intelligent woman and, on my return to Cape Town, I was most pleased to find a message from the JICA office in Pretoria, asking for a meeting to discuss a joint programme.

I met with Norio Shimomura, the regional representative of JICA, and he asked if we would arrange a five-day conference in Cape Town on transitional justice and human security. We invited people from all over the world to the conference in Somerset West. The papers were published under the title *Transitional Justice and Human Security*, made available internationally through the JICA and ICTJ offices. We also recorded the key speeches on DVD for use as a teaching tool during subsequent workshops on transitional justice.

As a result of the success of this conference, JICA also asked us to organise an eight-day training workshop on transitional justice and development. We were delighted to do so, because without economic development it is extremely difficult to have a just society, and the relationship between justice and development was still relatively unexplored in any substantive way. I was greatly assisted by Pieter le Roux, professor of development studies at the University of the Western Cape. Many outstanding speakers contributed to the success of the workshop, which was a demanding and tiring exercise but, I think, very worthwhile. In the latter half of 2007, we held a second conference on transitional justice and development, which was equally successful, and entered into discussions with JICA to jointly organise one more workshop. The relationship between the two organisations has deepened and we have learnt from each other. Mr Shimomura has since returned to Japan and has asked if he might translate my book on the TRC, *A Country Unmasked*, into Japanese.

My third visit to Japan was at the invitation of the UN, to participate in a round table discussion on transforming the organisation's structures and administration, as called for by the then secretary-general, Kofi Annan. Mrs Ogata was involved in this meeting, which brought together some twenty-five or thirty people from different countries. We made a number of recommendations to the UN Secretariat, and, as the result of our work and that of many others, some important shifts have taken place in the UN and there is a new approach to the Security Council. It is a cumbersome, bureaucratic organisation, and trying to galvanise the UN to action is like trying to move a huge liner around in a harbour; it takes a lot of effort and time, and there are still many reforms that the UN needs to implement. However, if we ever disbanded the organisation, we would have to invent something similar, because throughout the world the need for what the UN does and can offer shows no sign of diminishing.

One of the problems of going to countries that have been ravaged by war and violence is that they aren't always easy to get to, and, once you do arrive, the situation is not much better. My visit to Liberia in 2006 with Priscilla Hayner, a director of the ICTJ in New York, was a comedy of errors as far as the travel arrangements were concerned. The country had been decimated by more than twenty-five years of civil war. We went there in response to an invitation to help train commissioners who had been appointed to the Liberian TRC.

The terrifying conflict in the West African country accounted for many casualties and a great deal of the infrastructure was destroyed. When Priscilla and I made our trip, few airlines were flying to the capital, Monrovia, though this will doubtless change as the country's new democracy grows. At the time, however, the only way to get to Liberia was from London's Gatwick airport. Priscilla and I linked up there and flew to Freetown in Sierra Leone, then on to Monrovia.

The airline was virtually a no-name operation, with seating offered on a first come-first served basis. As we walked up the steps into the aircraft, I thought to myself, 'This is a very ancient plane and I hope it can fly!' After sitting on the runway for half an hour, the pilot announced that we were ready for takeoff. He switched on the engines, there was silence and then the pilot said, 'Oh my God, oil is pouring out all over the tarmac! This plane is not going anywhere!'

I wondered if it was safe to stay on board while oil spilled from the aircraft, and the pilot must eventually have thought the same, as all the passengers were told to disembark as quickly as possible. We went back to the terminal and waited for several hours before being taken by bus to a different aircraft. To my consternation, however, technicians seemed to be working on the tail of this one while we were boarding. We finally took off and got as far as Freetown, where we were told that there was a problem with the on-board electronics and there would be yet another delay. We were not allowed to leave the aircraft and no refreshments were served while we waited. We were exhausted, annoyed and felt utterly hopeless. Some hours later, we finally flew to Monrovia, arriving at about 3 a.m. I had begun to think we were never going to make it, so I was extremely relieved to get off that aircraft.

The airport in Monrovia is small and decrepit and it was in virtual darkness, but we still had to go through three official checkpoints before collecting our luggage. One man, looking at my passport, said: 'Ah, South Africa! Krugerrands. We welcome that in this country.' I said I was terribly sorry, but I didn't have any krugerrands, to which he promptly responded, 'American dollars will do!' I was in no mood to surrender any of my hard currency. We collected our bags at about 3.45 a.m., but were stopped yet again by a very large gentleman who demanded to know where we thought we were going. I explained that we were going into Monrovia, where we had appointments to keep in just a few hours. I told him that we had been invited by the president of Liberia and he could check this with her office. He reluctantly stepped aside and we boarded a bus for the drive into the capital.

Monrovia was a city in shambles. The poverty is visible everywhere. There are potholes on every road, even in the city centre, and it is as hot as hell. Hospitals and clinics were barely functional, and the water was contaminated. To the great credit of the new president, Ellen Johnson-Sirleaf, elected as Africa's first woman head of state in January 2006, she is trying, with amazing courage and skill, to hold the country together and move it forward from being a failed state.

Charles Taylor, the former president and warlord who masterminded the war and dreadful atrocities in both Liberia and Sierra Leone, was arrested in March 2006 and handed over to the UN Special Court for Sierra Leone before being put on trial for war crimes in The Hague in mid-2007. Within Liberia, a truth and reconciliation commission was set up to investigate human rights violations that occurred between 1979 and 2003.

It was interesting to meet Liberia's newly appointed truth commissioners. Both they and their support staff had made a bad start. Instead of ironing out their difficulties and problems in private, these had become both public and the subject of extremely negative reporting by the media. The international diplomatic corps and the United Nations were not impressed; there was no executive director and, seemingly, no budget controls. With some exceptions, the commissioners appeared to be more concerned about their status than with doing the job they had been appointed to do.

Initially, we didn't seem to be making any progress, but that changed towards the end of our visit. We introduced a role-play scenario in which the commissioners were asked to imagine that this was the first day of the hearings. We had briefed a young man to be a 'victim' and someone else was at his side for support. The young man, who clearly knew a great deal about human rights violations perpetrated in the country, was most convincing, recounting a litany of horror as if from personal experience. The commissioners proceeded with some hesitancy at first. What we had not told them was that two members of our staff had also been briefed to interrupt the hearing.

The first disruption came when one of our 'hecklers' said he was the person being accused, and demanded to make a statement that the account by the 'victim' was a tissue of lies. The commissioners had a hard time trying to cope, and had no sooner got him to sit down when the second staff member stood up and said that as the lawyer for the alleged perpetrator, he insisted that his client should have the right of reply. The argument went to and fro and it was clear that the commissioners suddenly realised, for the very first time, the enormity of the task facing them, and that they had best forget any claim to status and focus on service instead. This finally brought home to them that they would have to work closely with the commission staff in preparation for the hearings. The hostility feigned by our staff shocked the entire audience, but I think that, by the time we left, those assigned to deal with Liberia's bloody past understood that there was no place for status and posturing in the process, and that they had to get down to the hard work of listening and caring for victims, as well as calling perpetrators to account.

While in Monrovia, we met with personnel from the UN and many of the foreign embassies. I was most impressed with Ellen Johnson-Sirleaf, who is an excellent role model. Dressed in a traditional Liberian outfit, she presents a stately figure and is clearly determined to lift her ravaged and deeply divided country out of abject poverty.

It was a tough week, made no easier by our return journey. We waited in the small, crowded and uncomfortable airport for about four hours. No sooner had we boarded the aircraft than the pilot and his crew started arguing in full hearing of the passengers, saying there was too much baggage and not enough fuel on board, and that we couldn't possibly reach Gatwick. They decided nevertheless to take off, but, once airborne, announced that we would have to land in Portugal to refuel. This was hardly reassuring but, despite the aircraft being tiny and extremely uncomfortable, I eventually fell asleep, only to be awakened by an announcement that we were not landing in Portugal after all, but in Spain. We refuelled and duly proceeded to Gatwick.

In January 2007, I was invited to speak at a conference in Taipei. I had visited Taiwan once before, as a member of a South African parliamentary delegation. Under apartheid, South Africa was on extremely favourable terms with Taiwan, recognising and dealing with the government of Chiang Kai-shek for decades in preference to that of communist mainland China. As members of parliament, we were made warmly welcome, were entertained royally, stayed in a beautiful hotel and were taken sightseeing. But Taiwan was under martial law and in the grip of authoritarian power.

One of the junior members of staff at the South African embassy in Taipei asked to see me privately. He confided that he was actually a supporter of the Progressive Federal Party but, as a foreign service employee, kept his allegiance to himself. He warned me that my hotel room was bugged, in accordance with arrangements between the governments in Pretoria and Taipei. He also told me that my request to visit the university and meet with faculty and students would be declined. His information proved correct. I don't know what they thought I was going to do that they needed to bug my room, and I was, indeed, refused permission to visit the university.

By the time of my next visit, Taiwan had held free and fair elections and the dictatorship had been replaced by a democracy. However, the elected president did not have a majority and the former right-wing regime was making it extremely difficult for him to introduce any real reform measures. A group of youngish academics was determined to build up a record of human rights violations, even though the state had not sanctioned a truth commission, so I was encouraged to accept an invitation to speak at a conference in this regard.

The visit was fascinating, and I met a range of people from all over Asia. I spent a fair amount of time with members of the Taiwanese academic and human rights community, which is small but vibrant. I was glad to be of some assistance to them. Before I left, they asked if I would act as an adviser to them on transitional justice and human rights. I agreed, although I pointed out that there wasn't a great deal I could do from a distance. I put them in touch with our office in New York so that we could send them material and offer assistance wherever possible.

Soon afterwards, I was approached by the Taiwanese ambassador in South Africa, Richard Shih, who invited Archbishop Desmond Tutu and me on what was virtually a state visit to Taiwan. We were hosted by the government in Taipei, under the auspices of the Institute for Democracy. Desmond and I both had punishing travel schedules, so it wasn't easy to find a date when we could make the trip together, but we finally managed to do so in April 2007, accompanied by Jenny as well as Desmond's wife, Leah. We had a ninety-minute meeting with Taiwan's president and met separately with the vice-president. The foreign minister hosted a luncheon for us; we met with religious leaders, particularly the Buddhists; we visited temples and training centres; we travelled inland and met mayors and various officials.

All in all, it was a fascinating experience. They treated us like royalty. Tutu's name is so well known around the world that the four of us were guests at two banquets a day, at least. We had sumptuous hotel accommodation and people accompanying us at all times to be of any assistance we required. It was endearing to see how they cared for Leah Tutu in particular. She had recently undergone knee surgery and found both standing and walking quite difficult. Our hosts noticed her discomfort immediately, and from then on, whenever we arrived at or departed from a building, there was a wheelchair waiting for her – even at a railway station and the presidential palace. I think she was deeply appreciative.

The Taiwanese were in awe of Desmond and he was marvellous in the way he responded to them. Being the kind of man he is, he was also amazingly generous to me. Every time we met anyone, he would make sure that I was given an opportunity to speak, particularly on transitional justice. What surprised us was that our meetings with the top government officials were not a mere formal exchange of pleasantries. We actually debated the issues of justice, the need to address the past, the needs of victims. This is not always the case when you visit a country and meet people in high office.

Since then, I have stayed in touch with several of the leading human rights activists and tried to be of some assistance to them. Taiwan is in a difficult position. It is a tiny island in the shadow of the mighty mainland, and the Republic of China will never grant the Taiwanese full sovereignty or independence. They are not recognised as a member of the United Nations or the World Health Organisation, and they feel that deeply. They also have strong feelings *vis-à-vis* their changed status with South Africa. The ANC government recognises the Republic of China, which has become extremely active and involved in Africa, and Taiwan has become very much a peripheral factor. However, it is not the job of the ICTJ to change that; our main concern is responding to Taiwan's requests for assistance in dealing with the past and helping it to become a truly just and democratic society. What the future holds for the little country is uncertain. Perhaps, like Hong Kong, Taiwan will become a capitalist enclave within a vast and powerful communist state.

Whenever I visit the ICTJ headquarters in New York, I enjoy seeing the remarkable developments and the enthusiasm and commitment of the staff. The intelligent and concerned contribution of the board makes me proud to be part of this organisation. On a recent visit, I delivered the Ashok Sani

Distinguished Scholars Lecture at New York University's Stern Business School and also addressed students and conducted a seminar at the Wagner Graduate School of Public Service. Having taught law students for five years, it was interesting to make the acquaintance of business students. Both their culture and approach are entirely different, and it was refreshing, in a way, to listen to their questions and responses to dealing with the past and trying to come to terms with serious violations of human rights. Clearly, in pursuit of profit, business has often contributed to injustices in certain countries, and this community, too, needs to be challenged.

An invitation from the Rockefeller Foundation to apply for a fellowship at Bellagio in Italy provided a welcome break. Fellows from all disciplines are invited to spend a month, with a partner or spouse, at a magnificent old house that was bequeathed to the foundation. I think my application was greatly helped by references from Desmond Tutu, Richard Goldstone and Ricky Revesz, dean of the NYU Law School.

The facility, overlooking Lake Como, is simply amazing. Jenny and I had a large bedroom and study, with all our meals taken care of. Guests are left alone to do research, writing, painting, music or whatever else they choose. It was a privilege to mix with people from around the world and so many different disciplines. We met and made many friends there and, in fact, it was at Bellagio that I started writing this book. I owe a real debt of gratitude to the Rockefeller Foundation for the opportunity to spend a month in idyllic surroundings, being cosseted and cared for, with the freedom to write and think and read. Laurie Ackermann, a former judge of South Africa's Constitutional Court, and his wife Denise were there at the same time and this also enhanced our enjoyment.

In March 2007, an invitation came from a German institute that is doing good work in Turkey. I was asked to deliver the keynote address at an international conference that the institute was hosting, on transitional justice not only as it applies to South Africa, but in general accordance with international law. This was my first visit to Turkey. I flew to Istanbul, waited a few hours and then took another flight to Diyarbakir, which is right on the border of Iraq's Kurdish region. I was astonished to find a large welcoming party of Kurds at the airport at about 10 p.m. We travelled in a convoy of cars to the hotel where we were to spend the night, but sleep was not the first item on my hosts' agenda.

We had a meeting, communicating through interpreters. They were animated and excited, but I was exhausted. After a while, I said that since it was quite late, perhaps we should wind up the meeting. My companions were clearly disappointed, explaining that a dinner had been laid on in my honour. I couldn't refuse, so we went to a beautiful, typically Turkish restaurant and had many courses and much wine. There was a great deal of discussion, and I was struck by the fact that every citizen of Diyarbakir, male or female, seemed to be a smoker. What astonished me was that they seemed to know a great deal about the work I had done and, indeed, about truth commissions and the situation in South Africa. I then discovered that my book, *A Country Unmasked*, had been translated into Turkish and many of them had read it!

It was almost midnight when I turned to the director of the institute and whispered to her: 'We simply have to go to bed.' She misunderstood completely and was quite vehement in her response: 'No, no! That's totally impossible. I'm a lesbian!' I had to explain that I meant going to bed separately, that I was completely exhausted. As soon as she grasped my intentions, we made our exit, slowly but surely, and went back to the hotel. We were up early for a day-long workshop on the problems facing the Kurds in Turkey, dealing with past atrocities and the need for a truth commission in that country. I had been told that the meeting would be small and in the form of a discussion, but more than two hundred people crowded into the hall. The Kurds have been severely oppressed by the Turkish majority and feel strongly about resisting and taking what they consider their rightful place in Turkey.

At the end of the day we raced to the airport and boarded a plane, by which time I was in dire need of a strong drink. When the air hostess came down the aisle offering refreshments, all I could see was some rather anaemic-looking orange juice, so I asked, 'Haven't you got anything a little stronger?' I had quite forgotten that this was a Muslim country and that no alcohol would be served. Fortunately, the man in the neighbouring seat, the president of the Bar Association who had attended the seminar, leaned over and whispered, 'You like whisky?' I nodded vigorous agreement and he pulled a bottle out of his hand luggage and asked the air hostess for glasses. They were plastic, but that whisky tasted wonderful. I had only one drink, but my resourceful neighbour and another lawyer sitting next to him finished the bottle before we landed in Istanbul.

The following day saw the opening of the conference, which was titled 'From the Burden of the Past to Societal Peace and Democracy'. There were about three hundred people in attendance; clearly, a growing number of intellectuals and civil society groups in Turkey were interested in learning more about how to address the legacy of human rights abuses in their country. In my view, this is in strong contrast to the lack of political will to address these questions officially.

During the conference, I was approached by a group of Kurds who wanted to talk to me privately. They told me they had a message from Abdullah Ocalan, the jailed leader of the Kurdistan Workers' Party (PKK). This group had been fighting for greater recognition and independence for the Kurds since 1984, resulting in clashes with the Turkish security forces in the south-east of the country. Captured in 1999, Ocalan was serving a life sentence in isolation on an island near Istanbul. What was particularly interesting was that Ocalan had read my book – in Turkish – and had then issued a statement calling on groups in Turkey to start working on a truth-seeking process. I found it quite astonishing that a book written more than seven years earlier, about the South African Truth and Reconciliation Commission, should have found its way to a remote prison outside Istanbul, be read there and change the view of someone who had been committed to the violent overthrow of the Turkish government, but had now made a commitment to truth and peace. Perhaps the best that one can hope for is that efforts made at some point in one's life fall on fertile soil every now and then.

The general feeling at the conference was that while there was a genuine commitment to a truth commission among people in Turkey, totalitarian measures designed to prevent remembering had been put in place. For that reason, people should first focus on raising awareness at a personal level, at NGO level, before including it in the process of democratisation, and perhaps only then extend it to the state. Turkey has long wanted to join the European Union and has come under pressure from France and other countries to put its house in order in respect of human rights. This might hasten the day when the country comes to terms with its past and commits itself to a new democracy and justice. Meanwhile, the Armenian genocide, which took place in 1915, remains a dark shadow hanging over Turkey. It is amazing that something that happened so long ago has never been resolved; somehow, it will have to be if Turkey is to be granted EU membership.

As recently as January 2007, the very deep divisions in Turkish society were illustrated by the murder of prominent Armenian journalist and human rights advocate Hrant Dink. Gunned down by a teenage nationalist, Ogun Samast, Dink's funeral was attended by an estimated 100 000 mourners who staged a protest march while chanting, 'We are all Hrant, we are all

Armenians.' Tragically, at a major soccer match not long afterwards, thousands of nationalist fans shouted in turn, 'We are all Ogun Samast.'

Closer to my home, a situation that evokes deep concern, anxiety and anger is the steady erosion of the rule of law and violation of human rights in neighbouring Zimbabwe. We have always had a special interest in that country because Jenny was born there when it was still Southern Rhodesia; we were married there on the family farm; visited many times and enjoyed much of the beauty of the country and its people. For a while after 1980, Robert Mugabe seemed to be what the newly independent Zimbabwe needed: he spoke of reconciliation and non-racialism, of working together and building up the country after almost two decades of civil war. The people, black and white, responded and during the first few years of Mr Mugabe's reign, it seemed that Zimbabwe could serve as a blueprint for South Africa and other countries yet to become democracies.

I met Mugabe in 1987, on my return from Dakar in Senegal. He asked me to visit Harare to tell him what our meeting with the ANC had been about. Mugabe wasn't keen on the ANC, which had not supported him during the Rhodesian war. We met at State House, in a beautiful room filled with vases of flowers. At that stage of his presidency, Mugabe appeared to me to be reasonable, intelligent and interested – a view generally shared by many Zimbabweans.

As soon as Mugabe was challenged, however, he confirmed, in the most vicious way, that power corrupts and absolute power corrupts absolutely. Over time, Jenny and I watched not only the personal harassment and suffering of her immediate family and the loss of their farm (which was seized in the post-2000 period), but also the awful treatment meted out to the people of Zimbabwe at the behest of Mugabe, his war veterans, police and others. The thugs surrounding Mugabe hold sway, and anyone who dares to take a strong stand against him is harshly dealt with. It has been deeply worrying to witness the transformation of such a beautiful country into a place of hardship, food shortages, desperation and economic meltdown, to the point where Zimbabwe has become a failed state. Inflation is impossible to measure, rising every day, and people are dying of hunger.

I tried to persuade the ICTJ to become involved in Zimbabwe, although it wasn't what we would normally categorise as a country in transition. However, my view was that if we wanted to be effective and available when the transition does come, as it surely will, we needed to be there while people were experiencing the agony. The management board finally relented and, towards the end of July 2006, I went to Zimbabwe on a fact-finding visit on behalf of the ICTJ. Jenny accompanied me, because her mother – a very old lady, resident in a nursing home after suffering a severe stroke – was still living in Harare.

We had been to Zimbabwe so often before that we were a little taken aback when we were stopped by customs at Harare International Airport, and our luggage was almost torn apart. Every single item in the cases was removed, including many quite personal items for Jenny's mother. While this was happening, we were approached by two men who told us they were from immigration and, in a very hostile manner, demanded to know what I was doing in their country. I explained that my wife was born there and that we had come to visit her mother and family and friends. They ignored that and repeated, 'What are you doing in Zimbabwe?' I explained that I was very interested in the country and its future and I was going to meet a wide cross-section of people. Again I was asked: 'What are you doing in Zimbabwe?' Then they demanded to see my small briefcase, which I hadn't surrendered to the customs officials. Rather foolishly, I had placed my programme of appointments in it, listing everyone I was going to see. The two men looked at it and told us to wait, then disappeared. They returned about twenty minutes later, saying they had photocopied the programme and that I was not to deviate from it in any way, because they would know where I was.

I explained that it was difficult to give such an assurance because, when I met one group of people, they might ask me to meet others, but the men from 'immigration' simply repeated like a mantra, 'Do not deviate from your programme.' They finally let us go but I was apprehensive, because very strange things, including motor accidents, had happened to opponents of the state in Zimbabwe.

I met with members of the Zimbabwe Congress of Trade Unions, the Independent Editors' Forum, the National Constitutional Assembly, the Crisis Coalition in Zimbabwe, the University of Zimbabwe Student Union, the Ecumenical Support Services, the Movement for Democratic Change, the Media Institute for Southern Africa and the Commercial Arbitration Centre, as well as the Friedrich Ebert Stiftung. A very impressive individual was Beatrice Mtetwa, a practising lawyer, very active in defending people facing political charges, particularly members of the media, who are constantly under threat from the state. She is extraordinarily able and very committed, and I would imagine that if she survives, and should she wish to go into politics, she could be a future leader in the new Zimbabwe.

Everywhere I went and in every group I met, it was clear that their efforts were severely handicapped by the harassment meted out by the state. One question was asked of me over and over again: 'What is South Africa doing about helping us to return to true democracy?' It was difficult for me to answer that and it remains so. President Mbeki had committed himself to a policy of quiet diplomacy, but clearly that had almost no effect on the very stubborn president of Zimbabwe. In 2007, Mbeki was appointed the official mediator between ZANU-PF and the MDC, as well as members of civil society, in an attempt to try to reach common ground that would enable free and fair elections to take place in 2008. As that year dawned, it seemed highly unlikely that the significant changes needed before a free and fair election could happen would actually materialise. In the absence of some or other intervention, or series of interventions, it seemed probable that the elections would take place, that many of the voters would be too frightened to vote against ZANU-PF and would either stay away or indeed vote for the ruling party, and that Mugabe would become president once again.

Sadly, much could happen in the interim. With the shortages of food, the soaring inflation rate and escalating persecution of political opponents, the situation could become even uglier. Meanwhile, South Africa, Botswana, Mozambique and Malawi have been inundated by Zimbabwean refugees pouring into their countries, with an estimated three million Zimbabweans already living in exile. Ironically, it is the remittances they send to their families that have helped to keep Zimbabwe afloat.

The ICTJ is committed to being a serious player in Zimbabwe once its transition to a return of democracy begins. Meanwhile, we stay in touch with the opposition MDC as well as significant civil society groups.

While it is true that the alternatives to ZANU-PF have not always been effective or united, and that civil society itself is often divided, there are nevertheless some extraordinarily brave and committed people in that small country. It would require massive assistance from the international community, but I have little doubt that if change comes and a new democracy is ushered in, Zimbabwe could once again become a country that is both economically secure and a place of safety and opportunity for all its people.

CHAPTER 23

Reflections on
justice and peace

DESPITE THE FACT THAT TRANSITIONAL JUSTICE HAS BECOME
a widely accepted term, there is still confusion about the concept. The
word *transitional* is readily understood; it signifies that an old order is dying
but that the new one has not yet been born. The *Shorter Oxford English
Dictionary on Historical Principles* defines transition as: 'A passing or passage
from one condition, action or (rarely) place to another. It is a journey –
never short – often precarious.'

A country in transition is one that is emerging from a particular order,
and is uncertain and unsure how to respond to the new. On the one hand,
there is the problem of dealing with the past; on the other, there is the
ushering in of a new dispensation to contend with, as well as the challenge
of ensuring a sustainable peace so that democracy and economic growth
can flourish.

When we come to the term *justice*, however, the issue becomes more
controversial, because there are different kinds of justice. Justice is often
referred to as retributive, restorative or distributive, or even – quite starkly
– economic or social transformation. For some who are committed to
criminal justice, there is a suspicion that transitional justice may be less than
that, and therefore should be clearly defined lest it detract from the strength
and legitimacy of criminal justice, both domestic and international.[1]

It is important to understand that, far from being a contradiction of
criminal justice, transitional justice is a convenient way of describing the
search for a just society in the wake of an undemocratic, often oppressive
and even violent political dispensation. It offers a deeper, richer and broader
vision of justice that seeks to confront perpetrators, address the needs of
victims and assist in starting a process of reconciliation and transformation.

The rule of law is fundamental to the existence of a free society. It is
what separates us from anarchy. In order to maintain the rule of law,
accountability for unlawful transgressions is imperative. Since the late 1990s
in particular, the prosecution of war criminals has featured prominently.
International criminal law has moved from a small number of instances, such

as the Nuremberg and Tokyo war crimes trials that followed the Second World War, to a much wider legal response. This shift from impunity to accountability in terms of prosecutions has become the defining feature of the international human rights movement.

It is quite understandable that supporters and advocates of these developments rejoice at the possibility of achieving justice for grave human rights abuses. For those whose hands and arms were amputated in Sierra Leone, for HIV-positive rape victims in Rwanda, and for families burnt out of their homes in East Timor and Bosnia, the day of reckoning for perpetrators brings enormous comfort. While the search for justice is often imperfect, it is clearly well worth the pursuit.

Professor Noah Novogrodsky, who worked in the Special Court for Sierra Leone, acknowledges that all international attempts at securing justice reflect very real political compromise. Most of us accept that the establishment of courts is a pale substitute for preventive action, and that prosecuting some – but not most – human rights violators simply constitutes a form of *realpolitik*. There are clearly limits to law, and whenever there are human rights violations on a huge scale, such as in the former Yugoslavia, Rwanda or Sierra Leone, it is impossible to prosecute everyone. International criminal law offers a measure of personal culpability in the face of grotesque crimes, but there are limits to what it can achieve, and the horror of Darfur suggests that it is not the deterrent that most of us had hoped for. Furthermore, there are considerable political restraints on what is or is not possible.

For example, the Extraordinary Chambers for Cambodia will examine crimes committed by the Khmer Rouge between 1975 and 1979 only. The Iraqi Special Tribunal has no jurisdiction to judge crimes committed since the invasion of that country by the USA and its allies in 2003. For its part, the International Criminal Court in The Hague labours under well-known US opposition and cannot begin to apply universal rules to fully half the countries of the world, including states like Russia, China and the Sudan.

All of this suggests that, while criminal justice is extremely important, societies in transition need other instruments and models as supplements for this form of justice. Advocating a holistic approach that attempts to apply restorative justice as a complement to the retributive kind is of considerable benefit in establishing a just society. But what is meant by a 'holistic' approach to justice in societies in transition? There are at least five key pillars on which this concept rests.

1. Accountability

The rule of law and the fair, even administration of justice deserve our greatest respect. No society can claim to be free or democratic without strict adherence to the rule of law. Dictators and authoritarian regimes abandon it at the first opportunity and resort to brazen power politics, leading to all manner of excess. It is of central importance, therefore, that as far as possible those who violate the law are punished.

Legal prosecutions have at least three additional advantages: firstly, in most cases, prosecutions prevent high-ranking perpetrators from returning to positions of authority; secondly, tribunals and special courts aim to punish those who bear the greatest responsibility for human rights violations, thus assisting to break the cycle of collective reprisals; thirdly, due process avoids summary justice. It is often forgotten that both Joseph Stalin and Winston Churchill initially advocated putting Nazi leaders against a wall and shooting them! The words of Justice Robert H Jackson, chief US prosecutor at the Nuremberg Trials, are salutary:

> The wrongs we seek to condemn and punish have been so calculated, so malignant and so devastating, that civilization cannot tolerate their being ignored because it cannot survive their being repeated. That four great nations, flushed with victory and stung with injury, stay the hand of vengeance and voluntarily submit their captive enemies to the judgment of the law is one of the most significant tributes that Power has ever paid to Reason.[2]

But there is only so much that law can do, and we need to embrace a broader notion of justice than retribution. Not only is it physically impossible to prosecute all offenders, but an over-zealous focus on punishment can also make the securing of sustainable peace and stability more difficult. More than punishment is required to achieve a just society. Documenting the truth about the past, restoring dignity to victims and embarking on a process of reconciliation are vital elements of a just society. Equally important is the need to begin transforming institutions; structures must not impede the commitment to consolidating democracy and establishing a culture of human rights. It follows that approaches to societies in transition will be multifaceted and will incorporate the need for serious consultation to realise the goal of a just society.

2. Truth recovery

According to former US secretary of state Madeleine Albright, 'Truth is the cornerstone of the rule of law, and it will point towards individuals, not peoples, as perpetrators of war crimes. And it is only the truth that can cleanse the ethnic and religious hatreds and begin the healing process.' One of the non-judicial mechanisms that has gained great prominence since the 1990s is the truth commission. It was first used in South America but has since spread to many other parts of the world. There have been at least twenty-eight such commissions, with varying degrees of success. At the time of writing, there were at least four commissions under way, in Morocco, Sierra Leone, East Timor and Liberia. Several others were in the offing, including the Democratic Republic of Congo, Nepal and Iraq. In fact, there is hardly a modern-day peace accord that doesn't refer to a truth commission as one option for dealing with the past.

As indicated by its name, a truth commission is concerned first and foremost with the recovery of truth. Through truth-telling, the commission attempts to document and analyse the structures and methods used to carry out illegal repression, taking into account the political, economic and social context in which these violations occurred. In some ways, it is unfortunate that the word 'truth' is used. Beyond its Orwellian overtones, many critics rightly feel that it is impossible for all the truth to ever be known.

In its final report, the South African Truth and Reconciliation Commission distinguished between four kinds of truth. The first is objective or factual or forensic truth. The legislation that governed the TRC's work required it to 'prepare a comprehensive report which sets out its activities and findings based on factual and objective information and evidence collected or received by it or placed at its disposal'.

The second is personal or narrative truth. Through the telling of their own stories, both victims and perpetrators gave meaning to their multi-layered experiences of the South African story. Through the media, these personal truths were communicated to the broader public. Oral tradition was a central feature of the TRC process. Explicit in the legislation was an affirmation of the healing potential of truth-telling. One of the objectives of the TRC was to 'restore the human and civil dignity of victims by granting them an opportunity to relate their own accounts of the violations of which they were the victims'.

It is important to underline that the stories we listened to didn't come to us as 'arguments' or claims, as in a court of law. They were often heart-wrenching, conveying unique insights into the pain of our past. To listen to one man relate how his wife and baby were cruelly murdered is much more powerful and moving than perusal of statistics that describe a massacre involving many victims. Through personal accounts, the conflict of the past is no longer a question of numbers and incidents; the human face shows itself, and the horror of murder and torture is painfully real.

The third is social or 'dialogical' truth. Even before the TRC began its work, Judge Albie Sachs talked about 'microscope truth' and 'dialogical truth'. The first is factual and verifiable, he said, and can be documented and proved. Dialogical truth, on the other hand, is social truth, truth of experience that is established through interaction, discussion and debate.

People from all walks of life were involved in the TRC process, including the religious community, the former South African Defence Force, NGOs, the media, the legal and health sectors, political parties and – obviously – the broad population through the media and public scrutiny. What I am emphasising is that almost as important as the process of establishing the truth was the process of acquiring it. The process of dialogue involved transparency, democracy and participation as the basis for affirming human dignity and integrity.

The fourth kind of truth is healing and restorative. The law required the TRC to look both at the past and the future. The truth that the TRC was required to establish had to contribute to the reparation of damage inflicted in the past as well as prevention of its ever happening again. But, for healing to be a possibility, knowledge in itself is not enough. It must be accompanied by acknowledgement and an acceptance of accountability. Public acknowledgement that thousands of South Africans paid a very high price for the attainment of democracy affirms the human dignity of victims and survivors and is an integral part of society's healing.

3. Reconciliation

A number of commissions have talked not only about truth but also about reconciliation. If the word 'truth' conjures up problems for many people, so does the word 'reconciliation'. It has religious connotations, especially in the Christian faith, and there are many who would prefer that neither the word nor the concept be used by those seeking to recover the truth and focus on victims. At its best, reconciliation involves commitment and sacrifice; at its worst, it is an excuse for passivity, for siding with the powerful against the weak and dispossessed. Religion, in many instances, has given reconciliation a bad name, because its representatives have often joined forces with those who exploited and impoverished entire populations, instead of showing solidarity with the oppressed.

When reconciliation calls for mere forgetting or for concealment, it is spurious. In Argentina, the concept of reconciliation is regarded with deep scepticism. In that country, the Catholic Church supported the military junta in large measure, and the perpetrators of human rights violations were always the first to call for reconciliation. The same is true of Rwanda, where religious groups, priests and nuns participated in the massacre of the Tutsis. In this context, talk about reconciliation is highly suspect and can be viewed as an excuse for amnesia. Unless the call for reconciliation is accompanied by acknowledgement of the past and acceptance of responsibility, it will be dismissed as cheap rhetoric.

Perhaps one of the ways in which to achieve at least a measure of reconciliation in a deeply divided society is to create a common memory that can be acknowledged by those who created and implemented the unjust system, those who fought against it, and the many more who were in the middle and claimed not to know what was happening in their country. The process of reconciliation is never cheap. It can, in fact, involve demilitarisation, the handing over of arms and the reintegration of former rebel armies. The process is never comfortable, and often dangerous.

Reconciliation can begin at different points in a country's transition from totalitarian state to a new form of democracy. For some, it starts at the negotiation table; for others, when perpetrators are indicted and prosecuted. The release of political prisoners or the acceptance of a new constitution that guarantees fundamental freedoms may facilitate the beginning of reconciliation, as can the holding of free and open elections in which all citizens can participate. There are many starting points, but it is never a one-step, short-term process.

The process of reconciliation is ongoing, especially in countries where oppression has been deep and lasting. If it is to succeed, reconciliation must have an impact on the life chances of ordinary people. If genuine coexistence is to take place, the building of trust is indispensable. If trust is absent, citizens will not be prepared to invest their energies in the consolidation of democracy. As an old man in Bosnia told me, 'The bridges are all destroyed. Not the bridges across our rivers, but the bridges between people. If we don't rebuild them, my grandchildren will be fighting another war.'

Reconciliation, both as a process and a means of seeking an often-elusive peace, must be understood through the lens of transitional justice. It stands a better chance and is better understood if victims believe that their grievances are being addressed and their cry is being heard; that the silence is being broken. Reconciliation can begin when perpetrators are held to account, when truth is sought openly and fearlessly, when institutional reform commences, or when the need for reparation is acknowledged and acted upon. The response by former victims to these initiatives can increase both the potential for greater stability and the chances of sustainable peace. The process has often been hindered by the silence or denial of political leaders concerning their own responsibility and failure of the state. On the other hand, when leaders are prepared to speak honestly and generously about their own involvement – or at least the involvement of their government or the previous regime – the door is opened for the possibility of some reconciliation among citizens.

Receiving the report of the Chilean National Truth and Reconciliation Commission, Patricio Aylwin, elected president of his country in 1989, highlighted what I believe is the irreducible minimum for reconciliation to have a chance, namely a commitment to truth and justice. In a statement broadcast live on television, he emphasised the following: 'This leaves the excruciating problem of human rights violations and other violent crimes which have created so many victims and caused so much suffering in the past. They are an open wound in our national soul that cannot be ignored; nor can it heal through mere forgetfulness. To close our eyes and pretend none of this ever happened would be to maintain at the core of our society a source of pain, division, hatred and violence. Only the disclosure of the truth and the search for justice can create the moral climate in which reconciliation and peace will flourish.'

4. Institutional reform

For truth and reconciliation to flourish, serious and focused attention must be given not only to individuals but also to institutions. Institutional reform should be at the very heart of any transformation.

The truth commission is an ideal model for holding together both retrospective truth and prospective needs. Unfortunately, most truth commissions have chosen to focus almost entirely on individual hearings. This is important and critical, but, if commissions were to hold institutional hearings, it would be possible to call to account those directly responsible for the breakdown of the state and the repressive measures imposed on citizens.

In South Africa, an opportunity was created for the security forces, politicians, religious communities, legal representatives, the media, business and labour to give an account of their role in the past and – importantly – how they saw their role in the future. In other words, it is simply not enough to be merely concerned about the past. We must deal with it, but we must not dwell in it. We deal with the past for the sake of the future.

On a recent visit to Serbia, it was quite clear to me that one of the major problems preventing that country from moving out of its dark and ominous past into a brighter democracy was the fact that the institutions had remained almost exactly the same. The same police officers were controlling law and order, the same generals were in charge of the army, and this proved to be the case with all major state institutions. As I moved from one group of leaders to another, it was clear that unless and until institutions were radically restructured, there would be little opportunity for growth, development and peace in Serbia. This is also true of the former Yugoslavia as a whole.

In all failed states that are in transition, institutions have to be transformed. In deeply divided societies where mistrust and fear still reign, there must be bridge-building and a commitment not only to criminal justice, but also to economic justice. For that to be a reality, institutions as well as individuals have to change.

Vetting of former repressive security establishments is an essential part of institutional reform, but it has to be carefully managed. Immediately after the invasion of Iraq, the Baath Party, Saddam Hussein's power base, was banned. This made no provision whatsoever for the security that is both essential to and needed for the pursuit of justice and peace, and allowed only for collective guilt rather than individual responsibility. There can be little doubt that many Iraqis joined the Baath Party for no other reason than to survive. There are many other instances of individuals being effectively forced to join a particular party in order to ensure that their children have access to education and even to food. It is well known that many Zimbabweans joined ZANU-PF for the sake of their personal security and the welfare of their children. In both Iraq and Zimbabwe, individual responsibility for human rights abuse would be the right approach.

5. Reparations

Reparations have a long history, but until the middle of the twentieth century they did not receive sufficient systematic attention. The individual reparations made by West Germany after the Second World War were a watershed. Until 1952, reparation was solely an inter-state affair – payments exacted from the vanquished by the victors, as with the Treaty of Versailles. Compensation to victims of the Nazi holocaust was the first instance of a massive, nationally sponsored reparations programme to individuals who had suffered gross abuse of their human rights.

It is worth emphasising that, from the standpoint of the victims, reparations occupy a special place in a transition to democracy. They are the most tangible manifestation of a state's efforts to remedy the harm that victims have suffered. Even if it were completely successful, both in terms of the number of accused – far from being the case in any transition – and in terms of results – which are always affected by the availability of evidence and the persistent weaknesses of judicial systems – criminal justice is, in the end, a struggle against perpetrators rather than an effort on behalf of victims. Truth-telling can offer victims significant benefits that may include a sense of closure derived from knowing the fate of loved ones, and a sense of satisfaction from the official acknowledgement of that fate. But, in the absence of other positive and tangible manifestations, truth can easily be considered an empty gesture, cheap and inconsequential talk. Institutional reform will always be a long-term project that affects the lives of the victims only indirectly.

Pablo de Greiff of the ICTJ reminds us that a freestanding reparations programme, unconnected to other transitional justice processes, is more likely to fail, despite its direct efforts on behalf of victims. Without documentation and the acknowledgement of truth, the provision of reparations can be interpreted as insincere – the payment of 'blood money'.[3]

In many ways, the dilemmas and challenges of reparations are a microcosm of the overall challenges of transitional justice. How does one balance competing legitimate interests in redressing the harm to victims and ensuring the democratic stability of the state? Similar to other areas of transitional justice, such as truth-telling or institutional reform, simple judicial decisions cannot provide the comprehensive solutions demanded by such interests. Rather, solutions must be found in the exercise of judgement and a creative combination of legal, political, social and economic approaches.

Indeed, the success of reparations programmes and transitional justice strategies in general depends on the ability to form broad political coalitions. By virtue of their resilience and strength, in coalitions that demonstrate the resolve and solidarity of society as a whole, victims can become, in Kahlil Gibran's words, 'a voice that causes the heavens to tremble'.

Our attempts to achieve a just society must needs involve a multifaceted – or holistic – approach. In his important foreword to the book *My Neighbor, My Enemy: Justice and Community in the Aftermath of Mass Atrocity*, South American novelist, playwright and human rights activist Ariel Dorfman – whom many will know for his remarkable play *Death and the Maiden*, which also became a successful film – writes:

> It is comforting to watch the trials afterwards.
>
> After the bombs and the machetes. After the war of brother against brother and neighbor against neighbor. After the torn bodies and the burnt-out villages. After the faces of grief and the faces of those who are so beyond grief they cannot speak and cannot cry. After the children blown up or hacked to death. After the rubble and the fires.
>
> After all of this and too much more, so much more than anybody should be expected to witness, let alone live, yes, it is comforting to hear about, see from time to time, the trial of the man, some of the men, held responsible for any one of these outrages against humanity.
>
> Comforting to watch the accusations, the evidence, the witnesses. Justice is being done, punishment will be meted out, a balance has been redressed to a universe gone mad.

However, he continues:

> And yet, crucial as these efforts to deal with the unspeakable may be, beneath my enthusiasm there has always lurked the suspicion that such performances of justice are not enough, that they do not answer by themselves, cannot answer, the really hard question left in the wake of destructive conflicts inside nations.
>
> How can survivors coexist with those who killed their most beloved kin? How can trust be restored to a community where our best friends betrayed us, refused us refuge? Can the needs of an international war crimes tribunal for forensic evidence be reconciled with the needs of families desperate to identify and bury their butchered relatives? Indeed, can reconciliation ever be truly achieved in a society where the perpetrators deny their crimes? How is the damage repaired? Through money? Through symbolic and moral acts? Person by person or collectively? By providing education to the children of the dead or providing resources to the group that was injured? And can the ruined fabric that once held a society together ever be sewn together again? How to change the obdurate conditions that led to these conflicts in the first place, how to

insure they will not recur? Can a different form of common identity, forged in tolerance and not in detestation, be built by former enemies who are now again neighbors? Are there ways in which trials and legal proceedings can be understood not as the ultimate solution to every horror that consumed that landscape but as part of an ongoing quest for long-term peace?

Are there alternative systems of restorative justice which more efficiently integrate the vast and still fearful community, taking into account the customs and traditions of its own members? And how to involve the victims in the definition of what is to be done, how to avoid imposing upon them formulas from afar and from above, how to make them true participants in the rebuilding of their lives?[4]

It is this 'and yet' which deserves vigorous debate as we attempt to work towards justice and peace. The questions Dorfman raises are both tough and disturbing. It is clear that we cannot let ourselves grow comfortable with easy explanations and simple solutions for human catastrophe.

There are enormous difficulties in pursuing justice in a normal situation, but when one attempts to do this in countries undergoing transition, the problems are intensified. There is a need to balance two imperatives: on the one hand, a return to the rule of law and the prosecution of offenders. On the other hand, the rebuilding of societies and embarking on the process of reconciliation. In helping to make states work, it is important, therefore, to balance accountability with the shoring up of fragile emerging democracies. The overall aim should be to ensure a sustainable peace that will encourage and make possible social and economic development.

But the answer is not either/or. Once it is agreed that there must be the balancing of imperatives, it is surely a case of both/and. In other words, we must deal with the past and not dwell in it, but the measures that are taken have to take into account the nature of each transition and the political space for accountability. For example, when the bombing stopped in Afghanistan, some advocated the immediate introduction of trials and prosecutions. However, it was clear that the major problem was not in the first instance accountability, but rather security, the return of the refugees, food for those who were in danger of starving and a measure of good governance, so that law and order could be introduced and maintained.

The same is true of Iraq. While it was imperative to prosecute those who committed human rights violations during Saddam Hussein's dictatorship, the first imperative should have been to stop the looting, return to some measure of law and order, and enable the Iraqi leaders and people to start taking part in future decision-making. In this way, some semblance of stability and peaceful coexistence could have been restored. It is only after this has happened that one can consider the options, judicial and non-judicial, that will meet the urgent needs of a state in conflict with occupying forces and a history of brutality and division. An awful price is being paid in Iraq as a consequence of the failure to apply the first imperative, and the killing continues unabated.

While every situation will be different, I am convinced that the holistic approach to transitional justice affords a genuine opportunity for at least some accountability, some truth, some reconciliation and healing, some transformation and some reparations for victims.

PART VII

Looking back, looking forward

CHAPTER 24

Face to face with mortality

WHEN JENNY AND I RETURNED TO SOUTH AFRICA IN OCTOBER 2005 after my seven-week teaching stint at New York University, I decided that I should have a medical check-up, including a prostate examination.

Annual check-ups had long formed part of my routine, so I wasn't too concerned about this one and went to see George Dommisse, who had been our family doctor for many years. Two days later, he called to say he was concerned that my PSA count was too high and advised me to consult a urologist for a second opinion. I did so immediately and, after yet again enduring the 'digital test', was told by Dr Nicol that he had felt a definite growth and strongly recommended a biopsy.

I was bowled over by this news, because I felt well and strong and was travelling, teaching and working normally. However, this walnut-sized prostate gland was obviously going to concentrate my mind for the foreseeable future.

The biopsy procedure is miserable, as anyone who has undergone it knows – six needles into the prostate. A few days later, I was given the sobering news that I had cancer of the prostate. Inevitably, my thoughts went back to my previous joust with cancer, many years before. Having endured and survived that experience, my thoughts were a mixture of dread and determination that I would overcome this fresh assault as well.

News of this nature changes one's whole life in an instant. You can't simply carry on as usual; you have to deal with this intruder. My family was equally distressed. It is amazing how the word 'cancer' frightens all of us, even though there have been so many advances in this field of medicine.

I was referred to Dr Neil Wilson, an oncologist, and Jenny went with me to talk to him about treatment. He is a strong, bluff man who doesn't pull his punches. He told me that the situation was serious, but that with the treatment available there was no cause for despair. After a long discussion, he advised a course of radiation rather than surgical removal of the prostate. After I digested this, I asked whether he thought it would make sense to get a second opinion. He responded with alacrity that if he were in my shoes he would certainly do so. I told him that when Archbishop Desmond Tutu had been diagnosed with prostate cancer, he had gone to the Memorial Sloan-Kettering Cancer Center in New York for treatment, and wondered if that might be a good idea for me. Dr Wilson said immediately that while we had the necessary medical skills in South Africa, we didn't have the equipment that would allow me to be given the highest possible radiation dosage. Neil was most encouraging and contacted Sloan-Kettering to furnish them with details of my diagnosis. He and the doctors in New York discussed my treatment in several e-mails and they indicated that they would be ready to accept me as a patient.

Sloan-Kettering is one of the best cancer treatment centres in the world, and as soon as some of my friends in New York heard about my illness, they urged me to go there. I tried to explain that it wasn't as easy as simply jumping on a plane. I felt a strong need to have family and friends around me during this time, and perhaps being at home was the best idea. Also, it is expensive to travel and I didn't want to go on my own, which meant we would have to find the money for two airfares. In addition, the treatment was also extremely expensive, I would have to be in New York for three or four months, and I had no accommodation there.

Vincent Mai, such a good friend, assured me that all of this could be taken care of. Jim McGarry at the ICTJ called me and said, 'I am not sure if you know this, but you are still a member of the Oxford Medical Scheme and they would cover a great deal of the expenses at Sloan.' This was wonderful news and even better tidings soon followed. Harvey Dale, a close friend, had contacted the dean of the NYU Law School, Ricky Revesz, and told him that I needed accommodation. Once again, the response was immediate and positive. There would be an apartment for Jenny and me for as long as we needed it, at no cost.

I was overwhelmed that people would respond in this way. I discussed the matter with Jenny and my children, and some good friends, including Desmond Tutu. Making the necessary arrangements and fixing dates with the hospital took several weeks, but by the end of the year everything was in place and I decided that we would go to New York in early January 2006.

We decided to have a picnic in Kirstenbosch Gardens on New Year's Day. We had a wonderful outing with our daughter Kathy, her partner Hardy, and their two girls, Tara and Maya. I remember it so well: it was a windless day, the sunshine glorious, the sky a vivid blue; Table Mountain was a comforting rather than overwhelming or threatening presence. After enjoying the picnic on the rolling lawns, we made our way back to the car park. As we moved towards the exit, I noticed what appeared to be a small wishing well tucked away from the main gardens, its fountain restrained. I wasn't sure if it actually was a wishing well, although it looked like one. It wasn't clear that it demanded some suggestion of commitment, but, to be sure, I took out a five-rand coin, held it over the slightly murky waters, slowly let the coin slip from my fingers and made a wish. Obviously, some six weeks after being diagnosed with cancer, I wished for good health! No surprise there. I didn't say anything to the family about my wish, and a few days later, after frantic packing of suitcases, last minute chores, phone calls, emotional farewells to family and friends, Jenny and I flew to New York.

I found it very difficult to sleep on the aircraft. It is a long way from Cape Town to New York and we droned on high over the continent of Africa, en route from Johannesburg to Dakar, and then on to the US. All around me, fellow passengers were cocooned in their blankets, sleeping away the seemingly endless flight. The thought kept repeating itself over and over in my mind: 'Is your journey really necessary?' After all, there are excellent doctors and medical facilities in Cape Town. Why was I tearing myself away from loved ones and the glorious summer to spend a cold and dark mid-winter in New York? There was really no answer to that, except that when you are in extreme circumstances you reach out for whatever help you can get.

Jenny and I went to Sloan-Kettering the day after we arrived. The reception from this huge international hospital was warm and friendly. I met with Dr Fuchs, head of the radiology department, a genial, experienced and re-assuring man, together with his nurse and another doctor. Yet another 'digital' procedure was performed and then something I hadn't anticipated – an MRI scan. Although there was a long waiting list, they managed to fit me in.

I went into a cold, clinical room. Everything seemed to be hard, steel and forbidding. Then came the real shock – the insertion of a rectal coil in order to try to assess the extent of the cancer. An MRI on most parts of the body is quite straightforward, though never pleasant. But when they are trying to determine what is happening in your prostate, they shove a huge coil up your bum. You lie there for more than an hour while all sorts of tests are carried out. It was a miserable and lonely experience.

The doctors didn't wait for the results of the MRI, but decided that I would have what they call a simulation, which starts with a starvation diet – the emptying of the stomach. I shuffled into a room at the hospital two days later and met a woman called Beverley, who gave me a cup of red liquid that I had to drink. She told me it was to 'brighten my insides'. Once again I had to lie on my stomach on a hard, cold surface, and, to my astonishment, one of the technicians said, 'Please make sure that your penis is pointing towards your feet, and whenever you have treatment here, make sure that happens.' They put a cast on my back, a catheter up my bum and tattooed my skin to make absolutely sure that, when they started the radiation, they didn't damage healthy cells but targeted only the cancerous cells.

Jenny and I spent the week recovering: sleeping, watching movies, eating one of our favourite dishes, spicy chicken wings. On Tuesday 10 January, we went to a cinema in Mercer Street. It was my seventy-fifth birthday. I received wonderful messages from our children, their families and our friends, mostly from Africa but also from New York; and flowers and cards from the ICTJ. But that afternoon I received some sombre news. The MRI scan had shown that the cancer had spread to almost the entire prostate. It was too swollen for radiation, so I would first have to undergo hormonal therapy, which would prolong my treatment to more than six months. I was also advised that I would need the most extreme radiation possible in order to try to destroy the cancer cells. I felt psychologically mugged. Happy birthday, Alex!

We then had to make a decision. Should we stay in New York while I underwent the hormone treatment, which could last up to three months, or go home, complete the hormone treatment and then return when the prostate had shrunk sufficiently? We decided to go home. It had been a ten-day roller-coaster ride. I felt hammered, but believed that being at home would give me the support and strength that I would need. I had to wait a few days for the first injection before we could leave, and felt as though I was marking time.

I also felt very old. The thought of the hormones suppressing my testosterone levels hung over me like a pall and my energy levels seemed to be low even before the treatment started taking effect. I felt as if I wanted to retreat from life, yet kept on persuading myself, with great encouragement from Jenny, that I had to get a grip and embrace life.

It wasn't easy to return home. We had still been finding our place again in Cape Town society after our previous stay in New York when the cancer sent us back there, unexpectedly. Many people were confused by our coming and going. We seemed to be flitting in and out of the country and this perplexed not only our friends but also our family. Perhaps there was even some resentment over our unsettled lifestyle. People who cared about us didn't know where they fitted into this uncertain pattern, or what was happening. But there was also much to be grateful for.

Many years before, Jenny and I had bought a small cottage at Scarborough that we used as a hideaway, particularly after I walked out of parliament. We spent many happy hours there, preparing meals for ourselves, our family and our friends. Scarborough had become a place of peace and serenity for us, despite the cold sea, the storms and the howling winds. It has nourished us during difficult times in our life, either individually, together, or as a family, and so it was during the first few months of 2006. The beauty of Cape Town is hard to exaggerate and Scarborough is a peaceful haven on the west coast of the peninsula. The birds fight for a place to drink and swim in the birdbath and I can watch them for hours on end.

I saw Dr Wilson again. He was very frank and reminded me that there was no guarantee that the treatment would result in total recovery. He also talked about the side effects of the hormone treatment, which include depression, the loss of testosterone, impotence, mood swings and the threat of enlarged breasts! Fortunately, my body responded well to the treatment and my PSA count came down fairly rapidly, which meant I could return to New York after eight weeks.

This time, I went alone, which I think was a mistake. Dealing with the situation and the treatment on my own was grim and I missed Jenny enormously. I was hugely relieved when she joined me a fortnight later. She had been in Morocco on a painting trip and had wanted to cancel it, but I insisted that she made full use of the opportunity.

After another MRI scan and simulation, as I sat in the waiting room before my first radiation treatment, I looked around and saw all these old men, in their short hospital gowns. They looked so worried, so aged, and I felt very sorry for them. Then I realised that they probably had the same sentiments about me. In fact, I was possibly an even sorrier sight, because at my height – 1.93 metres or 6′4″ – the tiny gown was barely decent. I kept trying to tug it down over my knees.

Finally, my name was called. I was greatly impressed with the people who would be with me for the next forty-eight treatments. You get very close to therapists who hold your future well-being in their hands. I don't know how they manage to maintain their good spirits, warmth and encouragement, faced daily as they are with life-threatening situations, but they were certainly a great comfort to me. I lay down on a cold, hard surface and they all left the room while I waited for the radiation to start. I'd imagined that there would be a huge bolt of lightning, accompanied by a terrible, searing pain, but it was nothing like that. There was an awful noise, and that was it. I tried very hard not to think of these powerful rays burning into my back.

After the first treatment, I felt dazed and somewhat overwhelmed. I decided to walk for a few blocks before taking the subway back to the West Village, where I was staying. Making my way slowly along a crowded and busy Second Avenue, I felt an acute pain in the back of my leg. I swung around to see an irate elderly man in a wheelchair. He glared at me and shouted, 'Get a move on, I don't want to run you over!' Being accosted by an old, disabled man in a wheelchair was one of the really low points of the entire experience. I decided to pull myself together and walk tall.

I recall having a conversation with a couple of our New York friends, Len and Ann Sands. He was a federal judge, a remarkable man, and his wife was also a superb person. One evening, she asked me: 'How do you cope with the treatment, particularly when there are painful procedures?' I told her that I didn't want to underestimate how invasive, how humiliating, how uncomfortable, how horrible it all was, but that I had learnt during previous operations and procedures, even in a dentist's chair, to invoke an 'out of body' experience, detaching my mind from my physical form and floating close to the ceiling. Ann said she did something similar at times of stress, focusing her conscious thoughts on skiing. She asked me what image came to my mind. I told her that I was mentally transported to the deck of our Scarborough home, where I saw Jenny and myself sitting quietly, a bottle of white wine and a couple of glasses on the table, and Sam, our golden retriever, gazing at me with his sad brown eyes. I could actually feel him pushing his head against my hand, triggering a whole flood of memories: the little golden bundle when he first arrived in our home, the wonderful walks on the slopes of Table Mountain and the beach at Scarborough. Sam and I really talked to one another. I would say something to him and he would make a noise from in his throat as if he were answering me.

Sam was an extremely vivid, physical presence and I felt that he was helping me during these long weeks of treatment, a strong and empathetic companion. How wonderfully strange it was to be so far away, and yet have Sam feel so close. Even more astonishing, Sam had died five or six years before, yet there is no doubt that he seemed to be very much alive, and helped me through an extremely difficult time.

As we moved towards the fortieth treatment, I began a countdown. I simply couldn't wait until it was all over. I was shocked to hear from Dr Fuchs and his staff that they wouldn't be able to tell me at the end of the treatment whether or not it had been successful. I would have to wait a couple of months for the outcome, and have further blood tests and continual checks on my PSA count to determine whether or not the cancer had been killed off. This was not great news, but I had to accept it.

With the first phase of the treatment finally over, there were wonderful farewells from the many friends in New York who had been so good and kind to me, but I was overjoyed to be on my way back to Cape Town at last, where I would be with family and friends.

About six weeks later, I was thrilled when the first PSA count was less than one. The tests continued at regular intervals and, unfortunately, the PSA count began to rise. In August 2007 I was put back on hormone treatment, with the same side effects as before. I realised that this would bring the count down, and that the treatment could then stop and I could have what they call 'a holiday', which would give me a break and hopefully allow the body's rhythm to return to normal. I assume that this is how the cycle will go. But the alternative is far worse.

A blood test in November 2007 showed that the PSA count was, indeed, down, but Neil Wilson advised me to continue the treatment for a further three months. In January 2008 I received the good news that the PSA count was 0.4. This meant I could stop the hormonal treatment but continue with regular blood tests.

I am glad to be alive and to have had such excellent treatment, counselling, and support from family and friends, and I see no reason why I shouldn't continue to live a full life. In fact, much against the advice of friends, I travelled extensively during September and October 2007. One of the highlights was a visit that Jenny and I made to Edinburgh to see our youngest son, Nick, in the play *Truth in Translation*. The production, by Paavo Tom Tammi in collaboration with Michael Lessac and with music by Hugh Masekela, portrays the experience of translators and interpreters at South Africa's Truth and Reconciliation Commission, and was well received at the Edinburgh Festival. From there we went to Dublin for a few days and then to the south of France for a week. Jenny then returned home, while I proceeded to New York and to Flint, Michigan, where I addressed the board of the Mott Foundation. Flint, once a prosperous city in the heartland of the American motor industry, is now in the throes of depression. Racism is rife and it is one of the most violent cities in America. I went to Flint at the request of the Mott Foundation's chairman. He had originally invited me five years earlier, but 9/11 intervened, with all aircraft being grounded. The foundation had supported the ICTJ from the beginning, and I was finally able to give the chairman a first-hand report on progress and developments. Coincidentally, Mott sponsored the play *Truth in Translation*, which played to packed houses in Flint. 'The most integrated audience ever seen in this town,' was the comment of several board members who attended the performance.

Just ten days after getting back to Cape Town, I was on my way to New York again, for ICTJ board meetings. So despite my treatment, I was able to continue my normal, indeed somewhat hectic, life. Desmond Tutu and I often exchange notes about our respective ups and downs and joke about the side effects of the treatment, especially the hot flushes! But we also try to convey to others who find themselves in a similar situation that there is, indeed, life beyond prostate cancer.

CHAPTER 25

South Africa in transition

S INCE THE TRC, MOST OF MY WORK HAS BEEN INVOLVED IN places other than my own country. But South Africa remains my first concern. Most of my adult life was spent fighting for democracy and against injustice – in the church, in parliament and through IDASA – and I played a part in the new democracy through my role in the TRC. Together with so many others, my hopes were high for a new South Africa, a democracy truly of the people, a just and caring society. Have our hopes and ideals been realised?

After meeting Thabo Mbeki when he was still in exile, I certainly saw him as a future president of South Africa and I felt confident about the future. Obviously, along with many millions of others, I wanted Nelson Mandela to be our first democratically elected president in those explosive, tense, uncertain times. But we knew that he was growing old; he had already indicated that he would serve only one term, and Thabo Mbeki was certainly one of the strong favourites to replace him. There were others, like Cyril Ramaphosa, originally Mandela's own choice, but I was delighted when Mbeki became our president. Van Zyl Slabbert and I were among the thousands who attended the inauguration of President Mandela and were deeply moved and inspired. We also attended Mbeki's inauguration, and his speech on that occasion was incredibly moving and very challenging, focusing on the great gap between the rich and the poor, the two South Africas and his commitment and determination to lead his government to alleviate that poverty.

Much has been written about some of the major mistakes and bad judgement that we have witnessed during Mbeki's presidency. He will never be allowed to forget, and nor will South Africa, his stance on HIV/AIDS. It is no exaggeration to say that thousands of lives would have been spared if he and his government had come to their senses earlier. This has been an albatross around his neck and will taint his legacy forever. He has also been strongly criticised for his low-key approach to the Zimbabwean crisis. This is more difficult; few of his critics offer meaningful, realistic alternatives and, while quiet diplomacy has not worked, one can but hope that the mediation which started in earnest in 2007 at the behest of the African

Union may yet bear fruit. But certainly he ought to have condemned the wide-ranging injustices in Zimbabwe.

On a more personal note, I have been baffled by the change that seems to have occurred in Mbeki's personality. Despite Mark Gevisser's brilliant and exhaustive analysis of his life and work,[1] Thabo Mbeki remains – for me at least – an enigma. I cannot understand the remoteness, the bad calls, his lack of wisdom and judgement in so many different ways, and even less can I grasp his coldness and aloofness, the attitude that has earned him the description of being a 'black Englishman'. He doesn't seem at home in the townships. There is an awkwardness about him. This is not the Thabo Mbeki some of us knew long before 1994. I find the changes inexplicable and I think it is tragic that he has become like this, because he has also done so much good.

While he was still in exile, it has been said, Mbeki conned the media and people like Van Zyl Slabbert, me and others because this was part of his job as a politician working towards the resolution of the conflict in his country and ours. I am sure that was part of it. I think we were seduced, deliberately so, but I bear no grudge. I think that it was part of his responsibility to try to attract as many people as possible, across the board, to a more sympathetic stance towards the ANC and its policies. What I find difficult to believe is that his warmth, charm, humour and intelligence were a mask. We were with him for long periods, for days on end and sometimes all night. It is my view that if he was wearing a mask throughout our meetings, it would surely have slipped at least once. We would have noticed; we would have sensed it.

After his resounding defeat at the 2007 ANC Polokwane conference and the appointment of Jacob Zuma as president of the ANC, Mbeki's critics and supporters alike hastened to outline the many good things he has done, including his invaluable contribution to a successful economy, without which you can't reduce poverty, provide clean water, or build houses and clinics and schools. Quite rightly, he has focused on sound economic principles. While some would argue that more should have been spent on delivery, it is my view that the money has been available, but that management, par- ticularly at local level, has been lacking. However, here too I think Mbeki has failed. Economic success notwithstanding, he has somehow developed an insecurity that has made it difficult for him to use people, particularly whites, who would have been more than willing to assist, to train, to help manage, not in a dictatorial, presumptuous way, but simply by serving the people. The expertise has certainly not been lacking. There are many whites who took a tough stand against apartheid and would have been more than willing and ready to be of assistance at every level, to narrow the gap, to make things work. But Mbeki seems to have been unable or unwilling to make use of many of us, and I deliberately include myself. It may be politically incorrect to say so, but I have little doubt that Van Zyl and I could have played a supportive role without taking anything away from his leadership. However, perhaps he knew instinctively that we would not be yes-men, that our loyalty to the ANC would not be absolute. One of the reasons why he has failed to harness the support of his own party is that he has surrounded himself with people who tell him what he wants to hear.

In Gevisser's book, particularly in the chapter entitled 'Seduction', the argument seems to be that many whites, including members of the business community, journalists like Max du Preez and many of us in IDASA, including Van Zyl Slabbert, were deeply impressed by Mbeki and admired his humour, his intelligence and his commitment to non-racial democracy. However, as time went on, some of those whites saw a new Mbeki, no longer approachable, and even racist. So they sulked and became ultra-critical of the man they once admired.

According to Gevisser, Mbeki sees things very differently. He argues that, as long as he was talking reconciliation, whites were happy. However, when he argued for transformation, those same whites were upset and accused him of playing them for useful idiots. I concede that there may well be many whites who were at first enchanted by Mbeki and put him on a pedestal but were later disturbed by his tough stance on the need for transformation, but it is nonsense to suggest that Du Preez or Slabbert or I was wedded to an idea of reconciliation without major substantial change. Those of us who were with Mbeki in Dakar acknowledged the absolute necessity for transformation. In the TRC recommendations, we declared that without economic justice, reconciliation would wither on the vine. It is insulting to suggest our disillusionment with Mbeki is the result of resistance to change. The change in Mbeki has not manifested in his political views, but rather in the man himself, and I can neither understand nor reconcile the man I knew then with the Thabo who now seems so defensive, isolated and remote. I wish we could sit down together and talk about this, but, of course, that won't happen.

At the initiative of Tony Heard from the communications department in President Mbeki's office, I met with Frank Chikane, his director-general, a few years ago. He is an old friend whom I had come to know well through the South African Council of Churches. He did brave work in the SACC and survived a close encounter with death when the state sought to poison him. We met in his office at first and then, over dinner, where we were joined at my invitation by Mike Savage, we talked at length about the obvious need for expertise in city and town councils to assist people to spend the money that was available for the care of the poor. Chikane told me that he would report back to the president, and in fact asked me to list the areas that I thought were important for the president to know about and consider.

In 2006, I arranged a dinner at the Cape Town Castle with a group of friends: Mike and Lucia Savage, Geoff Budlender and Aninka Claassens, André du Toit, Heribert Adam and Kogila Moodley, all of whom had been deeply involved in the anti-apartheid movement and were ready to assist in building the new democracy. We discussed what we would each say to the president if we had the opportunity. Together, we decided on a number of signals that we would urge Mbeki to send out to the country. Firstly, the fact that the judiciary was sacred, that the rule of law would always be observed, that everyone was equal before the law, and that, irrespective of race, colour, creed or gender, people could serve at the highest levels in our courts. This was a strong signal that we felt was needed, because many of us were beginning to wonder whether justice was sacrosanct or whether it was being controlled by the state. Other potential problem areas that we identified were the government's growing intolerance towards a media critical of official policies and inefficiencies; bad judgement in so many state departments; an urgent need for the real alleviation of poverty; the need for a public call to people, black and white, to offer their services in assisting local communities with delivery; an intensification of the struggle against AIDS and support for victims, which of course backfired very badly with Mbeki's decision in August 2007 to fire the deputy health minister, Nozizwe Madlala-Routledge, who took such a strong, refreshing stand in contrast to his health minister, Manto Tshabalala-Msimang.

There were two other areas that we felt required the president's serious attention. One was crime. I am appalled at Mbeki's attitude to those who have commented vigorously on the escalating crime rate; to the random violence, particularly towards women and children; to the fact that no one can really count on being safe and secure. When he said this was the racist attitude of affluent whites, I was so incensed that I wrote to him as follows, raising this issue as well as the government's quiet approach to Zimbabwe:

Dear President/Thabo

We haven't seen each other for a long time, but I often think of our first meeting in Lusaka and then subsequent meetings in London and New York, but most of all, our time together in Dakar, Senegal. I was appreciative of your leadership then and the warmth of spirit in which we discussed possible future scenarios for our country.

I am acutely aware of the heavy burden of office that you carry. I have often thought of contacting you but have hesitated, because you have so many people who are doing just that.

I am writing to you not as a whinging white man who seeks to put all the blame for any and all of our ills on your shoulders and/or a black government. In a small way, I worked towards the new democracy which we currently enjoy and have deep sympathy for the manifold problems which face us as a direct result of the legacy of apartheid.

There are, however, a couple of points I would like to bring to your attention, knowing full well that you have probably thought about these things many more times than I have and that you have the heavy responsibility of trying to address them.

Firstly, I think that the crime issue is much wider and broader than merely the bleating of white South Africans who are fearful of anything black. Almost every day we read of victims of crime and they are not white or black, but all South Africans. I agree with you entirely that many whites have almost a pathology about anything black and many will use the crime epidemic to blame black people in general, not merely some criminals who happen to be black. But I do think there is a deep-seated fear amongst black and white South Africans about the level of crime and a feeling of insecurity. I would urge you, therefore, to call together a national conference on crime, its causes and possible additional remedies other than those already in place.

I believe that South Africa as a whole would be very much in your debt if you called together such a conference as a matter of urgency, not because crime is out of control but because crime is a serious problem for all of us.

We cannot solve this problem with a conference alone, but psychologically it would mean an enormous amount to all South Africans. The conference I envisage would not only comprise the usual suspects – top policemen, top military people, top businessmen, top officials – but representatives of civil society, many of whom are very anxious to help. If you should take this step I would be more than happy to try to be of assistance in whatever way you think would be helpful.

The second issue I would like to raise with you relates to Zimbabwe. I know it's an extremely intractable problem, but having visited Zimbabwe often and Jenny being born in that country, I have followed the developments there very closely. I have met with Mr Mugabe in the past and I know how sensitive he is. I have also met with leaders of trade unions, student bodies, opposition parties, church leaders and others. The situation, as we all know, is grave and whilst I am appreciative of the comments you have made, the comments made by the ANC and by your Deputy Minister of Foreign Affairs, I think the situation is so serious that it warrants a much stronger condemnation and a direct appeal to Mr Mugabe and all the leaders in Zimbabwe to come together, possibly under your leadership. If that is too much for Mr Mugabe to bear, then some independent mediator could be brought in. The awful cruelty that is taking place needs to be stopped.

There are other issues which I would love to talk to you about some time, but if you have read this far, I hope you will understand that I write as someone who is sympathetic, supportive and well aware of the sensitivity and ambiguity which is at the heart of politics and governance.

I wish you well as you face a very difficult year and if you have a moment, would love to hear from you.

With warm regards

Yours sincerely

ALEX

Apart from an acknowledgement of receipt from the president's office, my letter was followed by a deafening silence.

One of the great mysteries of our political life is how Mbeki seemed to be unaware that Jacob Zuma was gaining support at a rate of knots throughout the country; how unaware he seemed to be that the shift was anti-Mbeki rather than massively pro-Zuma, although there was certainly a great deal of the latter. Some of the scenes at Polokwane were disgraceful, to say the least, but when we compare what subsequently happened in Kenya after its national elections, with more than a thousand people dying, or consider the awful situation in Pakistan and so many other countries that I have visited in the course of my work, we must not panic or become over-alarmed about what happened at the ANC conference. In some ways, the outcome was a step in the right direction in the sense that ordinary grassroots members were directly involved in the election of their party's president. What is worrying, however, is the indictment hanging over Jacob Zuma, the company he keeps, the statements he has made, the emphasis on the songs of the struggle. It is almost certain that those who supported him, in particular COSATU, the SACP and the ANC Youth League, will demand even further action during the remainder of Mbeki's presidency. It may be the wish of many Zuma supporters that heads should roll, that he and his new executive should play a more dominant role even before South Africans go to the polls in 2009.

Perhaps the greatest worry is whether the more extreme Zuma supporters will accept the fact that, in the end, the courts must decide whether or not he is guilty of the very serious fraud and corruption charges that he faces. Zuma and his lawyers have every right to seek any possible legal loophole to avoid a trial, but if that fails and the trial goes ahead, it will be an incredible test of social stability, of the rule of law and of the sacredness of the judiciary, as the country waits to see whether the rank and file of his supporters will actually accept whatever decision is reached. Zuma is innocent until proven guilty, but these are troubled times for South Africa.

The charges relating to organised crime brought against police commissioner Jackie Selebi following months of speculation were good news for our commitment to the rule of law. I liken the present situation not to the uncertainties before 1994, but rather to a series of very tricky rapids that have to and can be negotiated with wisdom and commitment. An awesome responsibility rests on the shoulders of Zuma and the national executive committee of the ANC, as well as on those of Mbeki and his ministers, to take us through these rapids into smoother waters.

The problem we are confronting is not so much the election of Jacob Zuma. The problem is that when we take a long, hard look at the ANC in all its formations, it is hard to recognise the party that came to power in 1994. The evidence of greed, of inconsistency, of jobs for pals, is writ large. Somewhere along the way it seems as though the moral compass has been thrown out of the window. It is up to the leadership of the ANC in all the regions to rediscover the spirit of generosity, reconciliation and democracy that characterised the presidency of Nelson Mandela.

Mandela's was not a perfect presidency, but there was a strong sense of morality and humanity in his words and actions. As recently as 2007 he was given the remarkable honour of having a larger-than-life statue of himself unveiled in London's Parliament Square, alongside statues of Winston Churchill, Benjamin Disraeli and Abraham Lincoln. Characteristically, he used the occasion to express the following powerful sentiment: 'Massive poverty and obscene inequality are such terrible scourges of our times – times in which the world boasts breathtaking advances in science, technology, industry and wealth accumulation – they have to rank alongside slavery and apartheid as social evils. Overcoming poverty is not a gesture of charity, it is an act of justice. It is the protection of a fundamental human right – the right to dignity and a decent life.'

To help achieve a culture of human rights, we need to have a parliamentary opposition which has a realistic chance of becoming the government. At present this is simply not possible, despite the good work done by the Democratic Alliance and other smaller parties.

When I walked out of parliament, I also resigned from the then Progressive Federal Party. I did this in order to try to see if there was a way of bringing different groups and parties together to focus on negotiation politics, which would have been difficult – if not impossible – to do as a member of one particular political party. Nonetheless, I maintained a great interest in the work of the PFP and its successors, the Democratic Party and the Democratic Alliance. I knew many of those who represented the party at different levels and admired their opposition to the then racist policies of the National Party. Furthermore, people like Colin Eglin and Ken Andrew deserve very high praise for the contribution they made to the negotiations that began in 1990.

Colin's successor was Tony Leon, a young, bright lawyer, very knowledgeable about politics, strong on strategy and totally unafraid to speak his mind and to offer alternatives, particularly to the new ANC government. Unfortunately, in his eagerness to propagate his strong liberal values, he often came across as abrasive and even shrill. As a result, he left himself wide open to the charge of racism. I have no doubt that he is no racist, but he certainly made it easy for his opponents to accuse him of being one. Until he resigned in 2007, Leon had a long spell as leader of the opposition – ten years – and during that time the party became much stronger and larger. In the 2004 general election, the ANC won 279 seats, an increase of 13, and the Democratic Alliance won 50, an increase of 12. After the statutory floor-crossing period, the ANC has 290 seats and the DA 47. The DA was also represented in many of the provinces and councils, and was – and remains – a strong voice in most parts of the country. Possibly the two low points during Leon's leadership were the formation of an alliance with the New National Party, which ended in disaster, and his populist call for the reintroduction of the death penalty. I don't think he is terribly proud of that, but there is no question that he was a very able opposition leader.

His successor, Helen Zille, I have known for many years, and I have a deep regard for her. She is smart, principled and courageous, though perhaps overly ambitious? It is such a pity that she is not twins! Helen has a huge capacity for work, and I suppose this influenced her to seek the national leadership of the party while remaining mayor of Cape Town. I think this was a grave mistake. Cape Town is an extremely difficult city to govern. Local politics, particularly at council level, is very messy. There is a great deal of back-stabbing, and all sorts of problems arise from the clash between blacks, coloureds and whites. A strong, consistent and permanent hand on the tiller is needed in order to run Cape Town, and it is impossible for Helen, despite her amazing abilities, to give all her attention to the city. There must be times when local government officials need her to be present or want to seek her advice and guidance, when she is preoccupied with national issues or is away from Cape Town.

Conversely, as national leader of the Democratic Alliance, the main opposition in parliament, she should be spending her every waking moment thinking about how to strategically confront the current crisis in the ANC – and indeed South Africa itself. Instead she is constantly caught up in local issues. Surely there must be good people in the DA who could take over as mayor? Helen should be in parliament. This is not to detract in any way from the highly impressive and able DA parliamentary leader, Sandra Botha, but that is where the leader of an official opposition party belongs in a democracy. In my opinion, it is vital that the DA, under the leadership of Helen Zille, should do everything in its power to consolidate the opposition. It is not a question of taking over, but it seems to me ludicrous that Helen Zille and Patricia de Lille, another very courageous woman and leader of the Independent Democrats, should be in separate parties. Between them, they could spearhead a combined effort to offer an even stronger, more coherent opposition to the ANC government.

But I don't think that our political future should stop at consolidation of the opposition. The crisis in the ANC and its impact on South Africa as a whole offers opportunities to think outside the box. We have experienced the politics of repression and resistance as well as the politics of negotiation. We are now a democracy, but a democracy that is faltering at very crucial points. We cannot allow the scenario of being a virtual one-party state to continue. The ruling party acts, sometimes wisely, sometimes not; the opposition opposes, sometimes wisely, sometimes for the sake of opposing. We need to break away from this. It is so predictable, so stale. There needs to be something fresh, something new.

I believe that the time has come to consider with deadly earnestness the politics of realignment. There is considerable disillusionment in the ruling party. There are many within that party who are asking the question, 'Is this what we fought for?' They are tired of inefficiencies, of the stop-start approach to the scourge of AIDS, of the nightmare of inadequate energy resources, bad judgement at local government level, the widening of the gap between rich and poor. This disillusionment is not something unique to people in opposition. I believe there is a growing number of people within the ANC who are deeply disappointed in the lost visions and discarded ideals that once characterised the ANC. Many watch with dismay as their ideals and values are trampled into dust.

These people have no other political home. There is no way they can join existing opposition parties. Black leadership is imperative. When we read the newspapers, we see the strong views of young blacks who are disillusioned with the current leadership. They are educated, widely travelled and well read, and they don't want to settle for mediocrity, inefficiency and corruption. It is true that they cannot be swayed by Helen Zille or any other current opposition politician. From within the ANC itself there need to emerge black leaders who are willing to stand up and be counted. One thinks of a man of integrity like Cyril Ramaphosa, and hopefully there will come a time – soon – when he will re-emerge and enter the political mainstream. He is on record saying that the constitution must be the yardstick by which we conduct our politics, and he knows the values which are enshrined in our constitution. It is a radical step and a tough ask: it would be like leaving his family! But I do hope that he and others will be equal to the task. This is not a blatant anti-Zuma approach; it would not be so much *against* as *for* something: for values, for the rule of law, for equality before the law, for poverty alleviation, for efficiency at all levels of government, for a new set of priorities to root out corruption, to work for genuine non-racialism, to take seriously the awfulness of AIDS.

Ramaphosa could never do anything so bold on his own, but the debate has to start somewhere. The politics of realignment is an idea whose time has come. There will be many who will pooh-pooh this, who will say it is sheer idealism. There will be many detractors. Ramaphosa might well distance himself from what I have suggested, but what is the alternative? Keeping the ANC together at all costs? Perpetuating a virtual one-party state? Holding on to an eternal opposition, always the bridesmaid, never the bride? Why can't we start a debate that will allow people who belong together in terms of strong democratic and moral values to find one another and start talking to one another about this possibility? Why can such a debate not become so loud a clamour that, in the end, people will cry out: 'Why the hell is my name not on that list? I too believe in a substantial and significant change. I want to be part of a new movement.'

It may be that these are the muddled and jumbled thoughts of an idealistic dreamer with his head in the clouds, perhaps even senile! Somewhere it is written: 'Young men shall dream dreams and old men shall see visions.' It is necessary to see a vision of South Africa very different from what it is today, and to work towards that end. Is it so bad, so wrong-headed, to have a vision of a South Africa with efficient, clean governance, where the freedom of the media and the rule of law are not at risk; a country of which we can be genuinely proud; where people can sleep safely in their beds without fear of violence; where women can be respected and protected; where children can be truly protected; where impoverished villages and towns and cities can receive genuine assistance to give meaning to life for so many millions who continue to live in poverty?

There are those who ask me, 'Are you an optimist or a pessimist in contemporary South Africa?' My reply is that I remain an optimist. I believe that there are sufficient good people – wise people – in this country who can bring it back from the edge of the precipice; that we can climb that mountain again and make a fresh start; that we can harness the energies and the skills of *all* South Africans to overcome the formidable challenges that we face. But, for this to happen, we need to break with the past and begin in earnest to work towards a realignment in politics, and while this should be inclusive, the lead must come from black South Africans, from within ANC ranks. Perhaps we should take a leaf out of Zimbabwe's book. A former minister of finance, Simba Makoni, has opted out of his own ruling party in order to oppose Mugabe. Whatever the outcome of his decision, he has at least broken the logjam, and that takes guts. Are there men and women in the ANC who will show similar courage? If there are, they will find many thousands from all parties who will follow their lead. But the time for talking and debating is over. The time for action is now.

Chapter 26

The journey never ends

W HEN I AM INVITED TO SPEAK AT CONFERENCES, LECTURES and workshops around the world, I am usually introduced to audiences along the following lines: 'Alex Boraine has had a varied life. He spent time in the church, in business, in politics, in civil society, in the South African Truth and Reconciliation Commission and as a professor of law at NYU, and was the founding president of the International Center for Transitional Justice.' I tend to respond by saying: 'Well, listening to the variety of occupations I have had over the years, you can see that I have had great difficulty in holding down a job!'

My work in the church, business, national politics, civil society, academia and transitional justice has been rewarding and extremely exciting, though often very demanding. I have often felt that I was only just managing to keep going, often flying by the seat of my pants. In truth, I lacked the formal qualifications for many of the jobs that I took on, and my youngest son, Nick, suggested at one point that the title of this book ought to be *An Unqualified Man*! But I think I have been fortunate in that the value system which developed during my period in the church endured and underpinned all my life's work.

Although I have had many jobs, they were all variations on a theme – always returning to the same set of values: a concern for the underdog, the unfairness of treating people badly. It was not enough to be concerned; I felt I had to do something, however small, to alleviate injustice. There are obvious dangers in this. One could so easily become the idealistic liberal, out of touch with reality. There is the danger of paternalism, of sometimes being taken for a ride, of bad decision-making, the risk of not knowing if one's actions make a difference. Yet, looking back, I have no regrets. Some of my life and work may have been misconstrued, misunderstood, but for the most part it seems that what I have tried to do has found resonance and a positive response among many different people.

As a result of the varied and overlapping nature of my work, I have developed great working relationships and friendships with many colleagues. Paddy Clark has been an inspiration to me in almost everything I have attempted to do. There is no question that, without her expertise, support and friendship, I would never have been able to succeed at any of the attempts I have made to try to shift the world a little closer to greater decency, humanity, justice, peace and reconciliation. I have had other great colleagues in the church, in business, in politics and in civil society. Some of those who continue to influence my life include Desmond Tutu, Van Zyl Slabbert, Michael Savage, Heribert Adam, Kogila Moodley, John de Gruchy and Charles Villa-Vicencio. The circle is very wide and includes Harvey Dale and Debra LaMorte, Vincent and Anne Mai. The list is endless. There are many others at the ICTJ who are great colleagues and good friends. They know who they are and I think they know how much they have meant to Jenny and me through good times and bad, and that our gratitude to all of them runs deep.

My life has been a series of transitions, from the TRC in South Africa to transitional justice in the international sphere; before that, from opposition politics to negotiation politics; and, earlier still, from the church to business to politics.

As I look back on the radical shift from being at the heart of the Christian church to a life in politics, I can trace the journey of many steps that affected my career and my personal beliefs. I began with the zealotry of the fundamentalist, with little or no awareness of the political, but I began to question dogma at university, and was influenced by the civil rights movement in the USA and the anti-apartheid movement in South Africa, and, when I led the Methodist Church as president, I was criticised by church and state for being too political.

Despite this fundamental change in my beliefs, I remain deeply moved by the beauty of much of the poetry in the Bible. I find the psalms particularly moving, while the challenge of the prophetic writings of Amos, Hosea and Isaiah has influenced many of my words and actions. The parables of Jesus, so simple and yet so profound, have unquestionably influenced my approach to communicating a shift from apartheid to reconciliation and justice in my country. The art and importance of storytelling cannot be exaggerated.

I remember a retreat we held at Firgrove when we were in the TRC. Father Francis Cull, a small priest of eighty-one, with white hair and beard, led the retreat. He was a lovely man, deeply spiritual, with a wisdom and compassion that were a mixture of spirituality and common sense. He was sensitive to the fact that not all of the commissioners were Christian or even religious, that we were from different faiths and that some were agnostic. But one story stood out for me. He referred to an old rabbi who was reported to have said: 'An angel walks before every human being saying, "Make way, make way for the image of God."' So the image of God stays with me, but now it is more about the reverence for the sacredness of my fellow human beings, the fact that no one dare violate that sacredness. It is not terribly logical and doesn't make a great deal of consistent reasonable sense; I realise that I am at odds with myself. There is no bedrock of certainty, but I am not uncomfortable with that. I am not desperately seeking to find meaning, and I have no desire to fall back on the certainties of religious faith. I know now that I have one life and that my purpose is to celebrate that, and perhaps the best way is to serve those who have been in the darkness of exclusion and poverty for so long.

It's been a strange transition, and there are many of my friends, I am sure, particularly from the old days of the church, who will look at me with pity and say, 'Ag shame, he's lost his faith.' But, in a strange way, it *is* my faith – if one can use that word – which drove me out of the church into the world of politics and economics, so I don't worry too much about those who feel I have lost anything. I think I have rediscovered my faith in a new way, and this life in transition is one that I celebrate. I am not keen on labels, but if I had to describe my current position, it would be that of a Christian agnostic. My reasons for retaining the adjective 'Christian' stem largely from my gratitude to the church that taught me the core values that have formed the basis of my career, both within the church and beyond its precincts. I think particularly of the values of recognising my responsibility to my fellow man, the need to focus on justice and peace and reconciliation. I appreciate that these values are not unique to the Christian religion, but it was in that milieu that I discovered them, and I am forever grateful.

While I am often disillusioned by the contradiction between profession and practice within the church, and while I sometimes find it despicable that people take on their lips the name of God and their love of Jesus yet have a total disregard for what is happening around them in the world of politics, I have met some amazing people who stood courageously for what they believed in. There is a long history of brave spirits within the Christian tradition who stood out and dared to defend their faith, even when they were being persecuted by those inside and outside the church. I remember with great affection and admiration the life and work of Archbishop Denis Hurley of the Catholic Church; of Desmond Tutu, who has become the conscience of South Africa; of Seth Mokotimi, who first challenged me to understand that love for God is impossible without love for man. I was strongly influenced by Beyers Naudé, who bravely took a stand against apartheid and thus invoked the wrath of family members, his church and the majority of Afrikaners. There are so many others who see themselves as Christian humanists, but still stand firmly rooted in the traditions of the church, and I suppose this is where my path diverges from theirs, even while my gratitude to them and so many others helps me to hold onto the word 'Christian', although I am an agnostic. My experience with the TRC was also salutary. I listened in amazement to many people who had been deeply hurt, offering to forgive those who were responsible. And most of them did so on the basis of their Christian faith.

A book I found very useful and informative is *The Spirit of Freedom: South African Leaders on Religion and Politics*, compiled by a long-time friend of mine, Charles Villa-Vicencio.[1] It contains interviews with South African leaders on religion and politics. It is fascinating to read the responses from a diverse group that includes Nadine Gordimer, Albertina Sisulu, Chris Hani, Joe Slovo, Desmond Tutu and Nelson Mandela. What I discerned from this book is that I am not alone in battling to come to terms with faith and religion. There seem to be many people, not only in politics but also in religion, who have serious reservations about many of the key doctrines of the church and of the religion to which they adhere. It seems that for many of us, including Christians, Hindus, Jews and Muslims, the core value is being part of a community, but often our own life and work experience transcend many of the central tenets of the faith that spawned us.

I found the work of John de Gruchy, a friend of many years whom I'd met and worked with while general secretary of the Methodist Church Youth Department, very helpful in trying to come to terms with where I really am. In a chapter on being secular in his book, *Being Human: Confessions of a Christian Humanist*, he wrote:

> How many have stopped being Christian, I wonder, because Christianity seems to have been taken over by Christian fundamentalism or imperialism and the God it portrays? Do I really want to be identified with that God? Bad religion is infinitely worse than no religion at all. Is it not true that many secular humanists live lives that are more compassionate, more concerned about human rights, more engaged in the struggle for justice and peace than many Christians? Would we rather not be in their company than amongst religious people, Christians among them, whose

view of God demonizes and dehumanizes others with whom they disagree? But as one of my former Christian friends turned neo-humanist once said to me, 'You are a believer and I am not.'[2]

De Gruchy argues that this is the nub of the matter, the critical difference between Christian and secular humanists, and I concur. I am no longer a believer in the doctrines that lie at the heart of the Christian religion. I sometimes catch myself longing for the old days of absolute certainty, with no ambiguity, no questioning. But then I realise that I could no longer live like that. For better or worse, I cannot return to those early fundamentalist days, nor can I even claim to be a Christian humanist. If anything, I would call myself a Christian agnostic.

When my mother said that I was born with a silver spoon in my mouth, she was wrong in many ways. Our family was not wealthy, and we suffered terrible tragedies: my brothers dying during the war, and my father dying soon afterwards. But in many ways, through a life that has taken many twists and turns and been punctuated by setbacks and successes, I have been extremely lucky, and I am left with an overwhelming sense of gratitude.

I was lucky enough to marry someone beautiful in character as well as looks. Our marriage has always been a partnership. We have stood together, moved forward together, and I think each of us has enriched the other's life. Certainly a duet makes for better music than a solo voice, and ours has been nothing if not a symphony. Jenny has been such a calming and yet challenging presence in my life. She has always asked the right questions, made insightful comments, and kept me sane when everyone around me seemed to be going mad! As I have grown older and become more cantankerous – slower – that calm and challenge has remained, perhaps a little more pointed, but necessarily so. In the midst of her art and writing, her love of her garden, the plants and flowers, her magical touch, her warm reaching out to so many people in different strata of life, she has been an enormous inspiration to me throughout our years together.

Jenny and I will celebrate our fiftieth, or golden, wedding anniversary in May 2008. It is difficult to believe that we have shared our lives for almost half a century. We are very lucky to have each other and to have travelled so far together. There have been many bumps in the road, countless lively debates and confrontations and peace-making, and none of that ends after the first or second or tenth or forty-ninth year! In a creative, warm relationship there are bound to be strong differences. Quite recently, there was some or other trifling incident, which I don't even recall, that resulted in our not speaking to one another for several hours afterwards. I was thinking along the lines of Rhett Butler's immortal words in *Gone With the Wind* – 'Frankly my dear, I don't give a damn' – when Jenny came into the living room and said, 'I want to propose a deal.' 'What's the deal?' I asked. 'I will be nice to you if you are nice to me,' she replied. 'That's a deal!' I said, and that's been the deal throughout our married life. We have sought to be nice to each other, and this has helped enormously to flood our lives with great riches, much humour and superb togetherness.

We have four wonderful children who have become as strong an influence in our lives as they have grown into adulthood as I hope we were for them when they were younger. I am so fortunate that none of them have decided to leave the country when the temptation to do so has been strong. We never tried to persuade them one way or the other, but their deep love for South Africa, warts and all – a sense of commitment – has kept them here. They have all found fulfilment in creative work: Andrew, with his constant focus on making the cities human, as executive director of the Cape Town Partnership; Kathy, with her special commitment to her children and her home under quite difficult circumstances, and her involvement in school and community work; Jeremy, a great lover of books since his university days, as a publisher; and Nicky, who even as a teenager had the ability to mimic the accents of many different people and always seemed destined for an acting career. Whether he is performing Shakespeare or has a role in a B-grade movie or a commercial for fried chicken, he is a consummate actor.

Our children have all found lovely partners, and our family has been enlarged by grandchildren who bring us great joy: Tara and Maya, daughters of Kathy and Hardy; Mano and Angie; sons of Andrew and his wife Nike; and Dan and Gracie, children of Jeremy and Jane. Nick and Lou, also an actor, are yet to embrace parenthood. The family is close and caring. We laugh a lot and constantly pull each other's legs. We are quite quick with words, and when we get together on special occasions, like a birthday, Christmas or New Year, either at Scarborough or at one of the children's homes, it is a pleasure, deep and pure. Our grandchildren live in a very different world from that of our childhood. The Internet features prominently, but they are patient with their grandparents and there is a wonderful bond between us.

We have quite an extended family. My parents have long since died, my father at the early age of fifty, but Jenny's mother still lives in Harare. She is ninety-seven and had a bad stroke a few years ago, which left her incapacitated and unable to talk, but, from the sounds she makes, Jenny understands what she is trying to convey. Jenny visits her as often as possible, as do I, though not nearly as frequently. Jenny's brother, Peter, who was dispossessed of the family farm a few years ago, also still lives in Harare, together with his wife Anne and their children, though their lifestyle is very different now. Jenny's sister, Bridgie, and her husband, Arie Tresise, had to leave Zimbabwe for a second time, and now live in KwaZulu-Natal.

I enjoy the simple pleasures of life, one of my favourites of which is cooking. When we were first married, neither Jenny nor I could cook in the accepted sense of the word. The first meal that she prepared on our return from honeymoon was boiled eggs and toast. The yolk and egg white ran out of the shell when I cracked it and the toast was burnt. I realised that we had a challenge on our hands, so we made a pact. I said, 'I'll give you three months. If you can't cook by then, I'll return you to your mother.' It was a joke, but we agreed that we would both learn to prepare some basic dishes. We slowly learnt and Jenny became an extraordinarily good cook.

My own love of cooking must have come from watching my father prepare some really tasty meals when I was a child. The demands of my work allowed me little time in the kitchen for much of my adult life, but in later years I was able to hone my culinary skills to a level way beyond presiding over the traditional South African braai. My 'signature dish' remains a spicy curry, but cooking became a form of relaxation for me, and I love to experiment and combine different ingredients and spices. I never follow a recipe, preferring to improvise, and take great delight in people enjoying the results.

When I was younger, sport – including rugby – played a large part in my life. After sustaining a knee injury, I played soccer, cricket and mostly tennis. In later life, I continued to play with a bunch of old crocks at Mary and Geoff Burton's court in Rondebosch. These days, I watch far more than I play, although I still try to run around the tennis court with a few fellow ageing men from time to time. Television has become a great boon in bringing sport into the living room. I do make occasional trips to Newlands for cricket and rugby matches, but most of my sports enjoyment comes from watching it on a large TV screen.

I spend much of my time in Scarborough, on the edge of the Cape Point Nature Reserve, about a forty-five-minute drive from Cape Town. We have had our cottage here for some twenty years and it is a retreat, a sanctuary, a place to which one can escape to write and to read, recharge the batteries, renew one's energy. Scarborough is a magical village, and many of our family and friends have enjoyed spending time with us, celebrating our beautiful home, modest but comfortable. The mountain is our backyard, and we overlook the vast expanse of the Atlantic Ocean. The sea is icy cold and few of us venture in for long, but the lagoon is warm and the beaches are a delight. Books remain a major source of joy for me. Many of them are political, legal and biographical, but I also devour detective novels. To keep up to date, I read the *New Yorker*, the *New York Review of Books*, *The Economist* and local newspapers, but there are days when I can do little else but gaze at the ever-changing natural vista that we call 'home' for hours on end. Best of all, perhaps, is that moment when the sun plunges majestically into the sea at around eight o'clock on a summer evening. We often see the green flash at that moment when the sun dips into the water, though those who haven't had this experience – the unbelievers – point to the drinks table instead as the possible source of this magical event!

When we first came to Scarborough, the beaches were reserved for whites, typical of apartheid South Africa. But now the sands are open to all, which gives us much greater pleasure. Quite a number of people stay in Scarborough for only part of the time, for the Christmas holidays and perhaps Easter, but there is also a group of residents who live here all year round. Scarborough is home to a myriad eccentrics – writers, poets, guitar-makers, surfers, divers, academics – as well as ordinary people, who have lived here for years. There are no streetlights, a lot of the roads are untarred and there is only one restaurant. Yes, the south-easter blows fiercely and often, but when you have a calm day, Scarborough is a little piece of heaven.

We share the space with the baboons. Some of the animals are an absolute menace and people are terrified of them, but there are those among us who acknowledge that the baboons were here long before we were, and who recognise their particular charm. They are part and parcel of Scarborough and of our daily life.

Hardly a year passes without some serious bush fires, and on at least two occasions the flames have been licking at our back fence before being quelled. In January 2008 we had one of the worst fires in many years and large parts of the nature reserve were destroyed. Five houses in our street were burnt down and the fire came so close to our home that it is astonishing it survived at all. In the aftermath, we battled a strong south-easter that blew grit and grime into the house, and several weeks later the smell of smoke was still apparent.

Unfortunately, fire and baboons are not the only threats to our little piece of paradise. We don't live in a cocoon or in isolation from the political events that shape our society and influence our future, and nor are residents of Scarborough exempt from the crime that occurs all over South Africa. A week before the fire in January, burglars broke into our home and stole most of our belongings that were not nailed down. In a rather unusual twist, the intruders also took meat out of the freezer, cooked it in the microwave, and had an early morning meal on our bed, leaving the bones strewn all over the floor. I don't know if they would have broken in had we been at home, but perhaps it was as well that we were spending the night in Cape Town.

I am trying very hard to retire. I have in particular tried to cut down on the amount of international travel I do, but it is not easy. The passion that I have had for many years is still with me, and my interest in transitional justice is as alive today as it was when I first went into politics. Looking ahead, in March I will chair the board meeting of the ICTJ in New York and speak at a conference in Istanbul. April should see me in Beirut, Lebanon, where there is a concerted six-month campaign to highlight fundamental human rights. I have been asked to open that and to be there for two or three days. There are also plans for a visit to Bali in Indonesia, fund-raising in London, a trip to Bogota in Colombia and a seminar on transitional justice in Rome, apart from further board meetings in May and October. I can't believe that all of this lies ahead because, as I keep telling people, I really *am* trying to retire.

Fortunately, the ICTJ's Cape Town office, of which I have been director for the past few years and which focuses on sub-Saharan Africa, is undergoing a major change. Dr Comfort Ero, a Nigerian who has worked for the United Nations, has become director in my stead. My only role is to support her during the initial settling-in period. There are some exciting initiatives planned for 2008. An assessment mission will take teams to Angola, Mozambique, Namibia and Zimbabwe to try to learn from their transitions, mistakes and successes, and will share some of our own attempts in South Africa to work towards a consolidation of democracy. The Fellows Programme will continue, with people coming to Cape Town for an intensive training course in transitional justice. They will be drawn mainly from Africa, but also from further afield. There is also the third in a series of seminars on transitional justice and development, and the ICTJ will almost certainly become more involved in Kenya in the aftermath of violence in that country. Dr Ero will have her hands full.

I am an old man now, having turned seventy-seven on 10 January 2008. Sometimes I feel the weight of those many years, especially when travelling long distances. At other times I feel as though I am in my forties, full of energy and ready to go to work. But, as I said, I really am trying to retire. I don't know when the final transition will come, but, until then, I want to be active and involved.

It is passing strange that someone who is so full of doubt and has so few answers should conclude this record of a life in transition with a prayer attributed to Sir Francis Drake in 1577:

Disturb us, Lord, when
We are too well pleased with ourselves,
When our dreams have come true
Because we have dreamed too little,
When we arrived safely
Because we sailed too close to the shore.

Disturb us, Lord, to dare more boldly,
To venture on wider seas
Where storms will show their mastery;
Where losing sight of land,
We shall find the stars.

We ask You to push back
The horizons of our hopes;
And to push into the future
In strength, courage, hope and love.

This is my hope and wish for my grandchildren in particular, and for all the children of South Africa.

APPENDICES

Appendix I

Delegates who attended the Dakar conference

Delegates from inside South Africa

Bedford, Tommy	Koopman, Albert
Boraine, Alex	Kriel, Jacques
Botha, Hardy	Lieberberg, Ian
Breytenbach, Breyten	Louw, Chris
Brink, André	Louw, Leon
Coetzee, Ampie	Mitchell, Wayne
Cronje, Pierre	Moorcroft, Errol
De Beer, Maresa	Naudé, Beyers
De Ridder, Trudi	Nel, Christo
Du Plessis, Braam	Odendaal, André
Du Plessis, Lourens	Savage, Andrew
Du Preez, Max	Savage, Michael
Du Randt, Jaap	Schlemmer, Lawrence
Du Toit, André	Serfontein, Hennie
Eloff, Theuns	Slabbert, Frederik Van Zyl
Enthoven, Adrian	Sonn, Franklin
Erasmus Gerhard	Van der Heever, Randall
Fox, Grethe	Van der Westhuizen, Johan
Fox, Revel	Van Rensburg, Manie
Gagiano, Jan	Van Vuuren, Willem
Gastrow, Peter	Verster, Phillip
Gerwel, Jakes	Viljoen, Braam
Giliomee, Hermann	Williamson, Tony

Delegates from outside Africa

Adam, Heribert	Hanf, Theo
Buch, Hans Christoph	Von der Ropp, Klaus

Delegates who were in exile

Asmal, Kader

Jordan, Pallo

Mabandla, Bridget

Mabuza, Lindiwe

Maduna, Penuell

Maharaj, Mac

Masekela, Barbara

Mbeki, Thabo

Mbongo, Reggie

Meli, Francis

Nzo, Alfred

Pahad, Aziz

Pahad, Essop

Sachs, Albie

Trew, Tony

Tshwete, Steve

Appendix II

The Dakar communique

1. A conference organised by IDASA took place in Dakar, Senegal, from 9 to 12 July 1987. Participants were made up of 61 South Africans of which the majority were Afrikaans-speaking persons who had come from South Africa and a 17 person delegation from the ANC.
2. His Excellency President Abdou Diouf welcomed the participants and gave them exceptional hospitality.
3. The participants from South Africa took part in their individual capacities. They shared a common commitment of having rejected both the ideology and practice of the apartheid system. They were drawn from the academic, professional, cultural, religious and business fields.
4. Although the group represented no organised formation within South Africa, their place within particularly the Afrikaans-speaking communities, and the fact that they were meeting with the ANC, invested the conference with an overwhelming atmosphere that this was part of the process of the South African people making history. In similar manner, the international community focused its attention on the conference. Participants could not but be aware that some of the adherents of apartheid regarded the participation of the group as an act of betrayal, not only to the apartheid state, but also to the community of Afrikanerdom.
5. The conference was organised around four principal topics:
   (a) Strategies for bringing about fundamental change in South Africa;
   (b) The building of national unity;
   (c) Perspectives with regard to the structures of the government of a free South Africa; and
   (d) The economy of a liberated South Africa.
6. The discussions took place in an atmosphere of cordiality and a unity of purpose arising from a shared commitment towards the removal of the apartheid system and the building of a united, democratic and a non-racial South Africa.
7. The group listened to and closely questioned the perspectives, goals, strategy and tactics of the ANC. The main areas of concern arose over the ANC's resolve to maintain and intensify the armed struggle. While the group accepted the historical reality of the armed struggle, although not

all could support it, they were deeply concerned over the proliferation of uncontrolled violence. However, all participants recognised that the source of violence in South Africa derives from the fact that the use of force is fundamental to the existence and practice of racial domination. The group developed an understanding of the conditions which have generated a widespread revolt of the black people and the deep resolve of the ANC.

8. Conference unanimously expressed preference for a negotiated resolution of the South African question. Participants recognised that the attitude of those in power in South Africa is the principal obstacle to progress in this regard. It was further accepted that the unconditional release of all political prisoners and the unbanning of organisations is a fundamental prerequisite for such negotiations to take place.

9. Proceeding from the common basis that there is an urgent necessity to realise the goal of a non-racial democracy, participants agreed that they all have an obligation to act for the achievement of this objective. They accepted that different strategies must be used in accordance with the possibilities available to the various forces opposed to the system of apartheid. They accepted that in its conduct, this struggle must assist in the furtherance both of democratic practice and in the building of a nation of all South Africa, black and white.

10. It was accepted between the two delegations that further contacts of this nature were necessary. Equally, it was important that such contacts should involve more and wider sections of the South African people in order to dispel misunderstanding and fear and to reinforce the broad democratic movement.

11. Conference expressed profound appreciation to His Excellency President Abdou Diouf, the government and people of Senegal, for the warm welcome extended to the delegates as well as the assistance afforded to them to ensure the success of the conference. It further expressed gratitude to Madame Danielle Mitterrand for her assistance in organising the conference and extended thanks to all other governments and individuals who contributed material resources to make the conference possible.

Appendix III

Letter from Beyers Naudé

Letter of Introduction and Recommendation for IDASA, South Africa

Oslo

11-09-1986

This letter serves as a statement of my evaluation of the importance of the IDASA Project as set up by Dr Van Zyl Slabbert, former leader of the Progressive Federal Party (PFP) and of Dr Alex Boraine, former senior leader of the same party. It also reflects my personal recommendation of the need for financial support for this venture.

During the past months a growing number of whites in South Africa have become increasingly disillusioned with the policy and promise of reform of the government of PW Botha. This has led to a situation of uncertainty regarding the future political direction they are seeking. For many the switch of political allegiance to the UDF is still traumatic and strategically they therefore need the involvement in dialogue and action within an organisation subscribing to the aim and objects of the UDF. I am convinced that IDASA under the leadership of Van Zyl Slabbert and Boraine could provide that platform and I therefore heartily recommend both moral and material support for this programme.

BEYERS NAUDÉ
General Secretary, SACC

Appendix IV

Letter from Nelson Mandela

The work of the Institute for a Democratic Alternative for South Africa in demystifying the ANC within the South African community is well known, dating from the first historic meeting in Dakar, Senegal, and a number of other projects since that time.

I am grateful for their insistence over several years that liberation movements should be unbanned and that political prisoners should be released in order that genuine negotiations towards a non-racial, democratic South Africa could begin.

Their efforts to break down the walls of division and to build bridges of reconciliation will stand South Africa in good stead as we move towards this goal.

Now there is an urgent need in this time of transition to develop a culture of democracy in South Africa. IDASA, because of its history and its involvement, is well placed to play a major role in creating opportunities for all South Africans to give expression to this concept.

I support the efforts of IDASA and hope that they will receive the financial and moral support they deserve in order to fulfil this vital role.

NELSON MANDELA
Deputy President
African National Congress

Appendix V

Objectives of the International Center for Transitional Justice[1]

The fundamental aim of the ICTJ is to help societies respond to a legacy of widespread human rights abuse through technical assistance, training, networking, documentation and strategic research. Working closely with related organisations, the ICTJ responds to requests for assistance and comparative information from non-governmental organisations and governments, in an effort to promote accountability after repressive rule or civil war. Depending on the context, our work focuses on strategies to document abuse or establish truth commissions, prosecute perpetrators, reform abusive institutions, provide reparations to victims of violence and/or promote reconciliation.

ICTJ missions, consisting of staff members and expert consultants, are sent to countries that are in need of comparative information, training or assistance in crafting transitional justice policies. This may include advice on or the drafting of legislation. Research in the field is stimulated by identifying gaps in existing scholarships, sponsorship of specific projects or support for development of larger initiatives. The ICTJ tracks the work of organisations and individuals around the world and facilitates communication and cooperation between them, with a view to strengthening the field of transitional justice.

Seminars and training courses are used to build capacity by providing information and analysis to assist the design and implementation of effective transitional justice programmes. In some cases, training is offered during the pre-transition period to allow the formulation of strategies in anticipation of change. There are also seminars for policy-makers, which offer high-level government officials, international organisations and multilateral institutions an overview of lessons learnt from past transitional justice experiences.

The ICTJ's core values are reflected in the following five operational guidelines:

- Input and recommendations are based on understanding and respecting national context and circumstances. Each transition responds to local and national circumstances, rather than being approached in terms of set guidelines that predetermine options.
- The interests and perspectives of victims and survivors take priority; this often requires close cooperation with organisations that represent victims and with human rights advocacy groups.

- Promotion of understanding and acceptance of state obligations in response to human rights violations and compliance with international law.
- Promotion of local involvement and empowerment with a view to transferring skills and expertise, thus allowing nationals to develop policy and shape initiatives.
- Facilitation of communication, networking and collaboration among those working in the field of transitional justice.

The ICTJ's long-term goals include prevention of future human rights violations by strengthening policies that effectively address the legacy of past abuse; increased international understanding of transitional justice; and establishment of an international centre through which information and expertise on transitional justice can be accessed easily and effectively.

Notes

Chapter 5

1. William Boyd, *Any Human Heart* (London: Hamish Hamilton, 2002), p. 109.

Chapter 8

1. HR Niebuhr, *The Responsible Self: An Essay in Christian Moral Philosophy* (New York: Harper and Row, 1963).
2. William Stringfellow, *Dissenter in a Great Society: A Christian View of America in Crisis* (New York: Holt, Rinehart and Winston, 1966).
3. William Temple, quoted by George Hunter III, *How to Reach Secular People* (Nashville: Abingdon Press, 1992), p. 60.
4. Dietrich Bonhoeffer, *Letters and Papers from Prison* (New York: Macmillan, 1966), p. 166.
5. Alan Walker, *A Ringing Call to Mission* (New York: Abingdon, 1966).

Chapter 13

1. Colin Eglin, *Crossing the Borders of Power* (Johannesburg: Jonathan Ball, 2007), p. 214.
2. *Ibid.*, p. 218.
3. Frederik Van Zyl Slabbert, *Tough Choices: Reflections of an Afrikaner African* (Cape Town: Tafelberg, 2000).

Chapter 18

1. TRC Report, Vol. 5, p. 243.
2. I included the original findings against De Klerk in *A Country Unmasked* (Cape Town: Oxford University Press, 2001), pp. 303–4. The findings against the ANC can be found on pp. 308–12 of *A Country Unmasked*.

Chapter 19

1. TRC Report, Vol. 5, p. 309.
2. Aryeh Neier, Review of the TRC report, *New York Review of Books*, January 1998.
3. Sandra Day O'Connor, address to the Library of Congress/NYU Law School symposium, 2000.
4. Ron Slye, 'The legitimacy of amnesties under international law and general principles of Anglo-American law', *Virginia Journal of International Law*, Vol. 43, pp. 173, 245.
5. Quoted in Yav Katshung Joseph, 'The Relationship between the International Criminal Court and Truth Commissions: Some Thoughts on How to Build a Bridge Across Retributive and Restorative Justices', p. 17, http://www.iccnow.org/documents/InterestofJustice_JosephYav_May05.pdf.

6. James L Gibson, *Overcoming Apartheid* (New York: Russell Sage Foundation, 2004).
7. TRC Report, Vol. 5, p. 308.
8. *Ibid.*, p. 309.
9. *Ibid.*, p. 352.
10. *Ibid.*, p. 353.
11. *Ibid.*, p. 354.
12. *Ibid.*, p. 366.
13. *Ibid.*, p. 377.
14. *Ibid.*, p. 378.
15. *Ibid.*, p. 392.

Chapter 23

1. Some of the material in this chapter first appeared in an article I wrote for the *Journal of International Affairs* in September 2006.
2. In Michael R Marrus, *The Nuremberg War Crimes Trial 1945–1946: A Documentary History* (Boston and New York: Bedford Books, 1997), pp. 79–85.
3. In 2007 Oxford University Press, in conjunction with the ICTJ, published the definitive work on reparations. Titled *The Handbook of Reparations*, this massive and important work was largely due to Pablo de Greiff, the research director at the ICTJ and a close friend. Many practitioners, including myself, are very much in his debt.
4. Ariel Dorfman, *My Neighbor, My Enemy: Justice and Community in the Aftermath of Mass Atrocity*, edited by Eric Stover and Harvey Weinstein (New York: Cambridge University Press, 2004).

Chapter 25

1. Mark Gevisser, *Thabo Mbeki: The Dream Deferred* (Johannesburg: Jonathan Ball, 2007).

Chapter 26

1. Charles Villa-Vicencio, *The Spirit of Freedom: South African Leaders on Religion and Politics* (Berkeley and London: University of California Press, 1996).
2. John de Gruchy, *Being Human: Confessions of a Christian Humanist* (London: SCM Press, 2006).

Appendix V

1. See: http://listserv.buffalo.edu/cgi-bin/wa?A2=ind0103&L=justwatch-l&D=1&O=D&P=101464.

Index

National Endowment for
  Democracy 150
National Party (NP) 14, 59, 90,
  103, 113, 125–7, 128, 132, 133,
  145, 148, 155, 157, 159, 163,
  165, 296
  AB opposes in parliament
  82–3, 87, 89, 90, 92, 93,
  95–6, 98, 104–5, 111, 113–14,
  116, 130–31
  and TRC 171, 172, 174, 178–9,
  180, 181, 190, 192–3, 194,
  205–6, 208
National Prosecuting
  Authority 191
National Reconciliation
  Commission
  (Ghana) 244
National Security
  Management System 160
national service 117
National Truth and Recon-
  ciliation Commission
  (Chile) 173, 200, 272
National Union of
  Mineworkers 139
National Union of South
  African Students
  see NUSAS
National Youth Leadership
  Training Programme
  54–5, 111
NATO 236
Naudé, Beyers 96, 146, 165, 303,
  312, 316
Naudé, Ilse 146
Navsa, Mohammed 173
Nazis 32, 130, 240, 268, 274
Ndebele, Njabulo 161
Neier, Aryeh 167, 202, 224
Nel, Dr Christo 143, 312
Nepal 250, 269
New National Party 296
New Republic Party (NRP)
  90, 91, 104, 130
Newton-Thompson, Ossie
  81, 83

New Yorker 307
New York Review of Books 307
New York Times 231
New York University 202,
  219–21, 222–4, 226, 252,
  260, 281, 282, 300
Ngewu, Cynthia 212
Ngubane, Dr Harriet 177, 180
Nicol, Dr 281
Niebuhr, HR 62
Nieuwoudt, Gideon 190–91
Norgaard, Prof. Carl 173
Norgaard, Helle 173
Northern Ireland 223, 224,
  232–4
Northern Ireland Association
  for the Care and
  Settlement of Offenders
  (NIACRO) 232
Norway 138–9, 140, 228,
  245, 247
Notre Dame University 224
Novogrodsky, Prof. Noah 267
Nqalunga, Brian 191
Ntsebeza, Dumisa 181
Nuremberg Trials 267, 268
NUSAS 96, 99, 108, 119, 121, 145
Nyanda, Zwele 191
Nzo, Alfred 313

Ocalan, Abdullah 262
O'Connor, Sandra Day 202–3
Odendaal, Dr André 143, 312
Oettle, Eric 81, 82
Ogata, Mrs Sadako 253, 254
Ogilvie-Thompson, Julian 71
O'Leary family 9, 15
Olivier, Prof. Nick 112
Omar, Dullah 123, 167, 168, 171,
  172, 173, 179, 183
Open Society Foundation 151
Open Society Institute 167,
  202, 224, 236
Oppenheimer, Bridget 72
Oppenheimer, Harry 70–71,
  72–4, 75–6, 82, 83, 86,
  88, 128

Oppenheimer, Mary 71, 76
Organisation for Security
  and Cooperation
  in Europe (OSCE) 240
Orr, Wendy 181
Orthodox Church 237, 243
Oswald, Lee Harvey 48
Ottaway, Jim 227
Oxford University 35–6, 37,
  41–5, 220

Pahad, Aziz 147, 148, 152, 313
Pahad, Essop 313
Pakistan 294
Palestine 251
Pan Africanist Congress (PAC)
  59, 110, 163, 177, 214
pass laws 41, 89, 108
Paton, Alan 162
Peace Corps (US) 54
Pebco Three 187–8
Peru 247
Pfuhl, Bert 19–20
Pitman, Harry 127
Plavšić, Biljana 238–43
Poland 166
Polokwane conference 290, 294
Popper, Karl 151
portfolio committee on justice
  173–80
Potgieter, Denzil 181
Power, Prof. Samantha 228
Programme to Combat
  Racism 58
Progressive Federal Party (PFP)
  history of 89–90
  AB as MP 89–94, 95–101,
  103–114, 115–16, 118,
  130–31, 147, 258
  opposes tricameral
  constitution 126–7
  Slabbert and AB resign from
  127–34, 296
Progressive Party (PP)
  89–90
  AB becomes member of
  71, 75

Do you have any comments, suggestions or
feedback about this book or any other Zebra Press titles?
Contact us at talkback@zebrapress.co.za